Love and Politics

POLITICAL THEORY AND CONTEMPORARY POLITICS

Series Editors: Richard Bellamy, University of Reading, Jeremy Jennings, University of Birmingham, and Paul Kelly, London School of Economics and Political Science

This series aims to examine the interplay of political theory and practical politics at the beginning of the twenty-first century. It explores the way that the concepts and ideologies that we have inherited from the past have been transformed or need to be rethought in the light of contemporary political debates. The series comprises concise single-authored books, each representing an original contribution to the literature on a key theme or concept.

Also published in this series:

Liberalism and Value Pluralism
George Crowder

Political Morality: A Theory of Liberal Democracy
Richard Vernon

Forthcoming titles:

Defending Liberal Neutrality
Jonathan Seglow

Democracy and Global Warming
Barry Holden

Political Theory and Media
Alan Finlayson

The Politics of Civil Society
James Martin

Seductive Virtue: The Socratic Art of Civic Education
Russell Bentley

Love and Politics

Women Politicians and the Ethics of Care

Fiona Mackay

CONTINUUM
London and New York

Continuum
The Tower Building, 11 York Road, London SE1 7NX
370 Lexington Avenue, New York, NY 10017–6503

First published 2001

British Library Cataloguing-in-Publication Data
A catalogue record for this book is available from the British Library.

ISBN 0–8264–4782–1 (hardback)
0–8264–4783–X (paperback)

Library of Congress Cataloguing-in-Publication Data
Mackay, Fiona.
    Love and politics: women politicians and the ethics of care / Fiona Mackay.
        p. cm — (Political theory and contemporary politics)
    Includes biographical references and index.
    ISBN 0–8264–4782–1 — ISBN 0–8264–4783–X (pbk.)
    1. Women in politics—Great Britain. 2. Women social reformers—Great Britain. 3. Women's rights—Great Britain. I. Title. II. Series.
    JQ1236.5G7 M3 2001
    320'.082'0941–dc21   00–069376

Typeset by YHT Ltd, London
Printed and bound in Great Britain by Biddles Ltd
www.biddles.co.uk

Contents

Acknowledgements

I would like to thank Alice Brown for her encouragement and intellectual support. She has been a generous mentor and is a valued colleague and friend. Much of the Scottish material in the book has been shaped and informed by her own work and by collaborative projects with her and with Esther Breitenbach. I have greatly benefited from their ideas and discussions. Esther's scepticism has helped me to sharpen my thinking about a non-essentialist ethics of care, at least I hope it has.

I greatly appreciate the time and co-operation given to me by 53 very busy women councillors and other political activists and council officials. Thank you.

The Politics Department at Edinburgh University has provided a stimulating and collegial environment. Special thanks there are due to Kim Hutchings, who read and commented on a number of chapters and whose confident encouragement kept me going when I felt discouraged. Thanks also to Richard Freeman, Nicola Meyrick, Lindsay Paterson and Sue Innes for their support and advice at various stages of this project.

Georgie Young read, listened, kept faith and proof-read. I could not have finished it without her.

I am grateful to two anonymous reviewers and to Richard Bellamy for their very constructive comments on the draft manuscript; any deficiencies that remain are my own. Thanks are also due to my editor at Continuum, Caroline Wintersgill, for her patience and enthusiasm.

For my mother, Ruth Mackay,
and in memory of my father, Robert Watt Mackay

1

Introduction

At the beginning of the twenty-first century, women have an unprecedented presence in the new political landscape of British politics and governance. The issue of women's political under-representation is not, of course, new. It has attracted growing attention over the past thirty years, largely as a result of feminist activism at local and national levels and increasingly through transnational and global institutions such as the European Union and the United Nations. In the UK it achieved particular political prominence in the 1990s in the context of Labour Party modernization, demands for constitutional change and concerns about the need for democratic renewal and the reformation of politics.

In 1997 a Labour landslide victory ended eighteen years of Conservative government. Overnight Britain went from 50th to 24th in the world league of women in parliament with 18 per cent female MPs. These results were eclipsed in 1999 with the election of a new parliament for Scotland and a National Assembly of Wales, in which women make up 37 per cent and 40 per cent of elected members, respectively.[1] In the elections to the London Assembly in 2000, women took 40 per cent of the seats. Although still a long way from parity, this represents remarkable progress in a country where, with one or two highly visible exceptions, women have long been noticeable by their absence – or their rarity.

Once the celebrations and congratulations were over, realism kicked in – and reality bit. The gains made are contested and

1

vulnerable to reversal. The increases in overall figures are largely due to the quotas policy of one political party, Labour, and its subsequent electoral success. That special measures, such as quotas, work is beyond doubt. However, huge problems of legitimacy and political acceptance remain. In Britain, dominant discourses of representation, equal opportunities and justice are rooted in formal 'gender-blind' constructions of equality. None of the other major political parties in Britain seems likely to accept mandatory quotas, and even within the Labour Party they are contentious and there has only ever been uneasy and temporary acquiescence of that policy. If the political pendulum swings the other way, it will cut a swathe through the ranks of women elected members. With selection rounds well underway for the general election of 2001, the indications are that few new women candidates from any party have been selected to fight safe or winnable seats.

Despite much talk of 'new politics', there are few signs that the underlying problems of traditional political culture and institutions have been tackled within political parties or at Westminster, although the creation of new political institutions in Scotland and Wales has allowed for certain 'women-friendly' practices to be built in from the start (Brown, 1999). Female members at Westminster, Edinburgh and Cardiff have found that they are damned if they act or organize as women within their respective assemblies and, sometimes, damned if they do not. Party discipline militates against women working across parties and political culture frowns upon explicit women's caucuses. However, when women 'play by the rules' and, for example, refuse to rebel in order to defend women's policy concerns, they can be derided by the media (Mactaggart, 2000) and written off by women's organizations. So, women are indeed there, but their voices are ambivalent and their place is uncertain.

Principles and Practices

The unstable, uneven and contested process of women's more equal inclusion in formal politics highlights the strategic importance of political discourse and rhetoric. Political parties readily accept the case of equality in principle, but do less in practice. In part, this is because positive action sits uncomfortably with dominant under-standings of equality. British feminist academics and party activists have similarly privileged arguments based on equality and justice and have avoided the riskier arguments of difference. Although this strategy has served women to a point, it will not be sufficient on its own to take forward the campaign for an equal presence in the polity. Nor do the current arguments and strategies do much to challenge existing political culture and practices. Current limitations in the ways of thinking, talking and arguing about gender and political representation have resulted in the faltering progress of gender equality in electoral politics, which can result in stalling and sudden reversals.

It is within these contexts that this book takes a fresh look at women's recruitment, representation and participation in politics. We take as our starting point the concrete problems of political equality in the specific context of national and local representative politics in Britain and we draw upon both empirical and theoretical literatures to explore different ways in which the debate can be taken forward. The 'common-sense' analysis of women politicians in Scotland of their political role and practice is offered as an important form of situated knowledge and a neglected resource. We also consider whether a strand of moral theory based on the 'ethics of care' has anything to offer to current academic and practical political debates.

Part I examines the current balance sheet in respect of women in British politics. It is centred upon the following questions relating to political recruitment and political representation: Why are there so few women in politics? What has been done so far? What needs to be done? Why should there be more women in politics? What difference do women make? We examine existing explanations relating to women's relative absence from parliaments and councils. We explore different rationales for women's representation and consider the comparative empirical evidence relating to the political roles of women. Issues of equality and difference impact upon women as political actors at both rhetorical and practical levels. We argue that we must give greater consideration to arguments of difference. However, neither equality nor difference stands alone as either an adequate explanation of political realities or as a powerful strategy for change.

The costs of 'care' feature prominently in both traditional and feminist accounts of the barriers to women's recruitment to political office. Domestic and family responsibilities are a major 'supply' factor preventing potential women candidates from coming forward.

3

In the case of traditional political science and, indeed, mainstream political accounts, the sexual division of labour is seen as natural or a matter of individual choice. Feminist approaches understand it as a structural gender injustice and chart the way in which it disadvantages women in political life and other forms of social and economic activity. Seldom has there been consideration within mainstream accounts that women's experience of care work might give rise to political competencies or political values. There are also concerns that to concentrate on difference *only* as disadvantage does not adequately reflect the more nuanced understandings of women themselves.

Dominant understandings of the nature, needs and limits of equality impact upon demands for action and upon the political support for various reform strategies. We argue that in order to maintain progress and to tackle underlying social and cultural issues there is a need to search for new arguments and new understandings of women's 'place' in power politics. There is also a need to 'tangle' with difference, to look at both the positive and the negative sides of care, and to explore ways in which difference and equality can be reconciled, if only provisionally.

In Part II we look at alternative discourses and move into dangerous territory. We consider the demands of care theorists that values traditionally associated with women should be revalued. Some claim that 'women's values' or the 'ethics of care' contain the potential to challenge and transform values and practices in the public and political spheres. These theoretical suggestions – which may loosely be called 'care thinking' – have been developed by feminists from a number of different traditions. These ideas are not well known in political science or in popular political debates, and what does filter through tends to be caricatured as crudely essentialist. Feminist activists and academics concerned with political representation are inclined to give these ideas short shrift and a wide berth. They are dismissed as the basis of a 'dangerous politics' celebratory of women's traditional self-sacrifice, which would make women somehow responsible for care in the public sphere as well as care in the private or domestic sphere.

To be sure, some expressions of care thinking are reactionary, populist and unpleasantly supremacist. However, more subtle versions exist which emphasize that caring is socially and historically contingent and that care thinking arises from the social practice of caring rather than from innate 'womanly virtues'. We examine versions of the ethics of care which have been applied to the public sphere and political citizenship. They suggest a different view of what politics ought to be about. We ask whether insights derived from this literature provide a different rationale for the role of political representatives and whether new potential discourses might be developed. Care thinkers have not explicitly focused upon the role of the political representative as a form of active citizenship, nor have they related their discussions to women's own experiences of political life. In Chapter 7, this theoretical work is compared and contrasted with women's own stories. By bringing together care theory and women's voices, we note some striking parallels. Common themes emerge: the way present political and social systems and value structures obscure the central importance of care; and the means by which certain powerful groups and actors benefit from, while simultaneously devaluing, care; recognition that practical strategies and intellectual skills which arise from the practice of caring can be 'transformed' and transferred to a wider context of politics; and demands that politics change, not only that women may fully participate, but also that politics may more fully reflect the needs and interests of diverse communities.

New directions

The final chapter concludes that an examination of care as a political practice and a political idea enables fresh thinking about the current situation in respect of women's under-representation and their political roles as well as offering a prescription and resource for change. In this sense 'care' can act as an explanatory tool, a strategic resource and a framework of political values. Multi-valued arguments are needed to maintain and progress women's presence in formal politics and to challenge and transform political institutions. Analyses which highlight both the costs of care and the political resources arising from care can potentially call upon arguments of both equality and difference to present powerful reasons for women and for marginalized men to 'be there'. Women politicians' stories of political life and insights from care theorists provide keys to a better understanding of gender and elected politics. They also offer a basis for creating powerful new discourses to promote political equality of access and to transform political values and practices.

The book offers a contribution to debates about women and political representation and the political ethics of care. It also seeks to show how theories generated in the academy have the potential to be developed into pragmatic political discourses. It does not claim to provide answers but it does suggest some future directions. The suggestions here will provide a basis for further reflection and empirical examination.

Constitutional change has fundamentally reshaped politics in the UK. The creation of new democratic institutions and the reform of existing ones have opened up new spaces and new opportunities for women. These structural changes, together with ongoing political concerns about the perceived 'crisis' of liberal welfare democracies and the need to reconnect political institutions with 'the people', provide conditions which make the debate about women's access, presence and influence in politics particularly acute. It is crucial to find ways to maintain momentum.

Women and political representation

Joni Lovenduski (1997) has noted that feminist interest in women's roles in public decision-making is founded upon ideas about citizenship, equality and representation and is grounded in discourses about power, democracy and gender. These issues are complex and, as the book demonstrates, theoretical and empirical work has sometimes developed in parallel rather than in an integrated way.

A feminist focus upon political institutions and representation is rather recent both in terms of activism and academic study. The 'second wave' women's movement, in different countries at different rates, moved from a position of non-engagement with the state and state agencies to one of increasing involvement, some would argue increasing co-option and incorporation. From the 1970s onwards feminists entered political and state institutions such as political parties, trade unions, state bureaucracies, equalities commissions and women's policy machinery and elected office at national, regional and local levels. British feminists, in contrast to activists in some other countries, particularly the USA and Australia, were slower to engage with the state (Gelb, 1990; Eisenstein, 1991; Watson, 1992; Lovenduski and Randall, 1993). This reflected both the New Left 'anti-state' roots of the movement and the closed nature of British state bureaucracy. In time the approach became more pragmatic and, from the 1980s onwards, feminists entered political parties (Rowbotham *et al.*, 1979; Wainwright, 1987; Perrigo, 1996), trade unions and employers' organizations (Cockburn, 1983, 1991), elected political office (Lovenduski and Norris, 1993), and the state bureaucracy, particularly through local government women's and equal opportunities committees (Goss, 1984; Halford, 1992; Lovenduski and Randall, 1993).

British feminist activists in the Labour Party reinvigorated separate women's sections within party structures, gained greater powers for the women's conference, and lobbied for targets and quotas to improve the representation of women as office-holders within the party and as candidates for public office (Lovenduski and Randall, 1993; Perrigo, 1995, 1996). In Scotland, a broad coalition of political and trades union activists together with feminist groupings and other women's networks mobilized around the campaign for gender balance in the proposed Scottish Parliament (Brown, 1996, 1998, 1999). This mirrors the pattern in many other liberal welfare democracies and is informed by a growing recognition by many feminists that, whatever the shortfalls, the trade-offs and the pitfalls, 'for practical politics the state is not just important, it is unavoidable' (Franzway *et al.*, 1989, p. ix). As Cockburn notes, 'some feminists have deplored this as signalling an institutionalization of the movement. Others, however, point out that by such "entrism" women have for the first time approached the places of power and begun to challenge powerful men and the way they operate' (1991, p. 2).

With this move through the institutions have come increasing demands for more women in electoral politics at all levels. There is by no means consensus on the strategy of increasing women's representation nor a uniform vision of its consequences. For some, the increased presence of women in political assemblies is an end in itself – of justice done and seen to be done; for others, there are expectations that once a 'critical mass' of women gains power, politics and political institutions will be transformed. Others have reservations: first, that feminists who enter the state face pressures of co-option and incorporation; and second, that non-feminist women may do little to empower other women or act for change. Margaret Thatcher is seen to provide a cautionary example in this respect. Finally, increasing attention to differences between different groups of women, and to the fragmented and multiple nature of individual identities has led some feminists to doubt that women can represent women in any meaningful sense at all.

Work on women and political elites at empirical level has tended to focus upon the causes of, and upon potential correctives to, women's under-representation in political assemblies, and the search for concrete evidence of difference or similarity between male and female politicians in terms of attitudes or behaviour. This has resulted in an emphasis, first of all, on recruitment studies which examine barriers to women's political participation and potential correctives. This work has greatly advanced our knowledge of the complex barriers which face aspirant women, although less progress has been made with remedies to tackle the underlying causes. There have also been a great many surveys of office-holders' and candidates' expressed attitudes and policy stances, and reported behaviour. Fewer political scientists have explored women's political role in depth or the way in which the discourses of difference and equality impact upon both political debate and upon practice – and the relationship between the two.

Differing concepts of justice and equality, and the vexed question of difference are circled intensively and contentiously within feminist theory, but the issues have perhaps been less well rehearsed within political science and hardly at all within contemporary political culture. We argue that these ideas are relevant to the understanding of women's roles in formal politics in a number of strategic, discursive, and practical ways, and inform different stances on political representation and equal opportunities. For female politicians, they can articulate some of their lived contradictions as women operating in the world of conventional power politics.

Equality and difference

Before moving on we need to define briefly what is meant by equality and difference, and why they should so often be placed in opposition to each other. The following discussion is brief and is drawn from more substantial debate and review found in Evans (1995) (see also Bacchi, 1990; Rhode, 1990, 1992; Bock and James, 1992). The equality–difference debate is seen as a central tension within feminism and a preoccupation in feminist politics. Why is the debate important? First, because current terms of political frameworks mean feminists often have to choose between arguments of equality or difference (rather than equality versus inequality); second, this choice has potential consequences in the pursuit of equal rights, treatment and opportunities for women; and third, concepts of difference pose theoretical challenges to universalist conceptions of justice, equality and citizenship.

Formal equality is based upon universalism, and the idea of treating all people as if they were alike (sameness). Difference is thus positioned in opposition to an equality premised on sameness. Judith Evans (1995) remarks that newcomers to the debate are often puzzled at this opposition. The terminology of equality–difference is confusing. 'Only if we link sameness to equality does it begin to make sense' (Evans, 1995, p. 5). The equality–difference debate is therefore based upon a particular understanding of equality and a particular strategy of seeking to minimize or eliminate difference.

Difference, in this context, stands in opposition to an equality which is premised upon undifferentiation. Some feminists argue that difference, whether biologically based (sex) or socially constructed (gender), is relevant to issues of equality and that 'gender-blind' constructions of equality and justice disadvantage women. Difference offers a practical critique of the shortcomings of formal equality which fails to deliver for women. Denying difference, particularly the gendered realities of women's lives, their reproductive work and their unequal burden of care for men, children, the sick and the elderly, leads to 'equality in form, not equality in fact' (Rhode, 1992, p. 151). It also poses a challenge to universalist paradigms. It is argued that ideas like equality and justice are premised upon male needs and interests, which then appear as standard, natural and rational – whereas women appear to need special treatment.

However, this is only one dimension of difference. The second main usage of difference relates to diversity. As Cockburn notes:

> Women do not come in one kind. Nor are women, by virtue of being oppressed, innocent of the oppression of others. Feminists have found their theory has to tangle with 'difference' – and not just women's difference from men but the things that differentiate them one from another. (1991, p. 207)

Confronting and recognizing the differences between groups of women (and men) constituted an important part of the debate in the 1980s and 1990s and led to the fragmentation of the women's movement in many countries. The false universalizing of a predominantly white, middle-class, heterosexual and able-bodied women's movement has been challenged by black women (for example, hooks, 1981; Carby, 1982), lesbians (for example, Rich, 1980) and, more recently disabled women (Morris, 1991). It is now accepted that some women, for example, white women, simultaneously occupy positions of subordination (through hierarchies of gender) and domination (through hierarchies of race). Women can oppress other women and, in some cases, can oppress men from marginalized social groups. Feminism no longer claims to speak for Woman, but recognizes that women have diverse experiences mediated through differences such as class, race and ethnicity, disability, sexual orientation and age, as well as through gender. This debate both recognizes the differences between women, and also uses insights drawn from post-modernism to acknowledge competing loyalties and shifting identities – the fragmentation of selves – within women as individuals. These senses of difference offer a critique of formal equality which is seen to fail to deliver equality for women and marginalized groups of men; and they give rise to demands for contextualized equality which takes account of gender and other differences: that is, to treat people as equals may require that they be treated differently.

The recognition of, and theorizing on, difference as diversity has brought rich insights and has led to the cross-fertilization of ideas especially within the equal opportunities movement (Cockburn, 1989). It presents strategic problems for political action: can feminists claim to speak for the category 'women'? Can we talk of women's concerns or women's needs without risking being essentialist on the one hand and falsely universalist on the other? At one level these preoccupations can seem to preclude the possibility of sustained political action based on any group identity and there is no ready resolution. In the meantime, we concur with Cockburn's assertion that we can still talk about women without necessarily considering them as a unitary category. Instead, we understand 'identity framed in gender processes that vary according to whether they are black or white, whether they are lesbian or heterosexual and whether or not they experience disabilities' (Cockburn, 1991, p. 3). Cockburn says, 'Women need to keep the idea of sexual and gender "difference" in play, but on their own terms. Women are the ones who must be able to say when "difference" is relevant' (ibid., pp. 9–10). This point is reinforced by

Bacchi who argues that feminist preoccupation with the legitimacy of the category 'women' is misplaced, ' "Women" is already a key political signifier', therefore, 'feminists have little option but to engage in contests over its signification' (1996, p. 10).

In addition, there are also two other common uses of difference in the vast literature. The first is the sense of difference as an autonomous rather than a relative concept. It is a *label* representing women's specific experience, rather than a description of women's degree of deviance from a male standard. This approach is exemplified by the work of Italian feminists such as Cavarero (1992) (see also Bono and Kemp, 1991), and is also found in conceptions of women's culture (Ås, 1975; Carroll, 1992) and women's politics. Finally, there is also a pragmatic, empirical use of difference in the literature – that of making a difference.

In this book we argue that we must 'tangle' with gender difference while trying to resist the tendency to homogenize women. This need not imply an uncritical acceptance of the category 'women', rather, it recognizes that in the context of current debates and struggles for presence in formal politics, the category 'women' is politically relevant. This is evidenced by alliances among different groups of women around a common interest of access to political decision-making.

A view from Scotland

Although this book takes as its focus debates about women, politics and representation at national, devolved and local levels in the UK, it draws upon wider debates and comparative literatures. It is also grounded in a specific set of political circumstances in Scotland. Debates and activity in relation to women and political representation have been particularly lively in recent years against a backdrop of renewed campaigning for a Scottish parliament. It has been argued that equal representation – under the rallying call of 50:50 – became an intrinsic part of the broader debates of democracy and accountability which drove demands for constitutional change in Scotland (Burness, 1995; Brown, 1998). A broad-based and pluralist movement of women activists grew up around the issue of women's historic political under-representation and the perception that women needed to be in at the start of a new political institution.

The dominant 'official' discourse was one based upon arguments about 'democratic deficit' and justice. However, the belief that women would 'make a difference' was instrumental in mobilizing women councillors and MPs, party activists, trade unionists and members of a wide range of feminist groups and women's organizations to campaign for gender equality and family friendly practices in the new Scottish Parliament. The Scottish Parliament was seen by many women to hold the promise of a more inclusive and appealing politics. Brown (1996) argues that it is this vision of difference which has been important in bringing women together in a coalition of interests. Difference here is meant in a pragmatic sense of having an impact. However, expectations of 'making a difference' rest at least in part on implicit assumptions of difference. Women are seen to have the potential to make a difference because they are, in some important ways, different. Thus we see alternative discourses of difference at play in the Scottish context although the contours, meanings or implications of any such difference have not been explicitly addressed or systematically scrutinized.

It is not the aim of this book to give an account of the complex and eventful contemporary campaign for devolution in Scotland (Brown *et al.* 1996; 1998) and the parallel struggle for equality of representation (Brown 1996, 1998, 1999; see also Breitenbach and Mackay, 2001). These events have been charted and analysed elsewhere. However, it is crucially informed by these contexts.

Approaches

The book draws upon existing British and comparative literature on women in elected politics at local and national levels and also examines key theoretical work on representation, democracy and the political ethics of care. The aim is to provide a bridge between these different literatures. We ask what moral and political theory can contribute to practical politics and its study and what practical knowledge and empirical research can offer to political and moral theory where, as Sevenhuijsen (1998) observes, 'normative images' can often substitute for empirical realities and experiences. So while, on the one hand, we argue that lessons for feminist political science and political activism on representation can be found in certain branches of theory and in women's own stories, we also argue that feminist theorists have too often overlooked and excluded political and state institutions and conventional power politics from their considerations. The book also draws upon the 'voices' of some Scottish women politicians and their own 'common-sense' analyses of their political role and practice. We offer an interpretation of how these experiences relate to the literature on women and politics in certain respects, and how they might inform future directions.

The use of women's accounts or narratives is informed by feminist approaches which argue that women's experience and everyday theorizing are important and credible forms of situated knowledge (see, for example, Code, 1991). Women's complicated relationship with public and private spheres gives rise to critical questions and new insights. On a daily basis women *as women* confront and negotiate the contradictions which arise from their position. In turn, these everyday practices can give rise to ways of thinking which 'provide the space or the possibility for a political intervention to construct an alternative hegemony, an alternative view of the world' (Showstack Sassoon, 1987, p. 20). Drawing upon this insight, Showstack Sassoon contends that women's 'common sense' will include embryonic analyses, explanatory frameworks and blueprints for political change alongside notions of dominant ideology which serve to reinforce their subordination.

This suggests it is necessary to take women's accounts of reality seriously, warts and all. Rather than dismissing them out of hand as the product of 'false consciousness' or 'feminine ideology', they should instead be viewed as a starting point and an empirical and theoretical resource (see also Harding, 1987). Women's concrete experience of fragmented lives, managing contradictory aspects of their work and identity as women, mothers, wives, workers and politicians can give rise to insights. These realities will also be crucially shaped by race, class and other social divisions. Thus the common-sense discussions of female politicians are valuable sites for exploring complex and contradictory understandings of gender and politics, and are potential sources of new political discourses and new political visions, albeit tentative, contradictory and contested. Women's stories are also shaped by dominant ideologies and social structures and therefore will be marbled through with strands of thinking which are reactionary, stereotypical and fatalist.

Selection rationale

The stories recounted in this book are largely based upon a series of in-depth semi-structured interviews with 53 Scottish women councillors carried out in the mid-1990s. Interviews were supplemented by informal conversation and small group discussions. The selection of this case study relates both to personal and academic interests and choices and to the evolution of the research project which provided the genesis for this book. It is Scottish because, as noted earlier, a particular set of circumstances in Scotland opened up a window of opportunity for intensive debate and campaigning on the issue of women and political representation and the mobilization of women outwith political parties to campaign on the issue. Researchers elsewhere are beginning to awaken to the realization that 'something has been going on' in Scotland, at once both distinctive and also part of broader global developments of political representation.

Why local government? Local government is significant as a political arena in its own right with powers and responsibilities which influence the quality of everyday life. It remains the primary interface between citizens and services such as education, social housing, social services and public transport. It is a major employer (particularly of women) in many local economies and increasingly, plays a strategic role in local economic development. As Goss notes, 'Local government which intervenes directly into women's lives is an important site for struggle and change' (1984, p. 128). Local government is also commonly perceived to be more responsive than central government to the demands of women and members of other under-represented social groups, and more accessible in terms of opportunities to compete for political office. Women constitute about 20 to 25 per cent of local councillors in the UK, which ranges from around 30 per cent in certain types of English authorities to only 14 per cent in Northern Ireland. Until the creation of devolved parliaments and assemblies in 1999 and 2000, this was the level of government at which women had the strongest presence.

Local government is also an important pathway to other levels of political office, particularly for women. Thus women councillors form a crucial part of the potential pool from which candidates for other levels of political office can be drawn. They are in a pivotal position, simultaneously serving politicians and potential candidates, which is likely to provide them with interesting insights. Women councillors are also arguably closer to 'ordinary' women with whom they are in daily contact in the course of their council business and therefore may have views as to the reasons which discourage many women from becoming active in formal politics.

Why these particular women? The design was shaped by the original conception and the primary purpose of the research which used a case study approach to examine the ways in which gender was relevant to women's experience as political actors in terms of their access, presence and agency in political institutions. It sought to explore these questions in a concrete context where 'gender politics' was on the agenda. The four local authorities were chosen because they, between them, covered the majority of the Scottish population; they all had women's and/or equal opportunities structures in place; and were all involved in a radical public education initiative concerned with combatting male violence against women. As noted above, the sample consisted of virtually all the female members of four local authorities (although the process was complicated by an intervening election). This grounded the women within an organizational context rather than as atomized individuals and allowed the study to capture a sense of process and of relationships between women. This book arises from one particular aspect of the study. Discussion related to other elements of the research can be found elsewhere (Mackay, 1996a; 1996b; 2001).

Questions of representation

How representative are these women? The approach was qualitative therefore the sample was not generated to be statistically representative. However, this raises questions as to the extent we can generalize about women, politics and caring on the basis of these findings. In terms of profile, the women varied in age from 30 to over 70 years; only two had never been married and six were childless. The majority of women had cared for dependent children at some stage in their political career. Around one in ten specifically mentioned other caring commitments. Around two-thirds were employed or had been employed in traditionally female 'pink-collar' jobs or professions: mostly teachers, secretaries, cleaners and retail workers. There was one black woman in the sample, at the time the only black female councillor in Scotland.[2] None of the women interviewed was openly lesbian nor did any identify themselves as experiencing a disability. Some were feminists, the majority were not.

Labour has dominated Scottish politics in the post-war period in contrast to the relative dominance of the Conservative Party at UK level.[3] All four authorities studied were Labour-controlled, although one changed to Scottish National Party (SNP) control during the course of the study. They comprised two large regional authorities – with a mixture of rural and urban wards – and two urban district councils.[4] Interviews were conducted with a total of eight Conservatives, five SNP, eleven Liberal Democrats and 29 Labour women. In comparison with their relative proportional strengths in Scottish local government as a whole, the sample slightly under-represented Labour and the SNP and over-represented the Liberal Democrats and Conservatives. In a wider UK context the sample under-represents Conservatives and over-represents Labour. Women made up between 12.5 per cent and 27 per cent of the councillors in their respective local authorities. Those interviewed included two council leaders, one civic leader, and three opposition group leaders. This is an unusually high proportion of women in leadership positions as compared with Scotland and Britain as a whole. All four case study authorities had a track record in equalities work, therefore the women councillors served on councils where gender politics was on the agenda, albeit in many cases contested. It is plausible to suggest that there is some correlation between the political presence and influence of women and the promotion of issues of gender equality.

It must also be noted, as discussed earlier, that the interviews took place within a context of sustained campaigning for constitutional change in Scotland and demands for a Scottish parliament (which has since been established). Gender balance of representation was a central component of debates, therefore we can surmise that issues of political representation may have had a higher profile in these women's minds than for their counterparts in England.

Although representative of women councillors more generally in some respects, the women interviewed differ in important ways. We cannot generalize in any straightforward way from these findings. However, we can argue that they present important suggestions in the context of women operating in a better-than-average case scenario. These women were reflecting upon their experiences and views in a general context of heightened awareness and public debate about women and representation; in councils in which women hold relatively high proportions of leadership roles; and where gender politics is reasonably high on the political agenda.

What emerges are not answers but suggestions, plausible suggestions, based on practical insights and theorizing 'from below', about new possible directions.

Don't let the facts get in the way of a good story?

It is widely acknowledged that research is to some extent shaped by the perspectives and specific social location of the researcher. This is written from the perspective of a white, middle-class, feminist academic who accepts that one of the goals of feminist research is to produce useful knowledge for women (Harding, 1987). The focus is also informed by personal commitment and activism. Therefore the research focus and the results of this study by someone else with another perspective might well have been different.

The attempt to integrate political theory with women politicians' own stories in this study brings with it the possible charge that a connection might have been assumed between women and care and then interviewees selected accordingly to show this. However, this was not the case. The women were asked to recount their personal life histories of 'getting there' and 'being there' as women in local politics; to reflect more generally upon the role of women within political structures and upon issues of political recruitment and representation at national and local levels; and to comment upon a policy case study. The interviews were organized around general themes, however, an attempt was made to allow space for women to take the interview in directions which they thought were important. Time was, however, always a tension and a restraint upon the development of a 'co-operative framework' (Kelly, 1988). However, this flexibility did lead to certain issues being highlighted in ways that had not been anticipated, such as the spontaneous raising of care as a resource as well as a burden, and the contention that women's experience as carers served as a justification for the inclusion of women in politics, and as a predictor of their impact upon the political agenda and political processes. These themes, although sometimes articulated in contradictory ways, were striking enough to merit further attention. Directed by the data, we went to the general 'care' literature where the work of Ruddick (1989), Tronto (1993) and, later, Sevenhuijsen (1998) struck a chord. In turn, the themes raised by care theorists have been more systematically compared and contrasted with the common-sense theorizing of women politicians.

New Suggestions

This book seeks to generate useful knowledge by contributing to new versions of political discourses which will promote the greater representation of women in political elites and support projects to transform politics. In particular it aims to further the project Anne Phillips (1993) has identified as 'making transparent' the needs of equality. It takes as its starting point the concrete contexts and political realities for women in the political institutions of Scotland and the UK. We argue that in order to maintain progress and to tackle underlying social and cultural issues, there is a need to search for new arguments and new understandings of women's 'place' in power politics, and new political vocabularies to express alternative visions of politics and political practices. We draw upon two key sources to find new ideas and alternatives: the recent theoretical work on the political ethics of care; and the stories of a group of women politicians.

The book also seeks to give value to women's concrete knowledge. It calls for the reassessment of care as a meaningful practice with application in the public–political sphere. A challenge to orthodox politics emerges from the women local politicians' discussions of politics, representation and power, and from the work of feminist theorists, which positions care as a central political idea. It is suggested that careful and selective use of some of these common insights could be used to promote re-invigorated discourses and political campaigning on women's more equal representation and to act as a lever for political change.

Notes

1. In Wales, this has since risen to 42 per cent. Women make up 13 per cent of members of the new Northern Ireland Assembly, which was elected in 1998. Although still relatively modest, these levels represent a marked improvement upon previous representation rates.
2. Although Scotland has a comparatively small black and ethnic population (1.3 per cent of the general population), it is grossly under-represented in

politics. This is particularly the case for black and ethnic minority women. There are no black and ethnic minority MSPs and less than a dozen councillors.

3. Scotland differs from the overall British picture in a number of respects. It has four major political parties: the Scottish Labour Party, the Scottish Conservative and Unionist Party; the Scottish Liberal Democrats and the party which stands on an independence platform, the Scottish National Party. Constitutional issues with respect to the political union of Scotland and England have been a recurring theme in Scottish politics since the nineteenth century, and home rule has been a key issue since the 1970s. Labour has been the strongest political party in both national and local Scottish politics since the late 1950s; achieving hegemonic status in certain parts of the country. Until the 1997 general election, Scottish voting trends had diverged from those of Britain as a whole: in particular, the decline of Conservative support in Scotland contrasted with their strength of support in England (Brown *et al.*, 1999b). In that period the main challenger to Labour became the Scottish National Party 'fighting on both nationalist and social democratic battlegrounds' (Brown *et al.* 1996, p. 136).

4. The study took place prior to local government reorganization in Scotland in 1996, which replaced the old two-tier system with a unitary system of all-purpose authorities.

PART I

Getting There, Being There – Making a Difference?

2

In the Way of Women: Barriers to Political Life

Why are there so few women in elected politics? Why is it so difficult for most women (and also some groups of men) to get involved – and stay involved – in parliamentary and local government politics? What, to use Cynthia Cockburn's phrase, stands in the way of women? This chapter considers existing explanations of women's relative absence from politics at different levels in Britain. It seeks to reinforce the message from empirical studies that barriers are complex and inter-related. In particular, it focuses upon the role of women's assumed and actual caring responsibilities and its interconnection with other factors which together constrain and disadvantage women as both potential candidates for elected office and as political actors within institutions. As noted earlier, the 1990s marked real progress for women. We seek to summarize the current position for women and future prospects in terms of further action. These developments are considered within the context of system-wide and party political factors. In addition to existing analyses we ask to what extent the scope for political action is shaped by dominant understandings of equality and fairness.

Models and Frameworks

First, we turn to look at explanatory models and frameworks which have been developed to study the complex processes of political

23

recruitment. Pippa Norris and Joni Lovenduski (1995) have developed a multi-dimensional model of comparative political recruitment process which they used to examine the interaction of gender, race and class in recruitment to the British House of Commons in the 1990s. They identify the three levels at which constraints or barriers to women may operate: *systematic*, *party political* and *individual*.

At the *systematic* level are factors which relate to legal system, the electoral system, the party system and the general structure of political opportunities. *Party political factors* relate to issues such as party organization, recruitment practices, party rules and party ideology and traditions. *Individual recruitment factors* relate to factors which may have an impact upon the recruitment of individual candidates.[1] These include individual resources and motivations of aspirants (supply-side factors) and attitudes and practices of the selectors or gatekeepers (demand-side factors). These levels correspond with Alice Brown and Yvonne Galligan's typology of macro, meso and micro level barriers (1995).

Supply and demand models

The individual political recruitment process works as a ladder with potential barriers at each stage of the process: at the first stage, people have to be available and willing to enter the pool of eligible candidates; at the second stage, hopefuls or aspirants have to get the support from the selectorate and other gatekeepers; and at the third stage they have to win the votes of the electorate (Norris, 1994, pp. 86–7). Norris and Lovenduski are among a number of people who use models of supply and demand to analyse factors affecting the recruitment process at the individual level (see also Randall, 1987). The supply side relates to the availability of eligible and aspirant women and the demand side relates to their recruitment. On the demand side is placed the selectorate, those within political parties who are empowered to choose candidates. Demand-side factors involve formal and informal criteria and expectations. For example, in the British context both party service and, increasingly, local government service are seen as important qualifying criteria for prospective parliamentary candidates.

Vicky Randall categorizes supply-side factors under general headings of socialization; and situational and structural factors

(1987, pp. 122–43). Socialization constraints refer to the effect of sex-role stereotyping and other socialization which may inhibit women from becoming aspirants, in particular a psychological conflict between domestic and political roles (Githens and Prestage, 1977). This is deemed to inhibit the development of politically desirable attributes such as confidence and ambition.

Situational factors include the impact of family responsibilities, particularly motherhood, on availability, together with the related constraint of time and lack of control over time. Some researchers have posited women's time constraints and unpredictability of time demands, as reasons for their preference for non-institutional forms of political participation (Lee, 1976; Hernes and Voje, 1980). Responsibility for children may be less of a barrier to participation in local politics than in national politics (Phillips, 1980; Randall, 1987).

Structural factors relate to the position of women within educational and professional opportunity structures, and the potential impact this has upon eligibility criteria. For example, if women are found in smaller proportions in influential brokerage professions from which many (particularly national) politicians are drawn, then this would decrease their chances of entering the pool of potential candidates.

Demand-side factors discussed by Randall come under the headings of institutional barriers: including electoral systems, traditions of appropriate occupational backgrounds, traditions of long political apprenticeships, the ethos and organization of political institutions at each level, and finally, direct discrimination in terms of expression of male prejudice and power (Randall, 1987, p. 132).

Recruitment in Practice: National Politics

Different pathways to national political office exist within different political systems. Each system has its own set of political opportunities which structure the composition of political elites and individual chances of success. For example, within the British context a 'narrow ladder' exists which is rarely deviated from, in which political careers begin with constituency office, and then standardly progress to local government experience, then parliamentary candidate to backbench MP and perhaps eventually a ministerial post (Norris, 1997, p. 4). In contrast, federalist systems such as the United States offer diverse pathways to political power with the opportunity for sideways moves between for instance, House and Senate as well as vertical moves between state and federal levels; and, in addition, brisk two-way traffic between elected office and careers as lobbyists and so on.[2] A comparative account of legislative recruitment covering 19 advanced industrial democracies concluded that, whatever the differences in the institutional and cultural elements of political opportunity structures, and the variation in selector demands and candidate supply from system to system, the under-representation of women was a persistent feature, together with the disproportionate representation of better educated, more affluent, middle-aged males usually from the majority ethnic group (Norris, 1997).

Focusing upon Britain, the electoral system is an important systematic factor in shaping patterns of political opportunities. Elections to different levels of government in mainland Britain have traditionally been conducted using a single member constituency, 'first past the post' (FPTP) majoritarian system which comparative research has demonstrated disadvantages women candidates. First, the opportunity to fight winnable seats is restricted in a majoritarian system which advantages sitting MPs, this is known as the 'incumbency problem'. Second, because the system means that 'the winner takes all', selectors are encouraged to choose standard or 'ideal' candidates who have traditionally been white males, rather than risk non-standard candidates such as women (Norris, 1994; Eagle and Lovenduski, 1998).

However, since the election of a Labour government in 1997, a number of new systems have been implemented and other reforms to the electoral system have been proposed. At time of writing, elections at Westminster and local government levels were still conducted by FPTP. The newly established Scottish Parliament and National Assembly of Wales were elected in 1999 using a modified majoritarian system, the Additional Member System (AMS). Under AMS a certain proportion of seats are elected using FPTP and a certain proportion of seats, known as Additional Members, are allocated through a list system to achieve greater proportionality in terms of the relationship between party support and number of seats gained. The Northern Ireland Assembly is elected using the Single Transferable Vote. The elections to the Parliament of the European Union were conducted using a multi-member constituency form of proportional representation for the first time in 1999. This presents the current framework within which the recruitment process takes place.

Norris and Lovenduski's (1995) survey of candidates in the 1992 general election, the British Candidate Study (BCS), is the most comprehensive British political recruitment study to date. Although the majority of candidates and MPs believed they personally had been treated fairly in the selection process, there were commonplace perceptions that political parties placed barriers in the way of women. Candidates were asked to rank possible reasons for the under-representation of women as MPs. Just over half (55 per cent) of the candidates thought that parties did not give women opportunities to stand, a demand-side explanation. The most popular explanation, however, was that not enough women put themselves forward (cited by 73 per cent of responding candidates), which is a supply-side factor. The third most common reason suggested was that women lacked the confidence to stand, a factor which also relates to supply.

Norris and Lovenduski remain sceptical about demand-side explanations of women's under-representation at Westminster (1995, pp. 14–15; see also Chapters 6 and 7), arguing that while explanations of selector gender discrimination are 'pervasive', only rarely are they substantiated in research. What they term the 'social-bias' outcome of the selection procedure may be attributed to two potential forms of discrimination operated by the selectorate: direct and imputed. Direct discrimination is defined as the positive or negative judgement of aspirants on the basis of characteristics seen as common to their group, rather than as individuals. 'Party selectors may rely upon background characteristics as a proxy measure of abilities and character; prejudice functions as an information short-cut' (1995, p. 14). Imputed discrimination describes a process whereby individual selectors without personal prejudice nevertheless do not select certain sorts of candidates because of the perceived electoral disadvantages of such a choice. For example, it may be believed that picking a female candidate or a black candidate in certain constituencies would lose votes.

If demand-side factors were significant, then one would expect to see marked differences between the characteristics of applicants and the characteristics of those who are selected as candidates. This was not the case, instead 'the most striking finding was that in most respects candidates were very similar to the total pool of applicants'

27

(Norris and Lovenduski, 1995, p. 122). Their survey of gatekeepers' attitudes revealed little discrimination by constituency party members against women candidates, and members expressed support for the idea of more women in parliament. Although women were less likely to score as highly as men in terms of campaigning qualities, Norris and Lovenduski argue that the difference was not great, which leads them to conclude: 'There is no evidence that gender stereotypes necessarily disadvantage women candidates; and members believe nowadays women are vote winners' (1995, p. 141).[3]

Instead, in line with earlier studies by Bochel and Denver (1983) and Rush (1969), they conclude that supply-side explanations, which contend that too few women come forward, are more plausible. Supply-side explanations focus on candidate resources (such as time, money, political connections, educational qualifications, experience, skills and career flexibility) and motivational factors (such as ambition, drive, confidence, stamina, dedication and interest) which are needed to sustain aspiring candidates on the 'risky, gruelling and unglamorous' pursuit of a political career (Norris and Lovenduski, 1995, p. 162). Motivation can be understood in terms of individual psychological factors but is also influenced by the institutional framework and political 'rules of the game' within which individuals operate (Norris, 1997). The vertical and horizontal segregation of women in employment, which disadvantages them in terms of access to high-status jobs and incomes, and their traditional domestic responsibilities which place constraints on their time, both impact adversely upon their 'political capital'. Norris and Lovenduski cite the importance of brokerage professions – those jobs which provide the connections, skills, status and flexibility, which benefit those pursuing political ambition. They see the relative absence of women in professions such as law, public administration, private sector management, academia and teaching, or their relatively low status within respective career hierarchies, as the key to understanding patterns of under-representation for women (and similarly for the under-representation of members of minority ethnic groups). Women do not have as much access as men to the 'traditional routes to political life' (Norris and Lovenduski, 1995). As Lovenduski points out: 'The argument is simple but the insight is important. To run for parliament an individual must have financial security, public networks, social status, policy experience, technical and social skills' (1996, p. 15).

Norris and Lovenduski accept that there is interaction between the demand and supply sides, for example, potential aspirants may fail to present themselves because of their perception of prejudice, the complexity of procedures or anticipated failure. However, there is little substantive discussion of the possible scale of what can be termed 'rational absenteeism', or the 'discouraged aspirant' that is, potential aspirants at various stages who do not present themselves. Brown and Galligan (1995) note that these findings counter previous research which has forwarded direct and indirect discrimination in the selection process of candidates as a key explanation for women's under-representation. They argue that, 'The findings sit somewhat at odds with the authors' three-dimensional explanatory model of recruitment; and with their previous conclusions about the complex and interactive nature of the recruitment process.' (1995, p. 3).

A qualitative study of women political activists in Scotland (Brown, 1996) found a combination of individual supply factors and certain demand, party and systematic factors operated as barriers to discourage women from pursuing political careers at Westminster. At the systematic level women identified the parliament's location and working practices as significant inhibitors for potential MPs from 'peripheral' regions and nations. The electoral system and the adversarial nature of the party system were also seen to work against women. Women activists considered that a macho adversarial political culture dominated both the Westminster and Scottish political arenas (1996, p. 33).

At the political party level, formal rules and informal practices were seen as alienating and discriminatory, although there were perceived differences between the parties. At the individual level, family responsibilities were viewed as a key supply factor. Traditional attitudes and gender-role stereotypes were seen to operate as both supply and demand factors, 'traditional attitudes towards women as home makers and men as decision makers continue to influence the expectations of both women and men' (Brown, 1996, pp. 31–2). In terms of personal resources, lack of confidence was highlighted as a crucial barrier. In terms of demand-side explanations, there were perceptions of discriminatory attitudes and practices by party gatekeepers, men and some women (particularly Conservative women). Again, response was conditioned by party. The survey reinforces Norris and Lovenduski's multi-dimensional model. It also highlighted the importance of political context in a particular country and the specific factors operating within the different political parties.

Recruitment in Practice: Local Politics

The previous section focused upon possible constraints operating at national level. Although women have traditionally had a stronger presence at local council level than at parliamentary level, they are still relatively under-represented. This relative absence is both an issue in its own right and also has implications for recruitment to devolved and UK political office. Local government is an increasingly important route to parliamentary careers. Vallance noted the importance of local government experience for women MPs in the 1970s, but by the 1990s it had become a key qualifying criterion.

The proportion of women councillors varies according to type of authority, its size, location, socio-economic character and political composition. A recent review of earlier studies (Brown *et al.*, 1999a) identified a range of demand- and supply-side factors at various levels, many of which parallel barriers identified at national political level. There was no evidence of voter bias (Studlar and Welch, 1987) although different studies have reached differing conclusions about the existence and degree of selectorate bias.

Most studies acknowledge that the main barriers to women's participation are structural and relate to the position of women in society, their domestic and caring responsibilities and cultural expectations and attitudes in respect of their role. Family responsibilities are seen as a major barrier to women's participation (Shaul, 1982; McGrew and Bristow, 1984; Martlew *et al.*, 1985; Barry, 1991). Hills (1983) stressed the importance of the role of lifestyle factors which may affect opportunities for participation. Lifestyle factors will include domestic and family responsibilities which may constrain participation in politics. Thus women's recruitment will be influenced by family attitudes and flexibility. Traditional perceptions of male and female roles were cited as inhibiting factors by Martlew *et al.* (1985), where politics was seen as a man's right but as a hobby for women. Caring responsibilities were identified as a major barrier for women councillors in Scotland (SLGIU, 1995) and in Northern Ireland (Wilford *et al.*, 1993). The central role of family life and the influence of both Catholic and

Protestant Churches in reinforcing the traditional role of women were seen as key inhibiting factors in respect of women's representation in Northern Ireland and the Republic of Ireland (Potter, 1998).

In terms of party political factors, a number of studies have shown that political parties, trades unions and local councils have formal rules and procedures and cultural norms and practices which operate to exclude and alienate women (Martlew *et al.*,1985; Halford, 1988; 1992; Cockburn, 1991). Brown (1996) argues that these political cultural factors can operate as both supply- and demand-side factors: on the demand-side, masculinist cultures and practices undermine women and thus reinforce under-confidence (a key supply explanation). Martlew *et al.* (1985) concluded that the 'macho basis of institutions' may deter women from entering politics and that anticipation of discrimination acts as a barrier to women presenting themselves as aspirants in the first place.

In addition to instances of direct discrimination, indirect discrimination has been identified in the form of the 'ideal candidate syndrome'. Chapman (1993) has concluded that the recruitment practices for the selection of local candidates within the main political parties can be seen as gender-specific. Her study demonstrates that each party has a set of recruitment criteria which disadvantages women. In each case, women's profiles resemble those of 'losing men'. The Conservative Party uses a 'standard recruitment' procedure of choosing people of higher socio-economic status. Women are disadvantaged in that they are less likely to be found in the category of highly educated and high occupational status. The Labour Party operates a 'modified recruitment' procedure where party organizational experience and socio-economic status are significant criteria. Labour Party selectors are more likely to choose from both high economic status and lower manufacturing and managerial occupations, both of which tend to exclude women. Studlar and Welch (1987) note that once selected to contest an election, women candidates are more likely to face an incumbent and less likely to be an incumbent, which further reduces their chance of success.

In terms of resources, family support is seen as crucial to women both when fighting elections and once they become councillors (Martlew *et al.*, 1985; Barron *et al.*, 1991). Juggling the triple demands of family, work and politics is seen as a major issue for those women considering entering local politics and remains a key problem for women as candidates and as councillors (Hills, 1983; Martlew *et al.*, 1985). A recent exit poll of English councillors (LGMB, 1998) summarizes the main reasons reported for councillors standing down. Overall, 'personal reasons' were cited as the most important reason for councillors standing down at 43.7 per cent, followed by 'competing work demands' at 20.4 per cent, 'competing family related demands' at 13.9 per cent, 'experience as a councillor' at 10.8 per cent and 'erosion of local government influence' at 11.4 per cent. In terms of gender, the most significant variations were the greater emphasis placed by male councillors on the 'erosion of local government influence' (13.4 per cent of men as compared with 5.5 per cent of women) and the relative importance placed by women councillors upon 'competing family related demands'; one in five women cited this as the most important reason for leaving politics as compared with one in ten men. A Scottish study found that, once elected, the proportion of men and women serving for only one term was the same. The most common constraints noted in terms of continuing to serve as councillors were balancing employment and council duties, and balancing council and family responsibilities. Men were more likely than women to see employment as a problem (36 per cent men to 21 per cent women) and negative financial impact (20 per cent men to 7 per cent women), while women identified family needs (20 per cent women to 13 per cent men) and being part of a minority party group (16 per cent women to 12 per cent men) (Bochel and Bochel, 1996). In addition, some research points to the ongoing process of constraint and exclusion which leaves women with less time for the politicking, the building and maintenance of networks of political support which sustain male political careers (see Shaul, 1982).

Common issues in practice

Barriers at different levels have been identified which impact upon women's access to politics. Other factors have been highlighted which serve to disadvantage women once they have gained a presence in decision-making institutions such as parliaments and councils. These work to limit women's influence and agency and, ultimately, may contribute to women leaving political office. While the preceding review demonstrates that there are differences dependent on the political context in different parts of the UK and at different levels of government, and the specific factors operating within the different political parties, there are also similarities and common links. The position of women in society, their domestic and caring responsibilities and cultural expectations and stereotypical attitudes in respect of their role figure prominently in explanations for the relative absence of women in politics at both national and local levels. Clearly, there are interconnections between structural and individual factors which operate in complex ways.

The barriers to women's participation in electoral politics are complex, which implies that action is needed on a number of levels: systematic, party political and individual. Additionally, long-term remedies would seem to require fundamental structural changes to gender relations and the gendered division of labour, on the one hand, and to political institutions, on the other. We next turn to consider proposals for change and progress made to date. Although the issue of women's under-representation has grown in prominence over the past twenty years or so, the 1990s was the key decade in terms of concerted action.

What Is to Be Done? What Has Been Done?

What is to be done? What measures and programmes of action are needed to remedy the under-representation of women in politics? What has been achieved so far? We consider the ways in which political parties have responded to demands for change. Political parties are the main actors in liberal democratic systems. As such, one would look to them as major agents and channels for action. Debates about what is to be done take place within political and organizational frameworks; they are also crucially shaped and constrained by existing systematic, structural and party political contexts and ideological hegemonies. In addition to surveying existing literature and policy proposals, we consider the ways in which dominant understandings of the nature, needs and limits of equality impact upon demands for action and upon political support for various reform strategies.

Given the complexity of the barriers which work to exclude women from politics, it is likely that a range of measures is needed. These may involve reforms to selection procedures which aim to make them fairer and more transparent and to ensure that equal opportunities are taken into consideration. Measures to promote women may involve active encouragement, the targeting of potential women candidates and the establishment of informal or formal mentoring and shadowing schemes. They may also include 'soft' or 'weak' positive action measures such as 'women-only' training or the provision of resources to sponsor individual women. Further along the continuum, although still classed as relatively weak, are positive action measures such as guaranteed places for women on shortlists and balanced selection panels. 'Strong' positive action measures involve mandatory quotas such as all-women shortlists, constituency 'twinning' and the 'zipping' or 'alternating' of female and male candidates on regional lists.[4] Experience in the UK and elsewhere demonstrates that 'strong' positive action measures are most likely to guarantee results (see, for example, Russell, 2000). In this regard, Russell (ibid., p. 14) argues that British political parties have been relatively late in adopting positive action for women compared with many of their European and international counterparts. It is also noticeable that the willingness of individual political parties in Britain to use positive action measures, particularly 'strong' positive action, remains limited.

How might we map the contemporary ideological and structural terrain upon which the under-representation of women in politics is discussed and tackled within the (mainland) British context?[5] Programmes of action, and their attendant justifications, are influenced by factors at system level, party level and individual level.

Political Parties and Models of Change

At the *system level*, the legal framework of equal opportunities presents difficulties. Sex discrimination and other equalities legislation in the UK are rooted in liberal ideology, with a focus on the individual and the protection of rights and enhancement of individual opportunities. Compared to strong 'affirmative action' policies on gender equality which can be found in other countries, British legislation is limited and weak. Affirmative action in employment or access to education as understood in US contexts is classed as positive discrimination and is illegal in UK law. Although, until recently, political candidacy was not understood to constitute employment under sex discrimination or race discrimination legislation, these definitions have in part shaped what is seen to be acceptable.[6]

At the *party political* level, influential factors include: the electoral or social salience of the issue of representation, party–state relations, party rhetoric, party organization, levels of internal debate and feminist activism and the political rules of the game. All political parties have made public statements about the need to encourage more women into political office, particularly to the Westminster Parliament. So the 'problem' of women's under-representation is recognized at a symbolic level. However, after that, parties have varied widely in the types of measures, if any, they have supported and the underlying reasonings for action (or their inaction).

Alice Brown and Yvonne Galligan (1993) stress the importance of party ideology in determining party strategy for women's representation. They note three types of political management concerning issues of women's representation: *promotional*, *active intervention* and *status quo*. Promotional strategies involve elite support, policies to encourage participation, the provision of resources and sponsorship of individual women; active intervention concerns the deliberate modification of party rules and structures to increase the representation of women, for example through statutory quotas; and status quo refers to resistance to change (1993, p. 167).

In their study of action on women's representation in political parties in Scotland and the Republic of Ireland they found that there was a broad pattern whereby liberal-orientated parties favoured promotional strategies; Left and radical parties – with a tradition of economic and social intervention – favoured active intervention, while parties of the Right tended to adopt the third strategy of status quo. In addition to matching strategy to ideology, Brown and Galligan introduce secondary explanatory factors such as processes of party modernization or changing patterns of party competition which can act to reinforce, or modify the pattern. For example, in the Republic of Ireland, they note growing support within Fianna Fáil for interventionist policies. In Britain, perceptions of electoral pressure have led the Conservative Party in Britain to become increasingly responsive in terms of promotional strategies (1993, p. 187).

Ideas and action

Parties differ considerably in their understanding of representation and equality and in their commitment to action. The notion of merit, allied to formal equality of opportunity (that is the absence of discriminatory rules and procedures), is particularly strong within the Conservative Party. It is argued that women of talent have a fair chance of success (Lovenduski and Norris, 1993; Brown *et al.*, 1999b). There is implacable opposition to positive action in terms of mandatory quotas, although there was a voluntary target, which failed miserably, of fielding equal numbers of male and female candidates in the 1997 general election.[7] It seems likely that there will be no new women candidates selected to fight Conservative 'inheritor' or 'winnable' seats in the 2001 general election.[8]

There is also a strong traditional 'difference' strand in Conservative thinking, which equates with Duverger's notion of feminine ideology (1955), which gives women party members and organizations considerable influence in limited areas, particularly matters to do with the family. Labour politician Clare Short has contrasted the 'women-friendly' image of the Conservative Party at the local level with Labour's local face which she calls 'massively more male, bureaucratic and off putting'. She sees the visibility of 'efficient, able and articulate' middle-aged women in local Conservative organizations as one of the reasons why 'the Conservative Party has a smaller number of women MPs, has opposed social reforms that have often benefited women and yet retains the women's vote' (Short, 1996, pp. 25–6). However, there is a tension between Conservatism, which stresses women's traditional role and neo-liberalism, within which equal rights to compete – particularly economically – are paramount (Campbell, 1987; Lovenduski and Randall, 1993).

The Liberal Democrats, and the nationalist parties, the Scottish National Party and Plaid Cymru, support equality of opportunity rather than equality of outcome. The parties stress the ideal of gender neutrality and argue that all individuals, including parents, will have a greater opportunity to participate in politics when a combination of electoral and institutional reforms are undertaken. There are women activists in all three parties campaigning for equality of representation, although they are usually less vocal then their Labour counterparts. Some limited or 'weak' positive action measures have been implemented, including women's training initiatives and, in some instances, 'balanced' shortlists.

The Labour Party, with a political goal of seeking social and economic equality as well as formal political equality and interventionist and redistributive traditions, goes furthest of all the major parties in moving towards equality of outcome. Activists successfully lobbied for a series of 'soft' positive action measures and voluntary targets for improving the proportion of women MPs and women office holders within the party in the 1980s and 1990s. Frustrated by the slow pace of change they succeeded in persuading the party to adopt 'hard' positive action in the form of the controversial 'all-women' shortlists in the run-up to the 1997 general election.

In 1993 a policy was agreed whereby all-women shortlists were to be introduced in contests for half of all 'inheritor' seats (where the sitting MP had stood down) and half of Labour's target seats (marginal seats held by other parties which Labour assessed were winnable). It began to be implemented in 1994–5 in the run-up to the 1997 general election in the teeth of bitter opposition and resentment in certain sections of the party. In 1996 an Industrial Tribunal in Leeds ruled that all-women shortlists were unlawful discrimination after a disgruntled male aspirant brought a case. Opponents of positive action did so on the grounds of 'merit', 'choice' and 'equality'. Until then it had not been thought that political candidate selection and recruitment came within the remit of the Sex Discrimination Act. Despite legal opinion that it was likely the judgment would be overturned on appeal, the party leadership chose not to challenge the ruling and dropped the policy, although selections already made under the system stood (Eagle and Lovenduski, 1998).

Since the early 1980s all the major parties have made some attempt to improve their performance and tackle the issue. Pressure has come from a number of different sources. The social salience of the issue has increased over the past twenty years or so and opinion polls and other social surveys now consistently register high degrees of public support for more women in politics and support for parties to take special measures to increase their numbers. The establishment of an all-party 300 Group (which campaigned to get 300 women MPs into the Westminster Parliament by 2000) acted as a lobby and a training, publicity and resource group. Crucially, feminists who had first moved into mainstream politics, particularly the Labour Party, after 1979 organized around the issue, and built and maintained internal pressure (Wainwright, 1987; Lovenduski and Randall, 1993). In the 1990s, the issue of gender balance in politics achieved prominence at national level, largely through feminist campaigns within the Labour Party. In Scotland, the issue of women's under-representation became a high-profile element of the campaign for constitutional reform and involved a broad coalition of female political activists, trade unionists and other feminist and women's groups. Campaigners linked arguments to the Labour Party's wider programme of modernization, the need to appeal to women voters, constitutional reform and social inclusion, and the need to develop policies responsive to different life experiences (Perrigo, 1995; Brown, 1998).

Justice, equality and political parties

A systematic factor seldom explicitly addressed within the literature is the shared legacy of dominant liberal democratic discourses of justice and equality. Although party stances differ, there are still significant commonalties, most notably notions of equality, which minimize difference and stress equal treatment. These notions are contested most within the Labour Party where positions can be markedly polarized. Similarly, the notion that impartial criteria and merit play the most important role in candidate selection is shared across the party lines. Equal opportunities, rather than equal outcomes, remain the predominant focus, and positive action is still largely characterized as 'unfair privileges'. It is opposed by the Conservatives and is a difficult and contested notion within the Liberal Democrat Party, the Scottish National Party and Plaid Cymru. Although it has gained greater acceptance within the Labour Party, it is still opposed and resented by sections, including some women candidates and MPs.

The 1997 general election

The 1997 general election saw the number of women in the House of Commons double from the 1992 figure of 60 to a total of 120. At 18.2 per cent, the representation of women at Westminster reached an all-time high and brought Britain into line with many other European Union member countries. However, it still fell far short of equal representation and well below the level of women's representation in Scandinavian countries at around 40 per cent. All but 18 of the female MPs were elected from the Labour Party (including the Speaker, Betty Boothroyd). Women accounted for almost one-quarter of Labour's MPs as compared with only 7.8 per cent of Conservative MPs and 6.5 per cent of Liberal Democrat members (see Table 2.1).

Table 2.1   House of Commons by party and gender, 1997 general election

Party	Women	Men	Total	Women as % of total
Labour	101	317	418	24.2
Conservative	13	152	165	7.8
Liberal Democrat	3	43	46	6.5
UUP	0	10	10	0.0
SNP	2	4	6	33.3
Plaid Cymru	0	4	4	0.0
SDLP	0	3	3	0.0
DUP	0	2	2	0.0
Sinn Fein	0	2	2	0.0
UKU	0	1	1	0.0
Independent	0	1	1	0.0
Speaker	1	0	1	100.0
Total	120	539	659	18.2

Source: Russell (2000)

The results can also be seen in terms of different party political responses to positive action. Eagle and Lovenduski argue that the dramatic increase of women MPs after the 1997 general election was not a result of Labour's landslide victory but instead largely the outcome of the party's controversial all-women shortlist policy. The proportion of Labour women MPs trebled. Without any such measures, the representation of both Conservative and Liberal Democrat women MPs actually fell. The success of the all-women shortlist policy, although only partially implemented, was demonstrated by the election results. Eagle and Lovenduski note that women candidates fared better in the target seats (50 per cent) and safe seats (34.4 per cent) than they did in other types of seats where no mechanism was in place. For example, they were only 16.7 per cent of women candidates in 'surprise gain' seats (1998, p. 9). There is also a large variation by region which may indicate entrenched resistance in some areas. The proportion of female Labour MPs varied from 48 per cent in the South West to 16 per cent in Scotland and only 12 per cent in Wales.

The Scottish Parliament and the Welsh Assembly

The creation of a Scottish Parliament and a National Assembly for Wales has provided opportunities for new institutions and processes to be designed which do not disadvantage women from the outset. The understanding that women needed to be in at the start was instrumental in campaigns for gender balance, most notably in Scotland.

There were changes at systematic level: the electoral system introduced elements of proportionality as discussed earlier in the chapter; modern working conditions and practices and 'family-friendly' policies were built in to the design of the new parliament and assembly (see, for example, CSG, 1998). The final report of the Scottish Constitutional Convention (1995)[9] included an electoral contract committed to gender equality signed by the Labour Party and the Liberal Democrats. The contract, which had been brokered by women activists in the two parties and by the umbrella women's organization, the Women's Co-ordination Group, committed the parties to accepting the principle that there should be an equal number of men and women members of the first Scottish Parliament. To achieve this, parties also committed themselves to selecting and fielding an equal number of male and female candidates; ensuring that candidates were fairly distributed; using an Additional Member System; and ensuring that the size of the parliament was large enough to facilitate effective democratic government (Brown, 1996).

All the Scottish political parties, with the exception of the Conservatives, offered some sort of training for potential women candidates in the run-up to the selections, in some cases with child care provided. The parties also introduced more professional recruitment procedures. Labour 'breaking radically with past practice' invited potential candidates to self-nominate. Model job descriptions and person specifications were drawn up outlining the skills needed for the role of MSP. A selections board, including independent advisers, was established and criteria-led selection procedures were undertaken to draw up a panel of candidates from which local constituency parties made their selections. The SNP also introduced self-nomination and used an assessment weekend to draw up a final approved list from which local constituencies were invited to select. The Liberal Democrats were encouraged by the party leadership to field an equal number of male and female candidates on their shortlists. The Conservative Party drew up an approved list from which local constituency associations made their choice (Brown *et al.*, 1999a, pp. 25–6). The tone was set by the government's White Paper *Scotland's Parliament* (Scottish Office, 1997) which emphasized the importance of equal opportunities for all, including women, members of minority ethnic communities and disabled people, and urged all political parties offering candidates for election to bear equal opportunities in mind in their internal candidate selection procedures.

It had been anticipated that the Labour Party, the Liberal Democrats and the SNP would all adopt some form of 'strong' positive action to ensure gender balance in their selection of candidates in the first-past-the-post side of the elections and/or the 'additional' seats in the first elections to the Scottish Parliament. In the end, however, the Scottish Labour Party was alone (of the major parties) in adopting a specific mechanism designed to produce gender balance. Under the new electoral system, the Labour Party stood to gain most of its seats via the FPTP or constituency elections unlike the other parties who stood to make their gains through the regional or 'top up' lists. It therefore adopted a 'pairing' or 'twinning' system for constituency selections. Neighbouring constituencies were paired together (taking into account various comparability factors including winnability of the seats) for the purposes of selection with members in two constituencies voting together to select a woman and a man to be the candidates for the two seats. The woman who received the highest number of votes on the list of women was selected to stand for one seat, and similarly the man who received the highest number of votes on the list of men was selected to stand for the other.

The Scottish Liberal Democrats had intended to invite two men and two women to stand for selection in each parliamentary constituency (a balanced shortlist) with local members determining the gender balance for the constituency elections. The party then intended to use a 'zipping' mechanism whereby women and men would be alternatively selected from the party list to redress any gender imbalance at constituency level. Despite the support of Scottish Liberal Democrat leaders, the policy was defeated at the party conference in 1998 on the grounds that it could be open to legal challenge. It was argued that the only secure way to ensure that any positive action mechanism was not subject to legal challenge was for the government to amend the Sex Discrimination Act to exempt the selection process of political parties. As Brown notes, campaigners also attempted to get a clause inserted in the Scotland Bill which would also provide such an exemption. Neither of these proposals were accepted by the government, and in these circumstances, it was the majority view at the Liberal Democrat conference that they were not prepared to endorse this policy until legal immunity was guaranteed. The formal policy of the party was still stated to be in line with the Electoral Agreement agreed with the Labour Party within the Scottish Constitutional Convention (Brown, 1999).

The SNP leadership had proposed to adopt a positive action measures in the form of a 'zipping' system on their regional 'top up' lists to ensure gender balance. However, these plans were also narrowly defeated at the party conference in 1998. Despite the setback, the party leadership continued to encourage women to stand and to be placed in favourable positions on party lists.

The Conservative and Unionist Party maintained its opposition to any mechanism for ensuring an equal number of male and female candidates. They argued that they would select candidates on the basis of merit, regardless of sex, race or religion.

In Wales, a similar twinning system was adopted by the Labour Party despite internal dissent and the threat by a male party member to take legal action. The Liberal Democrats used balanced candidate shortlists in constituencies but did not adopt any other form of positive action. Plaid Cymru rejected proposals to implement a twinning mechanism for constituency contests. Instead it used the additional member lists to attempt to partially correct under-representation in constituencies by selecting a woman to head up each of the five regional lists (Russell, 2000). The Conservatives opposed any form of positive action.

The Scottish and Welsh results

The first elections to the Scottish Parliament and the National Assembly for Wales marked new heights in terms of women's representation: 37 per cent of Scottish MSPs and 40 per cent of Welsh Assembly members. The results reflected the relative strengths of respective parties and also their stance upon positive action. In Scotland, the Labour Party was the only party to use positive action mechanisms, and the only party to achieve gender balance. Its strength as majority party in both Scotland and Wales ensured that overall proportions were high. The nationalist parties in both countries also achieved substantial proportions of women: 43 per cent in the case of the SNP and 35 per cent in the case of Plaid Cymru. Only 12 per cent of Liberal Democrat MSPs were women in Scotland although women were luckier in Wales where they made up three out of the six Liberal Democrat AMs. Women were 17 per cent of Conservative MSPs in Scotland whereas in Wales not a single Conservative women was elected. The difference between the overall proportions reflects the poorer showing of the Liberal Democrats and the Conservatives in Wales compared with Scotland (see Tables 2.2 and 2.3).

Table 2.2 Scottish Parliament by party and gender, 1999 election

Party	Women	Men	Total	Women as % of total
Labour	28	28	56	50.0
SNP	15	20	35	42.9
Con	3	15	18	16.7
Lib Dem	2	15	17	11.8
Independent	0	1	1	0.0
Scottish Socialist	0	1	1	0.0
Scottish Green Party	0	1	1	0.0
Total	48	81	129	37.2

Table 2.3 Welsh National Assembly by party and gender, 1999 election

Party	Women	Men	Total	Women as % of total
Labour	15	13	28	53.6
Plaid Cymru	6	11	17	35.3
Con	0	9	9	0.0
Lib Dem	3	3	6	50.0
Total	24	36	60	40.0

Local government and women's representation

At the local level, there has been comparatively little activism to date on women's political representation. This is in spite of a rich tradition of community politics and social movement activism on gender and other equality issues and the fact that, in many respects, local government has been at the forefront of equalities work in the UK.

A recent report on the social representativeness of councillors in British local government (Brown *et al.*, 1999) summarized the positions of the main political parties with respect to options for reform. While all the main political parties (Labour, Conservative, Liberal Democrat, SNP and Plaid Cymru) had stated their concern to address issues of under-representation and their desire to attract a greater diversity of candidates, specific proposals had been less forthcoming. The Labour Party had been most proactive with its Project 99, which included measures such as: targeting rank-and-file party members, in particular women, young people and members of minority groups, to invite them to consider putting themselves forward; taster events, training and more detailed information to explain the role of being a councillor; self-nomination; improved information about the selection and recruitment procedures; and general improvements in the selection procedure, including the training of selectors in the use of model assessment criteria (Brown *et al.*, 1999a, pp. 26–9). Mechanisms to ensure that there was at least one female councillor per branch were considered by the Labour Party but abandoned after the Leeds Industrial Tribunal decision in 1996 (Eagle and Lovenduski, 1998).

In 1999 there were elections to all local councils in Scotland and

Wales and some authorities in England. Initial impressions suggest that there has been little change in overall patterns. Details of the social composition of English and Welsh councils will not be confirmed until the next census or survey is undertaken. In Scotland, despite the intense interest in gender balance in the Scottish Parliamentary elections – which took place on the same day – the proportion of women councillors remained virtually unchanged at 22.6 per cent. No party or council came close to achieving gender balance. In the case of Labour, the proportion of female councillors actually fell slightly from 23.7 per cent in 1995 to 21.8 per cent in 1999. In addition, less than a dozen of Scotland's 1,222 councillors were from minority ethnic backgrounds (SLGIU, 1999). This provides a cautionary tale and illustrates that gains made at one level of governance may not necessarily translate into gains across the board.

Looking at the overall picture at each level, we can see the importance of a number of different factors in changing the structure of opportunities within which women operate. First, sustained pressure by feminist activists within parties and in the wider women's movement has been crucial to maintain momentum. Second, the adoption of 'strong' positive action measures by at least one major party is required in such a process. Improvements in the overall representation of women at Westminster, the Scottish Parliament and the Welsh Assembly have all been primarily due to 'strong' positive action measures – all-women shortlists in selected seats and the 'twinning' of constituency seats – introduced by the Labour Party, the majority party in each setting. Third, the particular pattern of party competition and systematic factors plays a part. In Scotland and Wales, the nationalist parties (SNP in Scotland and Plaid Cymru in Wales) managed to achieve good proportions of women elected members. In each case, as the main contender to Labour, neither party could afford to appear to be lukewarm on the issue of gender balance. The regional lists and the differing logic of choice which operates in list systems – that is, the need to be seen to present a balanced ticket – also undoubtedly helped activists and the party leaderships to deliver. Finally, systematic factors such as constitutional change offer opportunities for targeted activism.

Progress: 'High Time or High Tide'?

Progress has been made but what of future prospects? Eagle and Lovenduski have a nicely turned question, which we might repeat here: do the achievements of the late 1990s mark 'high time or high tide' for women's representation? (Eagle and Lovenduski, 1998). Will progress be reinforced or reversed? The form and nature of change so far may prove to be particularly susceptible to the two steps forward, one step back character of much of the history of women's struggle for equality.

A significant systematic inhibitor is the legal context within which political parties act. At the time of writing there was uncertainty and confusion about the legality of positive action and a reluctance on the part of parties to adopt further measures to promote women's representation. The uncertainty resulted from the successful legal challenge to Labour's all-women shortlist policy, already discussed, and, in another case, a decision by the Employment Appeal Tribunal which concluded that political candidacy should be regarded as employment and subject to the Race Relations Act (and, therefore, by implication, the Sex Discrimination Act). On the positive side, this has led to pressure on all political parties to incorporate standard equal opportunities practices into their recruitment procedures. On the negative side, all future positive action measures have been put into question – despite Labour's adoption of a 'twinning' mechanism in the Scottish and Welsh elections which was not challenged, despite dire predictions to the contrary. (Brown *et al.*, 1999a; Russell, 2000). Eagle and Lovenduski (1998) express doubt whether women would have made progress in the absence of such a compulsory mechanism. Without renewed commitment to positive action, they argue, representation levels may fall over the electoral cycle. Some campaigners and activists have argued for a change in the Sex Discrimination Act to allow political parties to take positive action without threat of legal challenge, although this course of action has so far been resisted by the government:

> In order to reintroduce all women short lists for Westminster and local government, to allow Zip lists for Europe and the new assemblies and to implement pairing without fear of a legal challenge, a change in the law will be necessary. Under current interpretation of the Sex Discrimination Act a reliance

upon weaker (and possible ineffective) mechanisms such as compulsory short lists could be subject to challenge. Ideally legal change would permit, but not require, widespread use of positive action strategies to achieve sex equality. Once positive action is permitted, then parties can decided what form, if any, they wish to adopt. All women short lists are the most effective way of securing fair representation of women. But narrower measures would also enable progress to be made. Clarification of the political parties exemption for the Sex Discrimination Act would ensure that this exemption applies to the selection of candidates. (Eagle and Lovenduski, 1998, p. 29)

Concern has been expressed by politicians and some lawyers that any such amendment to legislation might constitute a breach of European or human rights laws. However, a recent report concludes that in the context of recent European developments which are supportive of positive action, it is 'highly unlikely' that political quotas for women would be declared illegal under European law. Russell (2000) argues for a new electoral law to govern candidate selections which would require fair procedures but also explicitly enable parties to adopt quota systems.

The adaptation of electoral law could provide the type of legal framework necessary to overcome this significant barrier to change. However, it is important to note that even if the way were open in legal terms, it is unclear if the political will and political stomach for positive action would exist within Labour and other political parties. For example, positive action measures were only ever intended to be in place for the first elections to the Scottish Parliament and the Welsh Assembly.[10] This points to underlying resistance to radical reform.

A range of modest reforms, such as fairer and more transparent selection procedures which would improve representation and enhance the calibre of candidates selected, find wider support (Eagle and Lovenduski, 1998; Brown et al., 1999a). Eagle and Lovenduski are clear that these are necessary but not sufficient conditions for delivering women's political representation. Equal opportunities procedures, together with 'weak' positive action measures such as compulsory quotas for women on shortlists and balanced panels all act to 'make it more likely that selectors will consider well qualified women, but do not guarantee it' (Eagle and Lovenduski, 1998, p. 23).

Without cultural change in all political parties, modest reforms may result in little more than tokenism. Cultural norms and the attitudes and practices of individual men present enduring barriers in a number of respects. There is a need for commitment at the top, for political leaders and party managers to act as sponsors of change. To some degree we see this commitment at rhetorical level at least. Powerful men do sometimes sponsor change within organizations but, as Cockburn points out, it will usually be for the weakest of equalities measures. She argues that in reality most 'put energy into limiting any extension of the agenda beyond bias removal, an opening of doors and, at most, some remedial training for women' (1991, p. 217). Within political parties, those in positions of power are mostly men and mostly white. They have the power to define what are the norms and what is classed as problematic or 'other'. Even where there is commitment at the top, the capacity of the centre to deliver varies from party to party and from setting to setting. All the major political parties in the British political system have found that political will at the centre has encountered political 'won't' at grassroots level. There has been dogged resistance to change within political parties, largely from men but also from some women.

Eagle and Lovenduski note systematic resistance to women persists in some parts of the Labour Party and that there is little evidence that the political culture has changed in favour of selecting women candidates:

> There is abundant anecdotal evidence that in the last parliamentary selection round some constituencies deliberately overlooked well qualified women and shortlisted 'token' women who were clearly not of sufficient calibre to threaten favoured male candidates. Often highly qualified women were rejected in favour of unqualified women in ruthless attempts to resist women candidates. (1998, p. 19)

Winning Ideas

Political parties have improved recruitment and selection procedures, some have introduced 'weak' positive action, more controversially the Labour Party has adopted quotas. We argue that all but the most modest of measures bring attendant problems in terms of legitimacy. There are difficulties in imbuing the case for action with urgency and in building and maintaining constituencies of support. Most recently proposals have been made by campaigners to introduce a new electoral law to clear the way for 'strong' positive action. Activists, and to some extent feminist academics, are pinning their hopes on quotas. However, the barriers are complex, which implies that action is needed on a number of levels: systematic, party political and individual.

There is little evidence to suggest that there have been significant changes to gender relations and the gendered division of labour, on the one hand, and political institutions, values and practices on the other. Yet, if these remain untouched, it is unlikely that the fundamental barriers to women's participation will be permanently tackled.

If feminists are to succeed in keeping up the momentum for change and to withstand the backlash that inevitably follows progress,[11] there is a need to build a broad-based movement for cultural and institutional change as well as gaining the support of powerful sponsors. However, the experience in Britain in the 1990s raises some questions about the limits of support for measures and mechanisms for change. Given the demonstrated efficacy of positive action measures, why is there such resistance not just at level of political parties but also individual party members, candidates and elected politicians?

Phillips observes that where a situation is glaringly unjust, for example, when the levels of women representatives are very low, then it is relatively easy to persuade 'well intentioned' people that something needs to be done; proposals for modest reforms will gain support without difficulty.'[O]nce the stakes are raised, however, to include more decisive guarantees of political presence, the potential backing often drops away' (Phillips, 1995, p. 22).

A number of further points need to be made. First, all measures are potentially contentious because – within existing paradigms of equality – they are pleas for 'special treatment'. A continuum exists: although some weak promotional measures, such as encouragement, are relatively unproblematic; the 'stronger' the positive action measure, the more contentious and the more difficult it is to win support. In this respect, quotas are placed at the strongest end of the continuum and are seen as the most problematic.

Some resistance to positive action undoubtedly stems from entrenched attitudes and men's unwillingness to give up their power. However, cultural norms and everyday arguments about political equality and fairness also underpin resistance to change. Debates are currently framed in such a way that it is extremely difficult to get beyond arguments of merit versus special treatment. We now move from the level of party response to explore some of the popular debates and the discussions at an individual level. We need to better understand the reluctance and discomfort of some women in debates about measures. We need to ask how justifications can be strengthened at the level of discourse: how can we talk better about the needs of equality? In the following chapter we further explore some of these issues through the discussions of some women politicians.

Notes

1. There is little evidence to suggest that the British electorate discriminates against women candidates (Randall, 1987, pp. 140–1).

2. The creation of a new level of government in Britain in the 1990s with the establishment of the Scottish Parliament and the National Assembly of Wales may diversify the standard political career progression. For instance, a number of MPs and Life Peers have chosen to continue their political life at Scottish and Welsh levels in preference to the House of Commons and the House of Lords.

3. There is greater evidence to substantiate the claim that imputed discrimination may operate against black candidates than there is to claim it operates against (white) women candidates (Norris and Lovenduski, 1995, p. 142).

4. See Eagle and Lovenduski (1998) and Brown et al. (1999a) for a fuller discussion of possible measures.

5. For a discussion of the complexities of gender and party politics in Northern Ireland, see, for example, Wilford (1996) and Wilford and Galligan (1999).

6. See Bagilhole (1997) for a 'map' of equalities legislation and Gregory (1999) for a recent reassessment. See Russell (2000) for a discussion of the political quotas and the law.

7. Speaking in Opposition Debate on Women: 7 March 1995 , Jean Corston (Labour MP for Bristol East) countered Conservative jibes about gesture politics (mandatory quotas) by saying:

Is it not rich for a Conservative Member to criticise the Labour Party for ensuring that half our electoral representation will be women, when the vice chairman of the Conservative Party [Dame Angela Rumbold], spends half her life trying to persuade Conservative associations around the country to select female candidates because there is a 50 per cent target in the Conservative Party for candidates at the next election? (*Hansard*, 1995, col. 154)

8. News item reported on *The World Tonight*, BBC Radio 4, 17 November 2000.

9. The Scottish Constitutional Convention was a forum involving representatives from the Labour and Liberal Democrat parties, trade unions, local authorities and public bodies, professional and voluntary organizations, including women's groups, and church groups which convened from 1989–95 to discuss and plan the future government of Scotland. It produced two reports *Towards Scotland's Parliament* (1990) and *Scotland's Parliament, Scotland's Right* (1995).

10. Interestingly, the widely reported predictions that the overall number of women MPs would fall after the 2001 General Election has placed the Labour Party under increasing pressure to include proposals in its Manifesto for a change in the law to permit political parties to take positive action in their candidate selection and recruitment procedures.

11. Policies which challenge existing power relations are likely to provoke resistance and 'backlash'. Kelly *et al.* contend that 'backlash' should be understood, in this context, as 'a short hand for an inevitable and persistent element in any struggle for liberation' (1994, p. 1).

3

Speaking from Experience: Barriers to Political Life

In this chapter we draw upon in-depth interviews with women councillors in Scotland to explore how women 'on the inside' explain why they are such a rare breed. They reflect upon their own and other women's experiences within political parties, as candidates to local office and as potential candidates at national level. The aim is to explore some of the themes raised in the existing literature and to consider how differing ideas of equality and difference might play out in the concrete realities of political life.

These are not the voices of 'ordinary' women who are outside the system, they are incorporated, at least partially, having gained local elected office. However, they have an interesting perspective and a pivotal position. In most cases, they have a history of activism and enduring connections with trade unions, party politics and community groups, all of which act as pools from which to draw political candidates. They are also 'plugged in' to local organizations, school boards, tenants associations, and so on and therefore have had an opportunity to gauge what 'ordinary' women in their communities might think of formal politics.

As local councillors they also form part of the pool from which potential candidates might be drawn for seats at Westminster and now the Scottish Parliament. In some cases, they represent 'discouraged' aspirants or unsuccessful parliamentary candidates. Since the study several have gone on to become members of the Scottish Parliament. Around a quarter of the women councillors had at some stage taken some steps to stand for a Westminster

Parliamentary seat. This may have involved getting onto an approved list or panel of candidates, fighting selection contests for parliamentary seats, or actually fighting in a by-election or general election. At the time of the interviews few women were interested in pursuing Westminster politics, compared with the three-quarters who stated they would be interested in standing for a Scottish parliament, should power be devolved from Westminster.

In addition, as noted earlier, these women have reflected upon their own and other women's perceptions and experiences within a political climate in which the relative exclusion of women from politics was a prominent issue of Scottish public debate and gender balance was a strong strand of campaigns for constitutional reform.

We start by examining the reasons these women councillors put forward as to why there were so few women in politics. To what extent do their discussions reinforce or undermine the standard explanations? Women councillors described and discussed a complex layer of barriers which intertwine and serve to inhibit potential 'hopefuls' at party and candidate level, while also disadvantaging women as political players within the system. This is followed by an account of what are seen as appropriate and effective strategies for change. We end by drawing together themes from Chapters 2 and 3 to argue that current ways in which we think, talk and argue about equality exert a powerful hold on political debate and in some senses make it difficult to see how lasting progress can be made. We suggest that a new vocabulary is needed with which to frame demands for action and change.

Patterns of Discrimination

Women politicians discussed their own experiences, if any, of discrimination. They also gave their opinions as to the nature and incidence of discrimination, in general, to aspiring women. Two specific areas of personal discrimination were dealt with: first, experience of discrimination in any of the selection procedures in which the interviewees had participated, at both local government and parliamentary level; and, second, experience of discrimination within party structures. Definitions of discrimination are generally problematic and indeed proved to be so in this case for many women politicians.

Twelve of the 53 women felt they faced clear or probable

discrimination in terms of their own candidate selection procedures when fighting selection contests at council and parliamentary level or competing for political posts within their parties:

> My selection [in 1990] had 23 men and no women all sitting in a circle and I had to sit on a seat and face them all and be questioned; and the questions were, of course, 'How does your man feel about you doing this?' and 'You've got a wean, how will you manage?' and that stuff. All the kind of traditional views were around. There was discrimination and there still is. (Labour)

> Oh yes, yes – quite definitely, certainly in terms of selection for parliamentary seats. I have actually been told on more than one occasion, where I have been on the shortlist, that: 'The trouble was you were a woman'; and 'People are more comfortable with a man'; and 'The wife is expected to do a lot in the constituency'. (Conservative)

> I felt very definitely that being a woman was not helpful. Women did other things in the party and men fought the glamorous seats ... The SDP, when I first joined it, was a very new party and people thought they could walk into council seats. And there were some very ambitious, very arrogant people coming in who suddenly thought, like Labour, like the Tories, there were going to be safe SDP seats. (Liberal Democrat)

Several women at selection and party political level identified other women as a source of opposition and resistance. The phenomenon of women party members discriminating against women seeking political office, particularly in the Conservative Party but also in the Labour Party, has been noted by others (Gallagher and Marsh, 1988). The current study noted examples of resistance or friction between women party members and women elected members within the Conservative, Labour and Scottish National Parties. Both the following cases are the experiences of Labour women involved in parliamentary candidate selection procedures some 15 years apart:

> I got a derisory vote even though I was chairman of the constituency ... and the person who is the MP now is an excellent first class MP but he was a trade unionist who came

down from Dundee ... and I think I got about six votes out of 79. I think it had *everything* to do with being a woman because we had a very strong Women's Section, as they were then, people who really *did* make the tea and run the socials and I obviously didn't get their votes. I felt very bitter about that at the time, we'd really done a good job of changing it into a really active constituency – I felt the women should have given me more support. (Labour: 1970s)

Certainly one of the questions I was asked was, 'Had I thought about the effect this was going to have on my kids?', which I thought was totally outrageous and I think I replied: 'Well, I hope you're going to ask [the male candidate] the same question because I really don't think that's an issue.' And certainly, coming from the Women's Section, this was the Women's Section selection meeting, I thought it was really rich! (Labour: 1980s)

Although only one in four women believed they had experienced personal discrimination, many more perceived that political parties discriminated against women and considered it to be a reason why there were so few women in politics. This widespread perception of discrimination reinforces Martlew *et al.*'s (1985) suggestion that *anticipation of discrimination* may deter some women from stepping forward:

I would say there are still 90 per cent of the men in Labour Party who say publicly that they support women – who don't given a secret ballot. And I think that becomes quite clear when you look at the Shadow Cabinet elections right down to your wee local who will stand for the treasurer of this branch ... and I think that has to be faced up all the time and men have to be challenged all the time. (Labour)

Other women discussed the case of political parties which claimed to be gender-neutral but, in failing to see unconscious discrimination, were, in reality, 'gender-blind':

The SNP likes to think of itself as non-discriminatory, which basically means you find in the party what you find outside – so, I can't remember the percentage, but practically all the convenors of the constituencies are men and the secretaries are ... women! But if you say to these people, 'See, you are discriminating against women', they would deny it. It's not deliberate, it's a subconscious thing, almost. (SNP)

A number of women, notably Conservative women, spoke about indirect discrimination against female aspirants in the form of the 'ideal candidate' syndrome. Although there may be little overt discrimination against women, they argued that informal 'eligibility' and 'suitability' criteria benefited men.

> It's the same with all the men from all the parties – with one's own party, they will not choose a woman candidate if there is a male candidate. He somehow appears in their mind to be a more suitable candidate and that will probably just be on the basis that he is married with a wife and two children – the standard boy–girl and a dog! (Conservative)

The ideal candidate syndrome was seen as operating in the Conservative Party and also the Labour Party where it was argued that trade union links, rather than merit, were the more persuasive qualifications. It was dubbed by some Labour women as the 'Ah, but . . . ' syndrome. 'There's always this feeling of ah, but. There is this image of an MP or a politician as being a man, white, middle class and so on' (Labour):

> There were three candidates who were at the selection conference, of whom two were women and one was a man and the man romped home on it. And I'm still convinced it was because he *looked* like a candidate. He had the right qualifications, one of which was undoubtedly that he was a man. I don't think many of the people who voted would have even realized that, it was more a mental image of what a candidate is. It is rather like young children saying men can't be nurses because they've only ever seen pictures of nurses with skirts and aprons and things. (Labour)

In contrast, Liberal Democrats and Scottish National women tended to believe that their parties were less likely to have in-built notions about ideal candidates because they did not have traditional 'interest' constituencies such as organized labour, business or farming. The ideal candidate syndrome was seen to be more likely to operate at parliamentary candidate rather than local authority candidate level, although it was also discussed in relation to office-holding within political parties, and in competition for committee convenorships and the like.

There were also a small number of women who felt very strongly that there was no discrimination now in politics:

> I've seen some very abrasive women in politics who I did not like one little bit. I think they were the ones who had to fight from the back all the time. That shouldn't happen now ... If you want my *honest* opinion, for the last twenty years, if a woman's *wanted* into politics she should have been able to get in. (Conservative)

Supply-side Factors – A Question of Resources?

Turning now to supply-side factors. Some explanations of under-representation point to women's relative lack of resources to engage in politics. Personal *resources* include time, confidence, support, experience, skills, finance and motivation. A lack of personal resources presents a constraint on women coming forward.

Only one woman believed that women lacked the skills to be politicians. Four believed that women lacked the interest. There was a clear belief that women met all the necessary criteria to be politicians, although it was perceived that they often lack confidence or are not aware that their skills are transferable. A few women made a distinction between local government and national government and thought they personally lacked the necessary skills to be an MP – particularly public speaking skills.

Time for families, time for politics

Three-quarters of the interviewees cited family responsibilities – that is, women's traditional role in the home, the sexual division of domestic labour, and women's caring responsibilities, primarily but not exclusively, for young children – as the major reason for women's relative absence from politics:

> The majority of women have, at some stage, some kind of care issue, be it children or elderly relatives. We still have a society that sees it as being the woman's responsibility. (Labour)

Family responsibilities were seen to inhibit political activity at most levels. Westminster was seen as particularly problematic, both in terms of practical difficulties, and also in terms of women's ideas and values. There was also a sense in which women felt a system which forces female – and male – politicians to be separated from their families is undesirable at both a personal and a more general level. Caring responsibilities were seen as important and valuable as well as onerous and limiting. The experience of bringing up families was seen as a resource for politics as well as a constraint. 'Because you've always got to care for the overall view – the household or the family – women give a far more open consideration to political issues, far broader aspects.' The dual nature of caring work is explored in more depth in Part II.

In the study, the interlocking triangle of practical and psychological disadvantage – family responsibilities, time poverty and lack of confidence – was cited as the major barrier to women's increased representation in decision-making elites. Women's lack of time or *time poverty* was discussed as an explanation for their under-representation in both local and national government. This was explained in terms of both overall lack of time and also lack of flexibility, or unpredictability, of time budgets.[1] Time poverty and the constraints of time budgets were usually explained with reference to women's traditional family and caring responsibilities:

> I know of at least four mums who would love to [get involved] and are quite good at speaking up for their areas. ... I've actually got one on the Community Council and she speaks up well for the people in the area – but every time I say to her, 'Would you like to take it further?', she says, 'I don't have time, I have the family.' And that's the whole problem. (Liberal Democrat)

The issue of women's 'double-shift', that is, the dual burden for women who combine domestic and caring labour with paid work was also widely discussed. It was considered to be extremely difficult for women to take on a third major time commitment. Around a quarter of the councillors worked full-time in addition to their council duties; a further 11 did some form of part-time paid work. Only one of the councillors interviewed juggled the care of an under school-age family with a full-time paid job and council duties. She was contemplating trying to negotiate a job-share at work if she was to continue as a councillor:

I think for women in particular, if they've got children, they feel that they have a full-time job. Small children and being a councillor is all too much for them. Because I was a councillor before I had children I suppose I was perhaps in a better position to carry on – because you're always in a better position to carry on something than to start something off. (Labour)

Around half of the councillors interviewed did no paid work, most classing themselves as full-time councillors. Forty-seven of the 53 women had children, around a third of whom were still dependent. The majority of councillors had combined the care of dependent children with politics at some stage of their council career. Others spoke of additional care commitments in the form of elderly parents or grandchildren. Many commented on the difficulties of combining work, family responsibilities and elected politics. This was more often an issue for younger women from all parties, which reflects child care commitments. It was also more generally an issue for Labour, Liberal Democrat and SNP councillors, which may reflect higher levels of constituency work (Barron *et al.*, 1991):

I find it hard enough to find time for my kids, never mind my Mum and my Gran – time commitments are the worst. (Labour)

I couldn't do the level of work that I'm doing if I didn't have somebody else at home who was bringing in a decent wage so that I didn't need to have to go out and earn a lot of money. I couldn't support my family on what I earn as a councillor – definitely not – and I think if you were working full-time, or even more hours part-time than I do, it would be extremely difficult to maintain the level of work. (Labour)

To say you can be a councillor in your spare time and have a job is just nonsense if you're going to do it properly. It's absolute nonsense, especially in areas like this – I have a meeting nearly every night. (Labour)

Family responsibilities and work patterns were also seen as part of wider gendered social structures which constrain women at both a practical and psychological level. These find parallel with discussion of constraints in the general literature:

I talk to a lot of older women who now express regrets, my mother being one of them. What she could have done? Realizing now what she could have done and she didn't, she just accepted a role. (Labour)

It's a circular argument, if you keep thinking that the children are the women's responsibility, then obviously that's why employers look on men in a different light than they look on women employees. And that is why a man is able – even in quite a low and menial type of work – on average to earn more than women is. We really need a *quantum leap* – everybody's whole mental focus on everything needs to change – not only in this arena but in many arenas.

Here we're back to the fact that there are so few women MPs and really although there are many more women councillors, still percentage-wise there's only one woman to every nine or ten men on this council and that's pretty par for the course. And it's for all these in-built reasons that I think people have very deep inside their psyche, men and women – women are often their own worst enemies and they don't *recognize* that they are, so they can't do a re-think because they don't even *realize* that they are thinking in that old stereotyped way. (Conservative)

Tracing Connections

Women in this study identified substantive demand- and supply-side factors as barriers to the recruitment of women in local and national politics. It is clear from the councillors' opinions and their own experiences that demand-side discrimination works at a multi-levelled and in a multi-faceted way. In this study an inter-locking triangle of practical and psychological disadvantage – family responsibilities, time poverty and under-confidence – was identified as the root cause of women's under-representation. However, in common with the findings from other research discussed in the previous chapter, barriers intertwine and inter-connect in complex ways. Women identified factors which can be classified as systematic or party political as well as individual as acting to exclude women.

About a third of interviewees spoke of political institutions such as councils, political parties and parliament as 'male structures', by which they understood that, at formal and informal levels, they operated on 'men's terms'. Several women spoke about the Westminster Parliament as a 'boy's club' or a 'gentlemen's club', and spoke about politics at national and local level in terms of 'boys' games'. They identified exclusionary elements integral to the structure of politics, for example, its formality, bureaucracy, inflexibility and inconvenient times of meetings, and so on. The style of politics was also seen as alienating and was characterized as adversarial, competitive, unfriendly and non-consultative. The structure and style of politics, together with the content of politics were seen to lead to 'the creation of an atmosphere that women don't feel comfortable in', or 'can't be bothered with'. They argued that many women in the community did not see their concerns and interests as political – because the system did not recognize or promote them as such. These factors were all seen as substantive in inhibiting women from becoming party members and party officials and also from aspiring to be candidates.

It is important to 'unpick' the nature and meaning of constraints. Alienation can be seen to be a systematic barrier relating to structure, culture and embedded practices. On the other hand, it can be characterized as an individual reason. As an individual reason, alienation can be interpreted in a number of ways, for example, traditional recruitment studies would tend to explain it in terms of a lack of ambition, drive and interest, whereas a feminist interpretation might trace the inter-connection between exclusionary structures and values, on the one hand, and, on the other, individuals' reactions to them. The complexity of factors can also be illustrated using the example of confidence. Lack of confidence is seen as key factor which explains why more women do not come forward in politics at both national and local levels. In this study it was cited as a major barrier by four out of every ten women. In traditional recruitment studies, confidence would be seen as a part of motivational resources. However, in this study women made a distinction between motivation and confidence. Whereas women are traditionally deemed as lacking in motivation, they argued that women potential aspirants may be motivated but are dissuaded by lack of confidence, sometimes described as a socially constructed or conditioned modesty:

I think it's automatic in how we either bring up men or gender imprinting – for men to say, 'I can do that'; and it's automatic for women to say, 'I can't.' And I do it myself, immediately go 'Ooop! I can't do that.' Whereas the men, who are possibly less talented or able or capable, will say, 'Yes, I'll do that!' and thrust themselves forward – I think what happens is that women are more likely to wait until they're absolutely sure in their mind that they will be completely successful. (SNP)

In addition, a number of women discussed the complex links between women's confidence and discrimination. One women, who as a miner's wife in the Kent coalfields had became politicized during the miners' strike of 1983–84, spoke about her struggle to be heard:

Women like myself – it took the miners' strike for me to have confidence. It's just lack of confidence, a lack of belief in themselves and fear of being laughed at – that's one of things that put me off as well ... Years ago, if I was sitting in the pub or miners' welfare club, and men were discussing politics – and if you said something men laughed at you, you immediately shut up. But now I let them laugh and then I turn round and say, 'Now, what was it you thought was funny about that? Tell me what you think', and that throws them and then they find they are actually in a discussion with you! But it's hard to overcome that, and that has a lot to do with the way women have always been treated as second-class citizens. (Labour)

The undermining of women's confidence is also highlighted as a continuing process, which constrains women after they enter politics. Some women spoke of feeling intimidated at an indirect level by being the only woman in a room full of male councillors and officers, or in a direct way by the aggression of individual men, 'there are examples throughout the country of women who have been intimidated by men'. Several spoke about the effect of verbal abuse, or 'tongue lashings', from male political opponents. One older woman said she considered some of the attacks as a 'form of male violence'. Others described it as the way that 'uppity women' were 'put in their place'. A young councillor discussed how the treatment meted out to her by her political opponents not only affected her own confidence but also acted to actively dissuade other women from coming forward as potential candidates:

> Oh, I've changed, yeah ... I think I was a bit thin-skinned to be honest. But the Provost said to me early on: 'You'll just have to learn to develop a thick skin and let it run off you and let it go.' Because if you take it all in, then it can eat away your confidence. But I find that women – non-political – have said, 'That's terrible what he said about you, how can you put up with that? Oh, I couldnae.' (SNP)

Groups of women councillors did provide each other with mutual support, however, many noted that this could engender negative reactions from male colleagues:

> It's OK, men can go to the pub and have their drinks and they can make their networks and make sure that whoever they want to get certain positions goes for it. But if women are seen as being supportive of each other, that's somehow more threatening. (Labour)

Another councillor, who was standing down after a long career in local politics, spoke about some of the complexities of discrimination and the links between an assessment of potential discrimination ('not putting my head above the parapet'), confidence ('I wasn't asked'), and feelings of alienation and disjuncture with politics – particularly Westminster politics ('It's a hell of a life'):

> One of my women colleagues was talking to me the other day about standing for Parliament and I said, 'Oh well, nobody had ever tried very hard to persuade me to do so.' And she said, 'But a man wouldn't have waited for that!' And so, to a certain extent, I think we discriminate against ourselves ... and I don't know how you get over that either, because I think – in business and politics – we do often put on our own glass ceiling, you know. I think I have become more aware of perhaps the limitations I've set on myself, and seeing that as a kind of discrimination ... You ask have I experienced discrimination, I haven't because I haven't actually put my head above the parapet. I think before I wouldn't have really been so much aware of that ... but I think now I feel that there are those areas where, if I had tried to get into, I would have then felt more discrimination ... I don't know, maybe

that's just an impression. I haven't held myself back from doing these things because I said, 'Goodness, if I tried to get into Parliament they would all be against me or people would try and stop me.' I haven't stood for Parliament because I just felt that was above and beyond the sacrifices I was willing to make. (Liberal Democrat)

These explanations are broadly similar to those found in the existing literature and give added support to earlier studies at local government level which identified family responsibilities, discrimination by the selectorate, women's alienation from the prevailing style of politics and political structures, and women's lack of confidence as reasons for the relative absence of women. These factors and processes intertwine to create a complex web which traps many aspirant women and which also, perhaps more significantly, acts to prevent some women from aspiring in the first place. Women, like the councillors interviewed in this study, do develop complex coping strategies to deal with the constraints and barriers and do become successful and effective politicians. However, they are further disadvantaged by an ongoing process of constraint and exclusion.

Supply-side explanations which propose women's assumed and actual caring responsibilities – that is, the clash between love and politics – as the major cause of their under-representation in political institutions are compelling on one level, but at another perhaps are too easy. As Brown notes, seeing family responsibilities as the whole picture may mean that issues of exclusion and discrimination need not be addressed (1996, p. 32). The unequal domestic and caring burden of women is so often remarked upon that it has become something of a truism but it needs attention because is a fundamental barrier to women. Family responsibilities represent a hurdle to women – they impede, restrict and shape women's entry and presence in both the world of work and of politics. However, these barriers are also inextricably linked to men's resistance as political players, as social actors and as partners to give up some of their power and with male-dominated political structures which assume political acitvists, candidates and politicians are 'unencumbered'.

Measures for Change

Chapter 2 outlined some of the measures proposed to improve the representation of women and charted the different party responses to demands for change. The following section examines the pattern of support for various measures first using data from the British Candidate Study and then qualitative data drawn from the current study of women councillors. As we noted earlier, all but the most modest of measures bring attendant problems in terms of legitimacy. There are difficulties in imbuing the case for action with urgency and in building and maintaining constituencies of support. We draw upon the model of long and short agendas of equal opportunities to discuss women politicians' discomfort with 'special measures'.

Cockburn uses the concept of the short and the long agendas for equality to analyse and describe strategies for equal opportunities in employment. The short agenda is premised on a notion of equality concerned with the assimilation of women (and other marginalized groups) within the status quo. It is formal and procedural, 'but nonetheless desirable'; while the longer agenda is concerned with 'equivalence' or 'parity', and seeks transformatory change within a system (society, work, politics) to take account of difference. She argues that, 'there is likely to be a greater potential constituency for such a concept of EO than for the pursuit of vested minority interests' (1989, p. 218).

Applying Cockburn's concept to the field of women and representation, the short agenda would in principle involve a public commitment by political parties and institutions towards increasing the number of women in politics as it is currently constituted. In practice, a short agenda for action would be characterized by practical concerns, generally acceptable measures to create a level playing field or a level starting point – such as standardizing selection interviews, eliminating discriminatory practices, and also some 'weak' positive action programmes like women's training. Quotas are more contentious, they are certainly not on everyone's short-term agenda but it is clear some women political activists, particularly in the Labour Party, characterize them as such. Short agenda measures especially those which seek to eliminate discriminatory practices, or to increase the number of women entering the candidate pool, are likely to be most acceptable to women (and men) across party. However, short agenda measures which use positive action, for example, special training and quotas, are likely to prove more difficult because of the tension between notions of merit and desirable outcomes.

All measures, whether 'weak' or 'strong', are contained within Cockburn's shorter agenda unless they contain the potential to fundamentally transform existing power relations and the gendered structures of families, organizations and political institutions.

The long agenda would involve radical changes. At a preliminary stage it would also need to be concerned with challenging ideology and dominant discourses. Long and short agendas tend to interconnect and are open to interpretation. It is difficult to argue precise definitions, but the long agenda might be said to contain elements of the following. First, societal changes would need to be effected in order that women and men were equally available to participate in politics. For instance, this could mean that measures be taken to ensure a more equal division of household and caring labour between women and men, or increased state support for people with caring responsibilities. Second, politics would be reframed to incorporate 'women's values', to assimilate their preferred ways of working, and to reflect their interests and concerns. These transformatory changes would constitute the *longest* agenda. Long agenda measures, which invoke difference and challenge male hegemonic values, are in opposition to dominant discourses within all the parties but may resonate with the contradictions of women politicians' lived realities. Women politicians, at the practical level, have to combine caring responsibilities with political lives and have to deal with the lack of 'fit' between their own experiences and personal political agendas, and the dominant political discourses. However, longer agenda measures are likely to cause problems in terms of, at an ideological level, finding the vocabulary to justify the type of radical political and cultural change needed in order to ensure women's equal access, presence and influence in political assemblies, and, on a practical level, in terms of political stomach for intervention.

Support for measures

Norris and Lovenduski's survey of parliamentary candidates in the 1992 British general election found that there were high levels of support across parties for measures such as party training for women;

child care in Parliament and change of parliamentary hours. There was markedly less support for all three measures from Conservative candidates. However, whereas three-quarters of Labour candidates, half of Liberal Democrats and two-fifths of Scottish National candidates supported quotas or other affirmative action, support among Conservatives dropped to 6 per cent. Similarly, Conservative candidates were least supportive of proposals to give financial assistance to women (Norris and Lovenduski, 1995, p. 243). The findings were not broken down by gender.[2]

In the current qualitative study there was widespread support for promotional measures to increase the representation of women at local government and national level. The greatest support was for encouragement, training and some sort of child care provision or allowance. There was also support at local level for councillor salaries. In addition, almost half of the women spoke about the need for change to the political system or party structure, sometimes radical. These ranged from changes in the style and ethos of political parties, especially the way in which meetings are conducted, to the overhaul of local councils and the House of Commons. Women from all parties, but most notably from the Labour, Liberal Democrat and SNP, spoke about the need for decentralization at all levels of government, and for the establishment of a Scottish parliament.

As noted earlier, significantly fewer of the women politicians were prepared to consider standing for Westminster than for a proposed Scottish parliament. Practical reasons such as travelling distances and the ability to combine their political and family lives were commonly cited, but strong themes also emerged about supporting decentralization, wanting to be part of a new forum which would do things differently and an optimism about a new sort of politics. Women politicians, whether involved in the Constitutional Convention debates or not, clearly felt a much greater sense of allegiance to and ownership of the planned Scottish Parliament than Westminster:

> It would be new, it would be modern and hopefully traditions have to start somewhere – so let's start one today. I think it would be groundbreaking and I would be very interested in being in at the beginning of that. I think Westminster's a hopeless case in as much as it's just an entrenched old boys' club. They have ways of doing things that they have been doing for hundreds of years. (Labour)

> I think a Scottish Assembly would be different because I think
> we really could effect real change. (Labour)

The possible establishment of a parliament in Edinburgh was seen as being more attractive to women than Westminster in terms of both removing certain practical barriers – and creating women-friendly structures. Women felt that members of a Scottish parliament (MSPs) would be better able to combine politics with family responsibilities than Westminster MPs in terms of travelling distance, but also that the blueprint for a Scottish parliament implicitly recognized the value of family life with its advocacy of sensible working hours.

In addition, some women, mostly Liberal Democrats, suggested that the reform of the electoral system and the introduction of some form of proportional representation would lead to more balanced representation of women and others. Support for quotas was limited to some Labour women in this study, with no support from councillors from other parties although a number of women from the Conservative and Scottish Nationalist parties expressed an understanding of the underlying frustration of Labour women.

To a greater or lesser degree all the women were uncomfortable with special measures which many perceived as either demeaning to women, or unfair to men. These findings are similar to those of Cockburn's research into the men's resistance to sex equality initiatives in organizations which found that women as well as men have ambivalent and contradictory attitudes towards equalities measures. She found that women saw some shorter agenda measures, particularly training, as tokenistic and unfair – but welcomed the idea of the longest agenda, that which promises transformatory change:

> Positive discrimination in favour of individual women is unpopular with women, who feel obscurely that it adds one more unfairness to an unfair organization. Yet they welcome the idea of transformative change that could improve things, they believe, for both women and men. (Cockburn, 1991, p. 216)

As in Cockburn's study, some women in the current study eschewed what they saw as 'special measures' for women but identified the need for transformatory change. While there is no doubt that sometimes this was a strategy for doing nothing (by reasoning that there is no point pursuing immediate short agenda measures when what is needed is some vague and far distant transformation of female–male relations); on the other hand, it can also be seen to illustrate the difficulties many women had in dealing with contradictory notions of equality and difference. The following discussion illustrates the complexities of individual women's stances. The Liberal Democrat councillor started off by appearing to argue that women had no need of positive action and invoked the discourse of merit and 'insulting' special treatment:

> Women shouldn't necessarily need these 'special' things. They should be standing on their own merits. We're here because we are quite capable of doing the job – we don't need all this cottonwool wrapped round us and gently urged along the way – we'll get there under our own steam. And it's almost insulting, if you like, to say we need these things.

However, she then developed her argument to suggest that it was men who need special measures in the form of some sort of 're-education' (a point made by several women). Therefore, she appeared to be pinpointing male resistance as a root cause of women's lack of confidence and as a contributory factor in their disadvantage as political players or aspiring politicians:

> It is men that need the education . . . I would really like to get the message home to them, somehow, that we are here because we are capable of doing the job . . . and if only they would *back off slightly and let us in* – they would find us a great asset. [my italics]

Although she alludes to discriminatory practices and attitudes which currently disadvantage women, she eschews short agenda measures such as training as unnecessary ('women will get there under their own steam'), unfair ('women should stand on their own merits') and demeaning (to women). Instead, she supports the idea of (future) transformatory change through the challenging of male attitudes and male behaviour. However, there is little sense of how and when this is going to be achieved. The problem (of men's resistance) is not directly characterized as an equality issue. There is an emphasis on fair play in terms of women not asking for, or being granted, special favours but there is also an incipient and more radical critique to be discerned in the imputed observation that men do not always 'play by the rules'.

Conservatives, Liberal Democrats and Scottish Nationalists were more likely to find short agenda, 'weak' positive action measures, such as training, a problem than were Labour women, although some Labour women were also concerned about what they saw as particularity. The issue of 'special treatment' was countered in several discussions by women councillors who argued that short agenda measures such as child care for councillors were needed in order to increase the presence of younger women with families in elected politics. 'You have to get more women into politics so they can get women's views over!' Once present they could then campaign to raise the priority of child care provision as a community-wide issue. Child care was thus characterized not just as a measure which would benefit individual women but as one which would act as a catalyst for greater change (the longer agenda).

It was also clear that in many cases thinking about how women's representation could be progressed was blocked by a lack of alternative common sense about equality. Many women felt they had to make a choice between love and politics – that is to decide upon political participation on men's terms or to save their energies for family life.

Thinking about Quotas

The greatest unease at tokenism is to be found in the debate over quotas. Some women who argued for the desirability – even urgent necessity – of women entering political institutions in greater numbers could not bring themselves to support a mechanism for achieving such change. This finds parallel with Cockburn's findings from research into sex-equality measures in organizations. She says the women she interviewed wanted 'full and fair representation' in their organizations but had difficulty in accepting measures which were seen to benefit individual women (1991, pp. 216–17). Her focus was not to investigate why women are unwilling to ally themselves with positive action but, rather, on the patterns of men's resistance. However, there are several clues and emerging discussions from her research. She outlines the ambivalence women feel about being granted 'mother's privileges' which men both resent but also offer in order to underline and delimit women as 'unreliable' workers (for example, maternity leave, career breaks, part-time working, and so on). She also stresses the limited nature of men's support (if any) for equality measures, which is characterized by a regard for the shortest agenda only.

Men's construction of positive action as 'privilege' which reinforces women as 'other' and delegitimizes them as either *real* workers or, in this case, as *real* political actors are powerful discourses which police women and constrain their actions and their understanding. These discourses also resonate with hegemonic interpretations of fairness – those of equality of opportunity, rather than equality of outcome.

A Labour councillor in the current study expressed the difficulty of presenting positive action in an arena where it is perceived as discrimination against men, in this particular instance the reaction of men in the Labour Party to the imposition of women-only shortlists:

> I would say that the majority of men don't accept that – they think that women ought to be there on their own merits and they shouldn't be discriminating in favour of women because they see that as a discrimination *against men.* And they can't seem to realize that women have other hurdles, other barriers, that they need to get over before they can actually *think* about joining either the council or becoming an MP or whatever. (Labour)

Women who did support mandatory quotas also worried that the sense of resentment and backlash they caused might make them counter-productive: 'It really does cause an awful lot of ill feeling, the reason given is that this is inhibiting lots of clever young men.' Women spoke of the difficulties in discussing the needs of equality, 'It comes down to men saying, "but I wash the dishes!" – that's what it's reduced to and once in people's minds it's reduced to that, they don't see inequality.' Resistance was explained, in part, as a result of lack of understanding, 'it's a baffling thing to them and, like anything else you don't understand, you're afraid of it and you resist.' These comments illustrate the ways in the 'needs of equality' (Phillips, 1993) are obscured by both dominant and common-sense notions of fairness and unfairness so that moves to promote effective equal opportunities can lead to resentment by those who, currently, have a marginal advantage. There is a need for positive action but there is also a need for it to be seen as 'fair', otherwise this can lead to paralysis and backlash.[3]

Among this group of female politicians, there was no support for

71

quotas by women from political parties other than Labour, and a great deal of opposition to quotas from some Labour women on much the same grounds: unfairness (to men); unworkability; and as patronizing to women. Indeed, many of those who supported quotas could not find easily the language of legitimacy in which to couch their demands. There was a sense in the discussions that formal equality was viewed as legitimate but contextualized equality was not. An equality which takes difference into account tended to be construed as partial. Even among those who supported quotas, few forwarded an argument which characterized quotas as 'fair' rather than expedient. Rather, they were seen as 'a pity but necessary', 'the last resort', 'unless it is enforced, then it won't happen. We do sadly need some sort of big stick.'

In addition, there was also a recognition, among both supporters of quotas and non-supporters, that some of the measures to increase the number of women in politics would benefit atypical women and there was a need for a more radical restructuring to include a wider cross-section of women and, indeed, marginalized groups of men. Thus, some women construed quotas as a contentious but short agenda measure. Several argued that atypical women, like themselves, who were already involved in politics, benefited from positive action but that such measures would not increase the number of women entering the pool of eligibles in the first place:

> The Labour Party have got it wrong in my view, not that I don't think we should continue with positive action in terms of women parliamentary candidates and women candidates in general – but that will only benefit women like me. It doesn't really benefit anyone else and what I think we need to do is to broaden out what we are about. Women in the tenants' associations, in the pre-five groups, in the pensioners' groups – every single group I can think about in my constituency, almost without exception, share my views – now why are they not joining the Labour Party? Because the political parties, in my view, are not user-friendly organizations. (Labour)

The implementation of quotas was viewed by some as a short agenda measure which does not tackle the long agenda – the long-term dismantling of discriminatory structures and thinking. The introduction of quotas may promote, but does not guarantee, gender parity in political elites. Women would still have hard decisions to make with regards to their caring responsibilities; and a great number of able women would make a rational assessment that they do not have the time resources to combine work, love and politics as it is currently constituted. Therefore quotas may only benefit atypical women who have few caring responsibilities or have sufficient resources to pay for their caring work to be done by others. To be sure, some women will be motivated enough, as at present, to do a double or treble shift, but they will remain disadvantaged political players.

Men and political parties would therefore be able to pay lip service to equality and the problem is individualized. Women and their 'baggage', that is, their children, their elderly parents, their homes and their relationships, are problematized – rather than dominant values and existing care-blind structures which serve to exclude. The result may well remain that of women fitting the system, rather than changing the system to achieve a better fit with women. Women who are most like men can be advanced in a gender-neutral system, other women have the 'choice' of coping with competing demands or, perhaps, the more rational decision of choosing not to engage.

The Long Agenda

Democracy theorist Anne Phillips, a staunch advocate of quotas, accepts that quotas 'may be a case of dealing with the symptoms rather than tackling the underlying cause' (1993, p. 106). She highlights three reasons underlying women's under-representation in parliaments and councils: first, the sexual division of labour in both the productive and reproductive spheres; second, the working conditions in decision-making assemblies are premised on un-encumbered individuals; and third, the prejudice of selectors. Thus, she argues, the worlds of work and family need to be restructured, and the decision-making assemblies should be reformed to allow parents to combine politics and caring responsibilities. These equate with Cockburn's long agenda. Finally she argues that quotas must be introduced to achieve gender parity of representation, 'The importance feminists currently attach to the third [quotas] reflects our sadly realistic assessment of the time it will take to alter the first two' (1993, p. 106).

Among women from all parties, whether they supported or opposed quotas, there were problems in constructing acceptable strategies for change. Few women saw easy answers or simple remedies. There was seen to be a need to think about care, families and their relation to the polity, and to re-characterize difference and equality. Many of the women councillors had difficulty in, as one councillor put it, 'working out how to get from *here* to *there*'. The 'here' is the male-dominated, women-unfriendly structures and practices of politics as currently constituted which impede women's access, disadvantage them in terms of presence and undermine their influence. The 'there' is a politics transformed. By no means a uniform or uncontested vision, but one which, across party, speaks of a politics which is more open, inclusive, and which embodies 'female' as well as 'male' values, needs and interests to the benefit of all.

Phillips underlines the need for ideological alternatives to dominant discourses when she speaks of need for a project to make 'transparent' the needs of equality, in order, 'To avoid the deafness of resentment' (1993, pp. 19–20). It is clear, using her own logic, that further work is needed to challenge existing conceptions of equality. Quotas cause discord and dissent. Those who defend quotas find themselves limited to justifications of expedience and of guaranteed results. Unfortunately neither of these defences tap into common-sense notions of fairness, nor do they challenge existing notions of criteria. Even 'weak' positive action measures like women's training cause some resentment.

The experiences and perceptions of the women in this study reinforce explanations found in the existing literature which relate women's political under-representation to, broadly speaking, the costs of care and the impact of inimical political culture and institutions. They also highlight the complexity and interconnection of different factors at different levels. To highlight the role that care responsibilities play in disadvantaging women is not to assume that only women have to combine caring responsibilities with politics. This would act as a constitutive reinforcement of the idea that male politicians do not. However, the weight it is given in previous studies and in this study reflects a number of practical and structural issues. First, it is still the case that women generally have primary responsibility for the care of children and other family members. Second, existing surveys and studies suggest that women politicians themselves see the combination of family and politics as a greater problem than do men (see for example, Barron *et al.*, 1991; LGMB, 1998). Third, expectations persist at the ideological level that women should be responsible. This plays out in stereotypical attitudes and social pressures. It may also be the case that internalized values present women with more acute problems of role conflict.

Although there is general support for the *idea* of women's equal presence in parliaments and councils, there is also resistance to measures which may be seen as 'unfair'. In this respect, standard understandings of equality exert a powerful hold on the political debate and in some senses make it difficult to see how lasting progress can be made. The pursuit of the short agenda and the marginalization of other discourses have resulted in a sense of closure in terms of progressing the debate and the reality of women's representation in political institutions. This has been the case particularly around issues of fairness in respect to positive action, and questions as to how to make politics more inclusive and more relevant to women – the long agenda project of transformatory change.

Chapters 2 and 3 considered explanations given as to why women are absent from power politics. In the rest of Part 1 we focus upon the arguments made as to why women *should* be present. In Chapter 4 we look to theoretical work on political representation and to comparative empirical work on the role and experience of women representatives. In Chapter 5 women politicians discuss their understandings of representation.

Notes

1. We borrow the phrase 'time budgets' from Martlew *et al.* (1985, p. 49).
2. Table: 13.1: 'Approval of Proposals by Candidates'. Party training: Con (71 per cent); Lab (97 per cent); Lib Dem (92 per cent); SNP (93 per cent). Childcare in Parliament: Con (62 per cent); Lab (99 per cent); Lib Dem (98 per cent); SNP (98 per cent). Change Hours: Con (58 per cent); Lab (92 per cent); Lib Dem (95 per cent); SNP (100 per cent). Quotas /Affirmative Action: Con (6 per cent); Lab (75 per cent); Lib Dem (49 per cent); SNP (42 per cent). Financial Support for Women: Con (6 per cent); Lab (59 per cent); Lib Dem (32 per cent) and SNP (47 per cent). The findings are not broken down by gender (Norris and Lovenduski, 1995, p. 43).
3. There has been a particularly acute white backlash or 'whitelash' in the United States against affirmative action programmes which promote women and black men. See, for example, Bacchi (1996).

4

Political Representation and the Rhetorics of Equality and Difference

The practical, political and ideological barriers facing women seeking political office were discussed in the preceding chapters. However, emphasis upon recruitment has often obscured or marginalized other issues. In particular, two further questions come to mind: the first is normative and asks why *should* there be more women in politics; the second is more pragmatic, although crucially linked with theory, and asks whether it matters, that is – what *difference* would more women in politics make? Why do we routinely talk of the low presence of women in mainstream politics as the *under-representation* of women? It is in this phrase that we become alert to the under-articulated but common-sense understandings of a connection between representativeness and political representation.

The chapter first sketches out some of the main ideas about political representation before moving on to examine the rationales developed to promote the greater presence of women in electoral politics. Theories of political representation and competing claims of equality and difference are then critically evaluated and discussed in relation to the comparative empirical literature on women in elected office. Anne Phillips is one of the few feminist democracy theorists to engage directly with the issue of women's political representation in liberal democratic assemblies. She notes that 'questions of voice or effective power have been far less fully addressed' in feminist democratic theory and there has been little thought given to the reformation of existing institutions (1995, p. 21). We therefore pay particular attention to her ideas about a politics of presence. In Chapter 5 we again pick up the themes of representation and presence when we move from the academic literature to consider further the meanings and implications of political representation through the practical experience of women politicians.

Ideas of Representation

Representation is a confusing concept with multiple, sometimes overlapping, sometimes contradictory, meanings. This lack of shared understanding or agreed definitions has led Iain McLean to remark, 'representation is one of the slippery core concepts of political theory' (1991, p. 172). The question of political representation raises numerous issues, problems and paradoxes. A recent review of the literature (Judge, 1999) examines the diversity of ideas on representation and the plurality of practical forms that political representation takes in contemporary representative democratic systems, with particular emphasis upon Britain. Judge highlights the paradox, first noted by Hanna Pitkin in her classic study (1967), around which political representation is centred: that citizens are both present and absent, 'simultaneously included and excluded from the process of decision' (Judge, 1999, p. 2). Representative democracy has evolved because the ideal of direct democracy is impracticable in all but the smallest of polities and each system performs a balancing act between popular control and other considerations such as efficacy. Different systems will display different degrees and types of democratization dependent upon differing democratic expectations and conventions, and variations in ideas about who the people are and the nature of their representatives' role (Judge, 1999; Beetham, 1992; Manin, 1997).

Pitkin distinguishes between two broad meanings of representation: 'standing for' and 'acting for'. Therefore political assemblies are representative if their elected members 'stand for' (resemble) the community; or if they 'act for' and on behalf of the community (Pitkin, 1967). 'Descriptive representation' requires that a decision-making body is a 'microcosm' of the population (Pitkin, 1967, Chapter 4). This sort of representation is variously described as descriptive, sociological, microcosm and proportionate. It is based upon a simple premise that it is desirable that the constitution of a representative body mirrors the community it represents in terms of relevant socio-economic characteristics such as gender, class and ethnicity (ibid., p. 61). Pitkin comments that descriptive representation engenders two problems: first, choosing which social characteristics are politically relevant and deserving of representation; and, second, that members of socially relevant groups may not share substantive opinions. Representatives may not vote as the majority of group members might wish. She argues that mirror representation diverts attention from what representatives do and that attention should rather be directed to issues of responsibility and responsiveness (ibid., p. 233). In a similar vein, Rao has argued that representation understood as 'resemblance' should be discounted in local politics and representation understood as responsiveness and responsibility (to electors and their interests and for the management of services) should be emphasized (1998, pp. 21–5). The alternative to demographic representation is that based upon the 'principal–agent' conception (McLean, 1991). Bodies are representative because they are made up of representatives elected to 'act' on behalf of their constituents. Political representation may involve either or both of these understandings but, as Rao notes, also involves a 'procedural character' and an 'acceptance of general responsibility for the interests of a group' (1998, p. 20). In addition, any relationship between representative and represented is crucially shaped and mediated by the party political system.

Judge (1999) identifies seven main sets of ideas about representation which he says exist in a potent mix in most representative democracies. They are: microcosmic, trustee, party, interest, functional, associational and territorial. These different ideas revolve around questions about how the people are represented: are they to be seen as individual citizens? Or as members of larger collectivities, for example, those of social class, geographical location or functional interest group? There are, then, different expectations as to who can represent whom, depending upon whether a 'standing for' or an 'acting for' definition is used. The focus and roles of representatives are similarly subject to competing definitions. For example, US political scientists Wahlke et al. (1962) argue that representative roles differ to the extent of the degree of discretion and independence allowed. Representative roles are placed along a continuum with the roles of delegate and trustee at either end (Wahlke et al., 1962, pp. 272–80; Gross, 1978, p. 259). A delegate has least discretion and regards her or his mandate as 'instructions from the community', while a trustee views her or himself as 'a free agent acting on the moralistic directives of his own conscience' (ibid., p. 360).

Judge argues that tension between competing notions of representation have been a persistent feature of the British political system since the mid-nineteenth century. Concern about the social representativeness (or rather unrepresentativeness) of political institutions can be seen as part of the impetus behind the formation of the Labour Party in the early twentieth century. Since then the skewed class and social background of MPs has been of intermittent concern to commentators (Mellors, 1978; Adonis, 1993). More recently the near-monopoly of white males in political institutions has given rise to calls for more proportionate understandings of representation. These concerns have been expressed in terms of a 'democratic deficit' and the idea of the need for a 'politics of presence':

> Many of the current arguments over democracy revolve around what we might call demands for political presence: demands for the equal representation of women with men; demands for a more even-handed balance between the different ethnic groups that make up each society; demands for the political inclusion of groups which have come to see themselves as marginalised or silenced or excluded. (Phillips, 1995, p. 5)

What is the connection between who our representatives are and what they do? Phillips (1995) characterizes two competing models of representation as the politics of ideas and the politics of presence. The politics of ideas is the standard model of representative democracies: here the emphasis is upon shared beliefs, ideas and values which are communicated and delivered through the vehicle of political parties. In the politics of ideas, it does not matter who our representatives are, rather what, in terms of policies and so on, they represent. Politics is understood as judgement and debate about ideas, rather than about personalities. The politics of ideas insists that it is possible that the social interests of one group can be looked after by members of another social group. So long as there is a sharing of ideas there is no need for personal experience. It is ideas, not experiences, that are the common link.

The politics of presence is born of an increasing sense of political exclusion, frustration at the slow pace of change and a contention that ideas cannot be wholly divorced from experience and identity, that is, who we are has an impact on what we think and what we do.

Contemporary claims for women's increased inclusion in political elites are based upon differing conceptions of political representation, differing ideas about the political relevance of gender and differing expectations in terms of end goals and outcomes. However, they may all be understood to fall within the framework of a politics of presence. We now turn to those theoretical and practical arguments.

The Justifications: Symbolic Arguments

Justifications for promoting the increased presence of women in political institutions can be categorized as resting upon either symbolic or substantive arguments (Skjeie, 1991a; 1991b; Norris and Lovenduski, 1995; Phillips, 1991, 1993, 1995). Symbolic arguments can in turn be divided into two distinct considerations: first, those of justice and equity, and, second, those of legitimacy and recognition.

In terms of justice, it is not acceptable or fair to exclude women (and other individuals from previously marginalized groups) from public life. All citizens should have an equal opportunity to participate in politics and stand for elected office. It is argued that if power were equitably distributed within a society, we would expect political representatives to be randomly distributed among relevant social groups. If that is not the case, there must be systematic obstacles which need to be removed if political equality is to be achieved. Political equality is seen to involve equality of access both to the state and to the policy-making process – that is to have both a 'voice' and a 'place'. Groups of individuals who are excluded do not have equal representation in terms of presence and influence and therefore suffer from political inequality (Phillips, 1991). Phillips does not argue for the institutionalized representation of groups but rather for the equalizing of political access for individual members of disadvantaged groups.

Phillips contends that arguments about justice and political equality can only be developed within concrete settings by identifying which groups have been systematically excluded from decision-making and examining the conditions for their political incusion. She also insists that the burden of proof needs to be reversed and men need to justify their virtual monopoly of political power. 'There is no argument from justice that can defend the current state of affairs; and in this more negative sense, there is an argument from justice for parity between women and men' (Phillips, 1995, p. 65).

For some, the justice argument also relies upon a feminist analysis that the current sexual division of labour represents gender injustice (for example, Okin, 1989; Phillips, 1995). For others, the argument is a more general one which posits women as another social group and locates their claims for justice within broader contentions that only if a parliament or any other decision-making assembly 'acts as a public forum for all points of view can it function democratically' (Judge, 1999, p. 37; Lovenduski and Norris, 1989; Brown *et al.* 1999). In both cases, structural discrimination needs to be established otherwise the justice argument is unable to deal with anything other than the most overt forms of discrimination.

The other dimensions of symbolic arguments centre upon legitimacy and recognition. Representative assemblies serve an important legitimizing function for political systems and governments. Characterized by Putnam (1976) as the 'Independence Model', the demographic representation of socially and politically relevant groups is seen in the context of underpinning the legitimacy of liberal democracies. If democratic bodies are 'seen' to be representative, they are therefore morally legitimate. Those favouring this argument see the symbolic presence of women (and members of other social groups) as acting as a kind of proxy measure or barometer for democracy. Conversely, the systematic exclusion of women is seen to undermine the democratic legitimacy of political assemblies and this in turn erodes public confidence and faith in political systems (Darcy *et al.* 1994; Norris and Lovenduski, 1995; Norris, 1996; Brown *et al.*, 1999a). As Anne Phillips observes, 'The extraordinary mismatch between the kind of people who get elected and the gender and ethnic composition of the population they claim to represent remains as a serious blot on the practices of democracy' (1993, p. 98).

The social composition of political institutions also plays a symbolic role in terms of the public recognition of social groups. The inclusion of marginalized groups as political representatives acts as a powerful symbolic reversal of historic exclusions and sends out strong messages that they are equally valued. Conversely, continued exclusion reinforces ideas that members of particular groups are 'lesser' or 'other' (Phillips, 1995).

These symbolic dimensions to arguments for proportionate

representation do not rest or fall on whether the inclusion of women will make a difference. No specific claims are made as to whether there is a direct correlation between the presence of individual members of specific groups and the representation of any group interests. The under-representation of women in political office is thus characterized primarily as a problem of the scarcity of women in the system rather than arguments about the consequences of their inclusion. 'The exclusion of women proves something peculiar is going on. Their subsequent inclusions does not guarantee a solution' (Phillips, 1995, p. 54).

Substantive arguments

In reality, however, symbolic arguments tend to become intertwined with ideas about the substantive consequences of women's inclusion in terms of impact on public policy and on politics itself. Substantive arguments predict that the increased presence of women (and members of other under-represented groups) will lead to a change in political agendas and policy outcomes. The inclusion of women is a means to achieve another goal, that of political and social change (Skjeie, 1991a). This 'rhetoric of difference' has been more commonly used in political debates in Scandinavian countries (Hedlund, 1988; Skjeie, 1991a, 1991b, 1993); however, it strikes a chord with popular expectations elsewhere. For example, the belief that more women politicians would 'make a difference' proved to be one of the key mobilizing factors for women activists to campaign for gender equality and 'women-friendly' practices in the new Scottish Parliament.

Substantive arguments are commonly classified into two types: those of interests, in which women's interests are seen as being different from men's and often in conflict, so that women need to be present to act in their own interests; and those of resources, which are based upon claims that women bring particular knowledge, values and skills to politics (Hedlund, 1988; Skjeie, 1991a, 1991b, 1993).

Substantive justifications: interests

Campaigners using interests reasonings argue that we need more women in politics to promote women's interests. At one level this is a pragmatic argument based on the observation of outcomes. In the British context, although legislation which provides for equal pay between women and men, and laws against discrimination on the grounds of sex, have existed since the 1970s, women and girls still experience considerable inequality and disadvantage in economic, social and political life when compared with men and boys. Gender and its complex interplay with other social divisions such as race and ethnicity, sexual orientation and disability work as a sensitive indicator of different life chances and multiple discrimination. Although these factors work in different combinations in different concrete settings, the overall picture suggests that political bodies which are overwhelmingly male and white have frequently failed to advance the interests, needs and concerns of the diverse communities they serve.

However, there are a number of theoretical issues or challenges to claims made upon this basis: first, we need to examine in what sense it can be argued that women have common interests, and, second, we need to interrogate claims that women can represent other women's interests. We draw here upon useful discussions by Phillips (1995) and Cockburn (1996).

There is, however, a prior question, which is whether we can talk about interests at all. 'Interests' has a common everyday usage which is seen as self-evident and non-problematic. However, interests are defined in political science as the instrumental goals of organized groups competing for power (pluralist model) or the objective interests of an economic class (Marxist model). Some feminist theorists have tried to adapt the frameworks of interests in relation to women, or gender. The classic debate in feminist literature around interests involved Virgina Sapiro (1981) who argued that women had interests as women, based upon relations of reproduction. She posited women as a reproductive class – or interest group – to which the political system should respond. In contrast, Irene Diamond and Nancy Hartsock urged that feminists should make 'a clean break' from the instrumental model of interests and interest groups rather than seek to incorporate women. (1981, p. 720). They argued that most women do not pursue the interests of women as a 'sectional' interest group. Instead many women understand their motivation as being to create a different and better world rather than gain individual or group advantage (Cockburn, 1996, pp. 12–13). Diamond and Hartsock and others have argued that 'needs' is a better framework than 'interests'. However, there is a caveat: needs talk can easily slip into paternalist talk. Nancy Fraser (1989) has demonstrated how those in authority have the power to interpret and define needs. Similarly, needs talk sounds passive in contrast to interests talk which has an edge of agency and activity and is crucially connected with ideas of political action and engagement (Jonasdottir, 1988; Phillips, 1995). At a pragmatic level some feminists now talk of both women's interests and women's needs (Phillips, 1995) and others prefer to use the phrase women's concerns (Cockburn, 1996).

Phillips (1995) suggests that it is relatively straightforward to suggest areas where women have distinct interests from men, for example, those related to child bearing. Jonasdottir suggests that women to a greater degree and different ways initiate, pursue and support issues concerning bio-social production and reproduction. To that extent a set of objective gender interests can be said to exist which results from women's biology and women's social location (Jonasdottir, 1988, p. 42). Others point to the shared experience of patriarchy, sexual inequality, sexual violence and oppression. Skjeie (1988) argues that women have shared socially constructed interests which arise out of their experiences of segregation (for example, in the workplace) and exclusion (from positions of economic, social and political power).

However, Phillips wonders whether these constitute a common set of interests which can be held up to systematic scrutiny. If interests are understood as a set of priorities and goals, then we see evidence of considerable disagreement between women, for example, the divergent views of women about abortion (Phillips, 1991, p. 73); we also see evidence, through social surveys and the like, of a convergence of opinion between women and men (ibid., pp. 68–9). There is a great deal of debate, and growing doubt, that women can share a unified and readily identifiable interest. Certainly simplistic assumptions about sisterhood have been demolished by recent feminist critique. Contemporary feminist analyses increasingly concentrate on the differences between groups of women and upon post-modern concerns about whether 'women' is a sufficiently stable category to have interests at all. In this respect, Pringle and Watson (1992) have discussed the complexity of women's experiences and questioned the utility of any unified notion of 'women's interests'.

Does the recognition of, and increasingly theorizing around, the diversity of women undermine the notion of gender parity in political representation? Cockburn argues that, if anything, the fact that women are not a unitary category strengthens rather than weakens their claims for presence:

> Women's demands for the representation of women are correctly legitimated by the difference between women and men. It is important that differences among women not be read as delegitimating that claim. The validity of special measures for representing women should, on the contrary, rest on the very diversity of the views and the needs that are being marginalized when 'women' are marginal. (Cockburn, 1996, pp. 17–18)

Phillips contends that the argument from interest does not necessarily rely upon demonstrating a common interest of all women: it depends, rather, on establishing that interests are gendered and that there is a difference between the interests of women and men. As she notes, although not all women bear children that does not mean to say that pregnancy can be understood as a gender-neutral event. Similarly, although women may indeed disagree about abortion, concern about reproductive rights is gendered. Women occupy very different socio-economic positions, however; their experiences are different from those of their male counterparts. Interests may also overlap with certain groups of men which may result in the potential for alliances around specific policy issues (Phillips, 1995, pp. 68–9). Similarly, Cockburn notes that although policy needs may display variation in respect of different groups of women they remain gendered, 'they are not arbitrary' (1996, p. 15).

Cockburn seeks to steer a course through some of the difficulties encountered in the debate about interests by using Jonasdottir's (1988) model of the 'political interests of gender' in which there are two dimensions to the concept of interests: first, in terms of form and, second, content (Cockburn, 1996, pp. 13–14). The form dimension involves the demand for presence and control – to be among the decision-makers. Cockburn argues that women can be seen to have an objective interest in access, that is 'over conditions of choice rather than the content of choice itself'(Jonasdottir, 1988, p. 40; Cockburn, 1996, p. 13). So women's interests can be seen in terms of agency, of engagement and of concrete presence.

The content dimension relates to the core ingredients of policy agendas, the substantive values that are debated within a political system and around which policy is made. In this respect the content refers to the needs, wishes and demands of various groups and subgroups of women. Cockburn follows Jonasdottir in arguing that it is inappropriate to consider women as an interest group because their policy concerns and goals often relate to others rather than themselves. These social values 'cannot be squeezed into the historically constructed masculine liberal notion of instrumental "rationality" or "interest"' (Cockburn, 1996, p. 14). She suggests we talk about women's concerns rather than women's interests. These are issues which have a bearing on women but about which no presumption is made as to the position any individual or group of women would take. This also recognizes that different groups of women might have different needs in respect of their concerns. The definition and interpretation of those needs would be the subject of negotiation and political alliances (ibid., pp. 14–15).

Women and men have sex-differentiated bodily experiences and gender-differentiated social life experiences, especially their experience of the sexual division of labour; these experiences are mediated through culture. Cockburn argues these 'aggregate differences' tend to generate 'distinguishable political perspectives' between women and men and account for women's greater support for social welfare policies and for 'the fairer sharing between men and women of responsibility for home and care, a new deal backed by changes in men's attitudes and practices' (ibid., p. 16).

Women's concerns cannot be taken for granted, they will be historically and culturally specific, but will cluster around substantive issues such as contraception, abortion, social provision of childcare, equal access to training and jobs and equal pay. Views are unlikely to be uniform and the policy demands eventually formed will be the end result of a process of prior public debate and the construction of consensus. Cockburn argues that these concerns need to be fought for in a system in which women's interests in terms of presence have been met.

Phillips makes a further less developed point about the relationship between interests and representation: if we argue that gender interests and needs and their policy implications are not immediately apparent, then we need women to be present in decision-making bodies to 'give further and fresh thinking' to the issues. In these situations, the sex of the representative as well as the political party will have a bearing (Phillips, 1995, p. 71).

Cockburn counters objections to the very possibility of articulating 'women's concerns'. It is possible to identify empirically that sets of women's 'interests' or 'concerns' or 'policies' (however constituted) emerge within specific concrete contexts. These agendas 'have been tested in argument and are the minimum around which it has proved possible to forge a substantial alliance' (Cockburn, 1996, p. 15). In respect of member states of the European Union she argues that women share core of concerns relating to the policy implications of their relation to reproduction and their disadvantaged position in labour market. We can also point to the common agendas for action, necessarily broad brush, which emerged from the UN Fourth World Conference on Women in 1995 where women's NGOs, working at global level, have collaborated to tap, consult, negotiate and construct common concerns.[1]

Phillips remains equivocal about the relationship between interests and presence. On an intuitive level she finds it plausible that certain issues will become more important if more women are present and accepts that this is borne out in part in Nordic systems where there are relatively high proportions of women in parliaments. On the other hand, she is chary of the implications of claims that women can speak for women, particularly in terms of accountability. She also reminds us that women, like men, are primarily elected to represent geographical constituencies and party policies:

> The shared experiences of women as women can only ever figure as a promise of shared concerns, and there is no obvious way of establishing strict accountability to women as a group. Changing the gender composition of elected assemblies is largely an enabling condition (a crucially important one, considering what is disabled at present) but it cannot present itself as a guarantee. It is, in some sense, a shot in the dark: far more likely to reach its target than when those shooting are predominantly male, but still open to all kinds of accident. (Phillips, 1995, p. 83)

A question of resources

Arguments based upon resources claim that women would bring distinctive skills, values and knowledge to politics. The source of difference is seldom systematically articulated in popular political discourse and can rest upon appeals to essentialist ideas about 'womanly virtues'. Women are seen to possess different but complementary resources to men which will benefit politics by making it more balanced. The thinking can be used to promote a specialist but limited role for women in politics in the fields of family policy and social welfare. This containment of women is still informed by 'feminine ideology', the distinctive but narrow viewpoint and expertise ascribed to women politicians by political scientists like Duverger in the 1950s and 1960s. Duverger contrasted the monovalence of women with the polyvalence of men (1955). This strand of thinking presents itself more often in parties of the Right.

Others argue that women bring different resources to politics because of their different life experiences, particularly relating to the sexual division of labour in society. The notion of 'women's culture' has been developed, mostly in Nordic countries and in the United States, to stand for a core of shared interests, common values and patterns of interaction which arise out of women's specific position as a result of the sexual division of labour in society. Carroll, in particular, stresses that this notion of commonality is loosely defined, it does not need to be based upon essentialist definitions of 'Woman' nor does it assume that the experience of all women is the same (1992, p. 26; also see Hedlund, 1988).

The nature, extent and implications of difference are in many respects ill-defined. Skjeie suggests, in the Norwegian context, this lack of specificity was of benefit because it allowed different parties to interpret difference according to their own 'ideological persuasions' (1991a, p. 237). She argues that the introduction of difference was a positive argument for change which brought results. Quotas are 'an end product of a line of political arguments that have forcefully maintained that gender constitutes an important political category that needs to be fully represented' (ibid., p. 236).

Explicit political arguments from interests and resources are seldom articulated in the British context although at a pragmatic level there is an argument which sees the exclusion of women from decision-making bodies as a waste of the individual talents of able women and there are popular expectations that women will 'make a difference'. Arguments from difference are seen as risky and essentialist and are at present marginalized and under-developed.

The preceding discussion highlights some of the theoretical anxieties about promoting the ideas of women's interests. However, it does seem plausible, as Cockburn suggests, that it is possible to identify empirically a common set of women's 'interests' or 'concerns' or 'policies' within a particular political system. It is then a matter of empirical investigation as to whether a case can be made that women political representatives work to promote those concerns.

The idea that women bring distinctive resources to politics receives still less serious attention in mainstream feminist debates concerned with women and political representation. Theoretical suggestions have been made by some moral and political theorists that women have distinctive skills, values and ways of thinking based upon their experience of care work. Some claim that 'women's values' or the 'ethics of care' contain the potential to challenge and transform values and practices in the public and political spheres. At present these ideas are not well known in political science and in popular political debates, and what does filter through tends to be caricatured as crudely essentialist. We will consider some of these ideas in more detail in Part II of this book.

A move from symbolic arguments to substantive arguments involves claims that the mobilization and integration of women into political decision-making bodies matter not only because it is fair but also because it will make a difference. Expectations vary, but include predictions of changes in political practices, political outputs and political outcomes. In terms of political practices it is claimed that politics would shift from adversarial traditions to more consensual and co-operative ways of working; in terms of political outputs, women are expected to mobilize the political agenda in favour of women's interests and previously marginal concerns, particularly social and moral issues; and third, changes in policy outcomes are expected which would progress gender equality and related issues and lead to the creation of a 'women-friendly society'.

Do Women Make a Difference? Some Evidence

In the following section we investigate whether substantive arguments of interests and resources can be substantiated in reality. Is there any empirical basis for these claims? We draw upon a range of comparative empirical work, both quantitative and qualitative, which explores the existence, extent and nature of any difference between female and male politicians. We ask what evidence there is, if any, that women politicians in current political systems operate in a gender-distinctive way? Do they promote 'women's interests'? Do they bring different skills and styles to politics? Empirical work so far has yielded ambiguous and inconclusive results about quantifiable differences between male and female politicians. However, research findings do suggest there may be substantive differences.

Power and process

First, research suggests that women view power and political process differently. Women politicians are more likely than male politicians to value citizen participation and consultation in the policy-making process and in service delivery (Bers, 1978; Neuse, 1978; Carroll, 1992; Thomas, 1994) and are likely to consult a wider and more diverse range of opinion when considering policy options than are men (Kathlene, 1998). However, women politicians do not see themselves as serving only women. For example, female politicians in the United States defined their primary role as that of a delegate representing the interests and general welfare of the whole community rather than solely women (CAWP, 1978; Merrit, 1980; Antolini, 1984; Githens, 1984). They were also less likely than men to put the interests of their district above the interests of their state as a whole (Carey *et al.*, 1998). Leijenaar and Mahon's cross-national survey found that women politicians in North America and Europe were more likely to be concerned with political action in terms of problem solving, service delivery and developing policy, whereas male politicians were more likely to see themselves as 'trustees', and measure their success by their bargaining position in power structures (Leijenaar and Mahon, 1992). Similarly, in an Italian study Marila Guadagnini found that working for the whole community was more important to local women politicians than either women's interests or party political interests (1990). Traditionally, the role of delegate has been seen as a politically passive and reactive, and women's preference for it seen as underlining their lack of confidence or competence to make independent decisions. Githens suggests that these characterizations do not accurately reflect women's conception of their role and function (1984, p. 57).

There is a strong and commonplace perception, among electors and amongst politicians alike, that women politicians have a more caring and collaborative leadership style than male politicians. This may say more about traditional feminine stereotypes than reality and there are notable counter-examples of adversarial women politicians. On the other hand, there is some evidence to suggest that these expectations may be borne out in practice (Rosenthal, 1998; Whicker and Jewell, 1998). Although more research is needed before firm conclusions can be drawn, the findings suggest that there are grounds to believe that women may have a different style of politics.

Agenda and outcomes

Second, it is argued that women have a distinctive impact on the political agenda and upon policy outcomes. Researchers in North America, Europe and elsewhere have looked at differences in political attitudes, policy stances and policy priorities to test this proposition. In terms of political attitudes, the picture is inconclusive although suggestive that women in local and national politics may 'operate within a gender-distinctive attitudinal framework that directs their policy decisions' (Antolini, 1984, p. 37). A survey of the literature by Norris (1997) reported that gender attitudinal differences had been detected within political parties in Germany and Sweden, mediated also by class, education and generation. Gender was also a significant (although not sole) predictor of political attitudes in studies in Britain (Norris and Lovenduski, 1995), Scandinavia (Karvonen and Selle, 1995) and the USA (Thomas, 1994). Some studies have suggested differences between male and female legislators or opinion leaders. For example, Norris (1986) and Welch (1985) both found that US female representatives were consistently more liberal in their voting preference than men, although the differences were small. A survey in the 1990s demonstrated that female state legislators in the USA were consistently more liberal than their male counterparts by party group and those differences were most pronounced in relation to social issues (Carey *et al.*, 1998). A study of US office-holders in the 1980s found women had a different orientation to men on issues such as economics, war, nuclear energy, capital punishment and abortion and the equal rights amendment (CAWP, 1983). Other studies have stressed the similarity in male and female politicians and opinion leaders in behaviour and policy stances. For example, Holsti and Rosenau (1982) found considerable similarities in the foreign and defence policy view of women and men in the American political elite. Recent research has indicated that there are increasing similarities in the way that male and female politicians in Scandinavia communicate in politics (Karvonen and Selle, 1995).

In terms of policy stances, women representatives whether identifying as feminist or not, tend to involve themselves in the promotion of women's concerns, including child care issues, funding for battered women's refuges and associated anti-violence work (Boneparth and Soper, 1988; Thomas, 1994). Various studies in the USA and Europe have shown that women are more likely to place a higher priority on social issues which relate to family, children and women than do men (Skard and Haavio-Mannila, 1985; Saint Germain, 1989; Thomas, 1991, 1994; Thomas and Welch, 1991). Where studies have found both women and men support an issue, the degree of support differs – that is, women tend to feel more strongly about issues of women's status than do their male colleagues.

Scandinavian empirical studies suggest small but significant differences between male and female politicians in terms of interests, policy orientation and style. Although Skjeie is careful to differentiate between what she calls conceptualizations of politics and political action (Haavio-Mannila *et al.*, 1985; Hedlund, 1988; Skeije, 1991a, 1993; Bystydzienski, 1992). In particular, 'care and career' politics, that is the range of issues which are concerned with the reconciliation of work and family life, achieved a prominence in Scandinavian politics long before it found a place on political agendas elsewhere.

Kari Skrede (1992) suggests that women share a common agenda but issues are then filtered through class and political ideology. So, for example, right-wing women will favour market-led solutions and left-wing women will favour collectivist or state solutions to commonly defined problems such as childcare (see also Skjeie,

1991a). A study of Swedish councillors found that both male and female politicians believed that women councillors better represented the interests of women voters than did their male counterparts. In addition, the majority of women surveyed defined themselves as changing the political culture of the council and representing issues of concern to women (Hedlund, 1988).

Making connections

Third, it is suggested that women politicians tend to recognize the connection between themselves and other women who either also aspire to office, or who want greater access to their government, or who want policy changes. Janet Flammang has characterized these features as a 'politics of connectedness' (1984, p. 12). Women are more likely than men to be active in encouraging women to come forward, although feminist-identified women are the group most likely to be involved in 'mentoring' (Dolan and Ford, 1998). Contemporary studies in Europe, North America and elsewhere suggest that a significant proportion of women politicians are 'pro-equality' and sympathetic about women's rights. For example, research, in both the United States, Scandinavia and the European Parliament indicates, with certain qualifications, that female elected representatives tend to speak on, intervene in and promote equality issues more often than their male counterparts (Carroll, 1985, 1992; Skard and Haavio-Mannila, 1985; Vallance and Davies, 1986; Hosykns, 1996); and that this proactive approach to sex equality matters increases as the proportion of female elected representatives has risen. However, these are not the only nor the primary activities of women politicians who are also active in other policy areas. There are also counter-examples of women politicians who display little attention to women's issues and do little to promote equalities issues. This led Joni Lovenduski, in her overview of women in European politics, to observe:

> The presence of women so far has not always guaranteed the taking into account of women's interests. The evidence is that many women politicians are surrogate men, and that they have no interest in pursuing women's rights, or questions of particular concern to their women electors. (1986, p. 243)

The UK picture

Turning to the UK, studies of MPs have yielded little evidence of gender difference in the House of Commons (Currell, 1974; Vallance, 1979). Virtually all the women MPs interviewed by Vallance in the late 1970s saw themselves as party politicians first and foremost and displayed little solidarity with other women MPs. This led Vallance to state, 'The women are too interested in and too divided by politics to contemplate any sort of a corporate identity' (1979, p. 96). Although Hills (1981) found evidence that female Labour MPs were more radical than their male counterparts, and Norris and Lovenduski (1989, 1995) found female parliamentary candidates in the 1987 and 1992 general elections to be more liberal than male, party still proved to be the strongest predictor of attitudes. Coote and Patullo, in an overview of women and British politics in 1990, argued that instances of women MPs working together within and across party groups were still 'straws in the wind'.

And yet there was ambiguity. Vallance (1979) noted that women MPs accepted, albeit reluctantly, that women expected them to represent their interests and that as such, they represented two constituencies: their geographical constituency, and the constituency of women. They also agreed that they tended to act more often than their male colleagues when sex equality issues arose. No formal caucus existed although Labour women worked closely together to combat the various challenges to abortion legislation during the 1970s (Vallance, 1979, pp. 83–90). Banks' (1993) study of the legislative activities of female MPs from 1918 to 1970 reached the conclusion that, whereas women operated for the most part along party lines, there were some gender-related issues on which women MPs would campaign as women: abortion, the marriage bar, sexual abuse and child abuse. This informal lobby, especially around abortion, was well established by the late 1980s (Coote and Patullo, 1990). Currell (1974), Vallance (1979) and Pugh (1992) have all noted that most, though by no means all, women MPs' activities were concentrated in traditional 'feminine' areas such as education, social welfare and health. The Labour MP, Fiona Mactaggart, commenting on Labour women's contribution to Labour's 'First 1000 days', argues that women ministers and backbenchers have moved forward on a 'women's agenda' in traditional areas relating to children and the family, work–life balance, domestic violence, and so on and have also worked to inject 'women's perspectives' into non-traditional policy areas. As a result she claims that, 'the fine detail of government policy reflects much greater sensitivity to the needs of women' (Mactaggart, 2000).

The most detailed empirical investigation of the political attitudes, roles and policy stances of politicians in the UK is the 1992 British Candidate Study, which surveyed all candidates, including standing MPs, in the 1992 general election (Norris and Lovenduski, 1995; Norris, 1996). Norris and Lovenduski found that within each party grouping women candidates were more feminist, more liberal and more left-wing in their attitudes than male candidates. There was also a gender gap within each party in terms of policy priorities with women candidates expressing stronger concern for social policy issues than men. Modest gender differences were evident across a range of issues but party still remained the best predictor of attitudes. However, in respect of women's rights, particularly in the fields of reproductive rights and domestic violence, clear gender gaps emerged which went beyond party. For example, Conservative women were more supportive of women's rights in respect of abortion and domestic violence than were male Liberal Democrats (Norris, 1996, p. 95). Norris and Lovenduski use three categories of legislative role in their analysis: constituency worker, parliamentarian and party loyalist. Gender proved significant across all three roles, with women giving greater priority to constituency work. Their estimates of both volume and time spent dealing with constituency case work exceeded those of men (Norris, 1996, pp. 100–3; see also Norris and Lovenduski, 1995).

In the UK, comparatively little work has been carried out a local authority level into the distinctive role and experience of women councillors. Barry's 1991 survey of London councillors found that women were slightly more oriented towards a community focus than were men which was broadly in line with the findings of earlier British surveys (see, for example, Bristow, 1980; Barron et al., 1991). Bochel and Bochel (1996) identified a similar gender gap in respect of motivation to stand for office among Scottish councillors. Men were more likely to stand because of a belief in public service (33 per cent men compared with 24 per cent women), to improve the local environment (19 per cent men to 12 per cent women) or because of concern over a specific issue (9 per cent men to 3 per cent women). Women were more likely to stress their interest in politics or community affairs (21 per cent women to 9 per cent men), and

8 per cent of women said they stood for election in order to get more women on the council.

A number of interviews and case study research have shown that, although women councillors do not generally identify themselves as feminist, many are 'pro-equality' and do act as agents or supporters of change (Barry, 1991, Kelly, 1995). London councillors generally recognized it was other female councillors who tended to give higher priority to issues specifically affecting women, but replies were highly conditioned by party (Barry, 1991, pp. 141–6).

The issue of violence against women is one area which provides more concrete examples of where the presence of women politicians can make a difference. Kelly (1992) argues that where women councillors have gained a strong presence over time, issues like violence against women gain prominence on the political agenda, along with an emphasis on gender-sensitive service delivery and effective community consultation. In the experience of workers within organizations such as Women's Aid, the presence of women local councillors and local government women's committees have provided support for feminist work. As Cuthbert and Irving note 'Although there have always been a wide spectrum of male politicians who have been sympathetic, and some who have been prepared to openly condemn male violence, women have, in the main, been more willing to be seen as supportive' (2001, p. 63). A case study of the Zero Tolerance campaign, a radical local government public education initiative on male violence against women and children, demonstrated that the success of the campaign in Scotland rested in part on the political support of women councillors, both feminist and non-feminist, across the party political divide (Mackay, 1996a; 1996b; 2001).

Although there are suggestive findings which might back claims of substantive difference, it is clear from the literature that differences should not be exaggerated and the impact of party should not be underestimated. David Judge argues that the behaviour of the (large) new intake of Labour women MPs into the British House of Commons post-1997 provides a 'forceful illustration' of the power of party over gender solidarity. The episode to which he refers concerns the Labour government's proposals to cut the total welfare benefit received by lone parents. Any expectations that the women MPs might work for a women-friendly polity were dashed when only eight Labour women voted against the proposed change compared with 39 Labour men. Just one out of the 64 new Labour women walked into the 'No' lobby (Judge, 1999, p. 40). Undoubtedly the lone parent benefit row has soured relationships between women's organizations and women MPs in the UK, confirmed the new intake of female MPs as 'Blair's Babes' to the media, and has provided ammunition to arguments that women do not make a difference in politics.[2] However, the incident may also be illustrative of the institutional constraints under which women politicians operate. Lovenduski (1986) observes as do Currell (1974) and Vallance (1979) that women politicians may be interested in women's issues but that interest is not converted into action because it is perceived as being a political and personal risk. There is a fear that women politicians may not be taken seriously if they become identified with a women's agenda. Vallance and Davies' (1986) study of women MEPs in the European Parliament reported the 'credibility' problems women faced upon becoming associated with 'feminism' or 'women's issues'. American political scientist Susan Carroll explains the discrepancy between women political candidates' high levels of attitudinal feminism, that is, their supportive attitudes to women's rights, and their low levels of behavioural feminism as rooted in women's perception of the political risk in becoming publicly associated with feminism. Carroll classifies such politicians as closet feminists. They may be committed to women's issues and the goals of the women's movement but 'their feminism remains hidden from public view' (1984, p. 319).

The constraints under which women politicians may operate at both national and sub-national levels have led some researchers to argue that it is unsurprising if women's presence in politics does not necessarily result in demonstrably different behaviour and outcomes. There is evidence to suggest that a certain proportion of women – a 'critical mass' – is needed within a political institution before they are able to 'make a difference' and to challenge and change traditional organizational cultures. Evidence from Scandinavian countries suggests that when women politicians constitute between 15 and 40 per cent of the membership of a political institution, changes can be detected in terms of the opening up of the political process and political agenda to new concerns and issues and at 40 per cent women achieve a breakthrough. Dahlerup terms this as the transition 'from a small to a large minority' (1988; see also Bystydzienski, 1992). When the levels of women are found at below 15 per cent, women are unlikely to have any marked impact.

In the context of minority presence, Antolini suggests three inter-connected factors which may act to inhibit women, and which may operate to suppress gender distinctive behaviour or orientation: realpolitik, institutional sexism and tokenism. The operation of realpolitik together with institutional sexism creates a system whereby women who want to advance must play by male-defined rules and identify with male-defined political goals. These inhibitors make it imprudent for women to be present as women in politics and thus potentially suppress any identification with issues which are seen as both marginal and, in some cases, subversive. Githens (1984) argues that the pressures to stay in the closet are such that attempts to evaluate women's performance on criteria such as feminist identification or public feminist platforms fail to take into account the structural pressures on women. Together with these two factors can be added structural rigidities, particularly in the British system, which act to both exclude many aspirant women from gaining entry to electoral politics at local and national level, and also to pressure women through party discipline and party loyalty to 'eschew both separate association and the search for solidarity across party lines' (Chapman, 1987, p. 318).

The third inhibitor suggested by Antolini and others is tokenism. This relates to the concepts of outgroups discussed by Kanter (1977) and marginality explored by Githens and Prestage (1977). These works discuss the pressures that face women, as an outgroup, in organizations and political structures. Women, and other outgroups, face hegemonic assessments of themselves as 'other' and 'lesser'. This leads women politicians to either disassociate themselves from other women and to embrace the (male) values, styles and goals of the system; or to accept a limited role within the system and to display what Vallance (1979) described in her study of women MPs in the British House of Commons as the 'conscientiousness' of 'good junior prefects'. Given the mass of structural, cultural and institutional inhibitors which operates within politics it is perhaps unsurprising if women's presence in politics does not necessarily result in markedly different behaviour and measurable outcomes. Or, to put it another way, perhaps it surprising to discern any differences at all.

To summarize, there is a growing body of evidence that women politicians may act in gender-distinctive ways. They appear to have different views of power and political process from their male counterparts. There is an apparent difference in terms of policy priorities which can result in an impact on political agendas and policy outcomes. Finally, there is some evidence of a politics of 'connectedness', relating to issues of communication, consultation and responsive responsibility. These differences are conditioned, sometimes dramatically, by political party. It is also the case that aggregate differences between women and men mask differences between different groups of women and different groups of men.

Standing for Women?

On the face of it, there is a plausible case that women politicians may represent women in both a symbolic and a substantive sense; to both 'stand for' women and 'act for' them. There is also a plausible case that women have common interests, albeit culturally and historically contingent. Why then do anxieties remain about moving from arguments of justice and democracy to incorporate arguments of difference?

Feminist academics and activists working on issues of women and representation privilege symbolic arguments. There are a number of good reasons for doing so. First, symbolic arguments are clearly understood and are seen as respectable and acceptable within dominant notions of gender-neutral equality in British political culture. Second, the justice strategy also avoids burdening women politicians with unrealistic expectations.

There are further grounds for concern, these relate to serious questions about accountability and identity. Claims that extend beyond the symbolic presence of women, those which more directly argue that women stand for women in a substantive sense are seen to bring the debate into the tricky area of group representation and identity politics. Phillips argues that the politics of presence is *not* an argument for group representation. Although she is in favour of mechanisms to ensure the equal numerical presence of women and men in all public decision-making bodies, she does not base her argument on 'any *substantial* notion of representing women' (Phillips, 1993, p. 92). Indeed, she continues:

> The argument is not strengthened – if anything it is weakened – by the more substantial notion of representing a new constituency or group. Accountability is always the other side of representation, and, in the absence of procedures for

establishing what any group want or thinks, we cannot usefully talk about their political representation. (1993, p. 99)

Her model of a politics of presence has been developed, in part, in response to the democracy theorist Iris Marion Young's model of group representation. Young has argued for new democratic mechanisms to recognize and institutionalize the representation of a wide range of oppressed social groups within the context of American politics (Young, 1989, 1990). Phillips (1993, 1995) has a number of democratic and practical concerns about notions of group representation. On democratic grounds, the institutionalization of group identities or interests leads to a 'freezing' of identity, to hostility and to a closure which can prevent the possibility of wider solidarities and more inclusive versions of citizenship. On practical grounds, she argues that there are intractable difficulties inherent in group identity. She raises the question of how people can choose between their different (and shifting) identities and group loyalties, for instance, when sex, race and class intersect, to decide to which group they should belong.

Phillips argues that group representation depends upon 'implausible essentialism' or 'impractical mechanisms' for creating sufficiently representative groups to establish common goals and interests. Furthermore, ensuring that group representatives are accountable to their groups is viewed as an 'almost impossible task':

It is hard to see what counts as 'representing' a group. For there are few mechanisms for establishing what each group wants. We cannot say, for example, that getting more women elected to local or national assemblies therefore secures the representation of women. Politicians are not elected by women's constituencies, and apart from canvassing opinion within their own parties and perhaps consulting their own coterie of friends, they do not have a basis for claiming to 'speak for women'. (Phillips, 1993, pp. 97–8)

Phillips raises important concerns about the implications of moving beyond symbolic arguments. We return to some of these issues in the following chapter.

Questions of Representation

The previous two chapters considered existing explanations as to the relative absence of women in politics. This chapter has focused upon questions of political presence. On what grounds is it argued that we need more women in politics? On what basis do they stake their claim? We examined the symbolic and substantive arguments relating to women's political representation. We also assessed the empirical evidence to support substantive notions that women may represent women's interests or bring distinctive resources to politics.

Symbolic arguments, those of justice and democracy, are dominant in British feminist debates on political representation. There are good reasons for this: symbolic arguments are less contentious and more acceptable in mainstream British political discourse. There are also fears that 'speaking difference' may unleash a dangerous politics which stereotypes women and is vulnerable to backlash. Furthermore, there are related problems connected with 'stronger' arguments about group representation and identity politics. Finally, feminists are justifiably anxious that women politicians will face unrealistic expectations.

In reality, symbolic and substantive arguments tend to intertwine and there is a plausible case that there are both symbolic and substantive reasons why gender parity of representation in politics is important. In addition to arguments about fairness, legitimacy and recognition, research suggests that the presence of women politicians in sufficient numbers, together with women in leadership roles in state bureaucracies, can lead to a change in political agendas, political culture and policy outcomes. Next we turn to examine the ways in which issues of representation and difference are negotiated in the 'common sense' of women politicians.

Notes

1. See, for example, the National Agenda for Action (1996) drawn up by the Equal Opportunities Commission and Women's National Commission in Britain, which is derived from the Beijing Platform for Action.
2. See Labour MP Fiona Mactaggart's discussion of this incident. She

argues that many women refused to engage in the 'virile' politics of a doomed rebellion. Instead, they worked assiduously behind the scenes to reduce the negative effects of the policy and to promote measures to further improve the position of lone parents (Mactaggart, 2000).

5

Representation in Practice

In the last chapter we surveyed debates about representation, equality and difference. Here we tap women councillors' understandings of their representative role and political practice. How do women politicians themselves talk about political representation and social representativeness? Do they perceive there to be a connection between who they are and what they do? As noted in the previous chapter, there are symbolic and substantive arguments for increasing the number of women in politics. Symbolic arguments draw a link between social representation and concerns about justice, democracy and recognition. Much of the emphasis has been on the under-representation of women, although the case can be applied to other socially relevant groups. The relative absence of women and members of marginalized social groups means they do not have equal representation in terms of presence and influence and, therefore, suffer from political inequality.

Substantive arguments make explicit links between social representation and the outcome of the political process. The relative absence of women is seen to leave politics the poorer. In short, it is proposed that the greater representation of women and others will not only enhance democracy but will 'make a difference' to the practice of politics.

Reasons to Be There

In the current study, the fact that women make up 50 per cent of the general population was seen by many to justify claims that they should make up 50 per cent of decision-making bodies. On an individual level it was seen to be a woman's right to participate in politics. 'Women are under-represented, that's just a bald statement of fact. I think a more balanced representation is better in a democratic society – it goes without saying, doesn't it?' (Conservative). The under-representation of women was also placed within a wider context:

> There should be more disabled people in politics, there should be more black people in politics – politics should reflect society as a whole – and as women constitute more than 50 per cent of the community then there should be more than 50 per cent women represented here. I don't see any other way of putting it, I think we can justify the fact that women should be wherever people are. (Labour)

As one woman noted, 'the equality point of view is my first and simple answer, frankly in lots of arguments that could just stand'. In a discussion which parallels Phillips (1993, 1995) she saw the under-representation of women in decision-making bodies as a serious problem for democracy which raised awkward and crucial questions about the distribution of power:

> The minute you find that in a population where gender is fairly equally distributed, yet when you get into power – which is politics – that it's largely dominated by one group then you have to start thinking: What does power mean? What do men mean by power? (Labour)

However, further justifications were also forwarded which clustered around ideas of women as a specific interest group. Thus it was reasoned that women have interests which differ from, and can potentially be in conflict with, men's interests. The argument continued that women would be better served by parliaments and councils with more female representatives in terms not only of identifying women's needs and putting them on the political agenda, but also in then giving those issues greater political priority than would men:

It would be ideal if the sex of representatives didn't matter – if women could feel that men would represent them equally well. But I don't think we are yet at that stage – that either women feel – or that men do. There are many women who will vote for men, but I think there are very few men who will truly, honestly represent everybody equally and impartially – the partiality will be subconscious. I don't think many men appreciate women's problems – a lot of them think women make a lot of fuss about nothing! (Liberal Democrat)

The third explanation rested upon ideas of resources. It was argued that women have either general or distinctive skills and experiences to bring to politics, or a mixture of the two. The argument embraces both ideas of 'special contribution', which claim women have gender-distinctive skills, and the 'equal opportunities' dimension which sees the exclusion of women from decision-making bodies as a waste of the individual talents of able women:

Women do have a unique understanding. They're the ones usually who go up to school, who get involved in their children's education and they're usually the ones who are looking after elderly parents and things like that. So it's really important to get more women in to represent the people out there. (Labour)

According to some of the councillors, women provided a counterpoint to men and together they provided a 'balanced ticket'.

Complex reasons

However, categorization of answers was not straightforward. Few women confined themselves to symbolic or substantive reasonings alone. Most invoked and interwove several strands of reasoning to create complex justifications for the increased presence of women in political institutions. Thus one explanation might contain themes of both equality and difference. Women argued on both gender-neutral and gendered grounds, explanations frequently overlapped and could be open to a variety of 'readings', including traditional and feminist variants. Discussions about specific women's interests or women's issues invariably broadened to include ideas of representing other marginal groups or, indeed, previously marginalized concerns for whole communities. As such, many women believed that they worked for the 'common good'. The 'common good' justification contained elements of both the justice/proportionality and the resource arguments. If justice/proportionality arguments argue for an ideal in terms of democratic representation, then 'common good' equates to an ideal in terms of outcome. It argues that the increased presence of women in political institutions would improve both political fora and political agendas, not for a narrow interest group, but for the 'common good'.

> I think there should be more women in politics because they represent, and are likely to represent, the views of women who are so many of the community. Things like, for instance, a road safety issue – it's very often women who are involved at that sort of community level because they see it as very important. It's very often women who see it on a day-to-day basis, they're the ones who are walking up the road to school with the kids. They see the dangers and they live it. (Labour)

Here, women's interests are equated with the wider issue of road safety in a community. In many instances women found it difficult to unpick women's interests from general care issues associated with their traditional place in families. Women often recast the argument to reflect the representation of the needs of a community rather than the pursuit of 'classic' interests.

Women's Perspectives

Women argued that because of their distinctive experiences they 'see' politics differently and have different agendas and different political priorities. It was commonly expressed as a women's perspective. 'It's not that women have separate issues, it's just they have a perspective on a whole range of issues which sometimes doesn't get a voice if you haven't got women there.' As one Conservative councillor put it, 'Women bring their own perspective to things and their own thoughts and their own experiences. They are different from men – whether the men like it or not.'

Ideas about women's perspectives and distinctive resources have been used in the past to promote a limited role for women in politics. The predominance of women in 'soft' specialisms such as health, education and family policy in legislatures around the world has been widely noted (see, for instance, Randall, 1987). To a degree, this containment of women is still informed by 'feminine ideology'. As one elderly Conservative councillor said, 'I think there is still that softness there. Well, women are the softer breed, aren't we? There's a kindness there – they can be bothered.' In a similar vein, a young Liberal Democrat explained her policy interests as follows:

> Because I am a woman that's where my natural interests lie: within the community with the womenfolk. In that, I'm interested in child care, I'm interested in women at work. I would probably be more interested in roads and transport if I was a man. (Liberal Democrat)

These examples of traditional thinking were not common. Although many women did, to some extent, accept they had a 'special' understanding of policy areas such as education and under-fives; two major shifts in thinking seem to have occurred since Duverger's work: first, women challenged the under-valuing of so-called 'soft' specialisms or women's issues; and second, they did not see themselves as limited to any specialism. Rather they saw their experience and their 'perspective' as transferable to any policy area. 'I think women are just as able to be Chancellor of the Exchequer as they are to be the Women's Officer or the Minister for the Family.' A former Finance Convenor – the first women to hold such a position in the history of her council – was seen to have 'proved' herself in a powerful 'male' post. However, she did not see that women had to 'choose between being equal or different'. Some women stressed the importance of women's experience in the traditionally 'soft' areas . They also argued that women's ordinary lives gave them an understanding of so-called 'hard' or 'male' areas, for instance, economics, although many women did not realize that was the case:

> It seems to me in the most simplistic of terms that if you have x number of pounds coming in a week and you've got certain things to do with it before the end of the week, then you certainly know a bit about the economy – I accept that's very basic. ... I mean one of the pictures that we will all remember about the horrible Margaret Thatcher was her shopping bag and that screamed out to me that all those hundreds of thousands of women out there who say they know nothing

about the economy do – and they do every time they step into a shop! (Labour)

In practice, many women's discussions contained elements of both traditional and 'transformed' thinking. For instance, the issue of child care was argued to be inextricably linked with economic development 'because it's one of the major barriers to economic regeneration'. At present the lack of women meant it was 'a hard job selling that understanding politically'. However, the increased presence of women in politics would transform the debate about child care and transform the agendas of 'hard' policy areas.

Doing Politics Differently?

The last major cluster of justifications centred around substantive differences in political behaviour or style. Two-thirds of the women in this study agreed with the statement that women politicians behaved differently to male politicians and a further fifth agreed with certain qualifications. Men and women were perceived to 'do' politics in different ways. In common with other empirical research many of the women in this study perceived themselves to be less formal and hierarchical and to prefer less status-seeking ways of 'doing' politics. Many felt they gave a greater emphasis to consultation and collaborative ways of working:

> I think women have a more civilized way of behaving towards people, listening to people and talking to them – rather than shouting at them – and discussing things. The area I represent is also represented by two Tory women councillors and I can communicate perfectly all right with them – although come the elections we will be fighting opposite sides. But I can still talk to them and, where action needs to be taken for the benefit of constituents by all of us, we are able to take action together for the good of the public, if you like, rather than feeling it always has to be some sort of political slanging match and that the public don't really matter. (Labour)

> It is dangerous to generalize, but I think on the whole men enjoy confrontation and conflict and women, on the whole, prefer to operate in a more co-operative way. (Liberal Democrat)

I wouldn't want to say it's necessarily universal because that is just to stereotype women but I think they tend to be more open to changing methods of working. Perhaps because the old methods of working simply haven't done all that well for women so it's been a necessity and from that necessity people discover that it is actually a worthwhile thing in itself. (Labour)

One Conservative councillor sounded a word of caution about the claim that women are more consensual, 'remember, women tend not to say things absolutely outright, and it sounds consensual – but they say a lot of things behind the scenes and that is less helpful. I think men are more direct.'

Some argued that if there were more women in politics it would lead to a general improvement in the way politics is conducted and in the public perception and estimation of politicians:

Politics would be done in a different way if there were more women, and I think it would be a great improvement over the other macho puerile way in which politics is conducted at the moment . I think it is the way in which men do politics which puts a lot of the public off politics ... Women don't do politics in that way – it doesn't mean to say that we don't have strong views about our opinions, or our determination to carry out what we feel is right, but we don't indulge in that sort of level of personal abuse. And I think it might well raise the profile, and the estimation of politicians in the public eye, if there were more women. (Labour)

Although perceptions differed, most of the women believed that the increased presence of women in political elites would change the political agenda and have an impact on policy. In general, younger women and Labour women were more likely to support this view and older Conservative women were the most sceptical.

Categorizing answers was not simple. Beliefs about the potential impact of (greater numbers of) women in politics frequently intertwined in interviews, with observations drawn from the everyday practice of female politicians. This sometimes led to deeply contradictory answers. Several women eschewed the relevance of gender when discussing recruitment, such as this Labour councillor, 'I would like to see more women in politics, but I would like to see them for their ability *not because they're women*'

(Labour) (our italics). However, when asked directly why there should be more women in politics, the same woman answered, 'Because I think we've got a lot to offer. We have a different insight into life, we have different problems, I think we're able to relate to women and the problems they have and the problems with child care'. These contradictions were not untypical. Several discussions emphasized the need for women to get elected on the same terms as men and drew upon arguments of equality and merit. However, they also invoked difference, in this case in terms of both interests (that is, women's problems and child care) and perspective (that is, a different insight). Similarly several women, in principle, espoused gender-neutral reasonings, that is equality or 'sameness' arguments. However, when discussing the daily practice of politics, they underscored the relevance of difference in terms of behaviour, or political agendas or policy development. The faultlines of internal contradiction were particularly clear in some accounts, but most women interviewed struggled with competing notions of equality and difference.

Representation as a Political Issue: A Sense of Connection?

As noted earlier, it is suggested that one of the ways in which women politicians have a distinctive politics is in their sense of connection to other women 'hopefuls' and their shared concerns with access. In the current study there were very high levels of support for the greater presence of women in political institutions and the issue of representation was seen as significant on a majority of the women's personal political agendas. In general, the issue had the greatest salience for Labour women, a larger proportion of whom were actively involved in promoting representation. This indicates the high level of internal debate experienced within the Labour Party at national (British) and Scottish level. A significant proportion of Liberal Democrat women were supportive of change, with smaller proportions of Conservative and SNP councillors perceiving under-representation as a priority issue for themselves.

The debates on representation were seen as legitimate and important to almost all the women in the current study. However, for one or two women, representation was understood solely in terms of agent principal – or 'acting for'. Therefore they perceived the proportion of women in politics to be irrelevant:

> The issue of women in politics is not at all important to me. What is important is decent representation of the population, competent government of the country, taxation, value for money and healthcare. They matter to me more than whether there are men or women MPs. (Conservative)

> I'm not here to represent the women in my constituency or the women in [the city] anymore than I am here to represent the men ... Women in the community think we're more sympathetic, but at the end of the day sex shouldn't come into it at all. (Liberal Democrat)

Most women councillors believed they had a personal responsibility, with varying degrees of commitment and activity, to encourage other women to seek political office. 'I have always encouraged other women whenever I can. I tell them, "I'm an ordinary woman. I haven't had a good education. If I can do it, you can do it" They can see me and think, "If she can do it, I can do it!" ' (Labour). In a number of instances young women with children felt a responsibility to stay on in politics in order to encourage others:

> We've got to encourage more women. To say, yes, you can do that, you can make a difference. You can do exactly what they're doing, despite having all the drawbacks of having to run off and pick up the kids in between meetings and then come back again and all that. But you can manage it – and one of the reasons I've decided to stay on is that I do think people have got to realize that an ordinary person like me can do it – so can they. (Labour)

In addition, a number of women talked about the need to keep links with women in the community and in women's organizations, 'to keep our feet out there':

> It's important to keep your links. Once you become a member of the council it's very easy to get drawn into the system. So it's vital to keep in contact with [women's groups] so that you know what women are expecting and to try and represent their views. (Labour)

111

Women Representing Women?

The contested meanings of representation and controversies about who can represent whom, and how, are explored in various ways within discussions. One or two women were sceptical about claims that went beyond the symbolic not only in terms of gender but also with respect to race and ethnicity:

> There's no reasoned argument for a gender balance of representation as far as I can see – just symbolic importance. The same as with your ethnic communities – ideally you have the same ratio and balance of representation there. But that doesn't mean that a Pakistani can represent an Indian. (Conservative)

In any event, few women were prepared to uncritically embrace the category 'Woman', and were clear that women are also divided by other factors such as class, race, ethnicity, religion, age – and perhaps most importantly in the case of female politicians, political party. Most women were careful to emphasize the complexity of identity and interests. Some women felt uncomfortable with the assumption that all women represented women better than men might. In particular, Margaret Thatcher was singled out as an example of a woman who had done little to represent women's interests, 'an aberration'. Women argued against simplistic assumptions that women politicians straightforwardly represent women's interests, 'the follow on to that would be that men can only represent men'. There were difficulties in how far to invoke or deny 'distinctive experience'. Some women saw the issue, neither in terms of symbolic equality nor a direct matching of group representatives with interests, but rather as a presence which would inform a notion of 'general thinking'. Others, again mostly Labour women, were prepared to argue that women across party shared a common outlook, 'women are more in tune with what other women are looking for no matter what their political beliefs or political make-up', and could form alliances around certain issues, particularly violence against women. This shared concern resulted in what one councillor described as 'a sort of solidarity'.

Perhaps the most striking evidence of common interests and understanding around issues of violence in this study was the crucial political support from women councillors, both feminist and non-feminist across the four major parties, for the ground-breaking anti-violence public education campaign Zero Tolerance in the 1990s. This support indicated not only the personal and political salience of the issue for the women councillors themselves but also a recognition of its significance to women in the community. The vast majority viewed the radical initiative as a legitimate part of politics and their own local political remit. They were also convinced that the campaign would not have happened, or was unlikely to have happened, without the presence of elected women members.

Women councillors perceived themselves to be more supportive and to place greater importance than did their male counterparts on a range of policy issues such as child care, nursery provision, community safety, community care, housing and transport policy, health, violence, equal opportunities and greater political representation for women. This commitment ranged from a recognition of the complexity of the issues and their place on the political agenda to active advocacy. Women across political parties found the term 'women's issues' problematic, in the main because they perceived these issues to be human or society issues rather than narrowly-defined women's issues. However, they recognized that without a 'label' many of these concerns could be rendered invisible.

Following Hedlund's study of Swedish councillors in the 1980s, the women councillors were asked whether they agreed with the view that women politicians represented the interests of women in the community better than men do. In Hedlund's study 83 per cent of female councillors thought women did represent other women better, with 17 per cent disagreeing. The Scottish findings are less clear: around a half agreed, although others agreed with certain qualifications and reservations. In total more than three-quarters wholly or partly agreed. The difference in findings may stem in part from the different ways in which the studies were conducted. Hedlund used a questionnaire which therefore would not reflect shades of opinion picked up in the semi-structured interviews used here. In addition, a number of women discussed the perceptions of women in the community who saw women councillors as having a special responsibility as women to represent them. Many interviewees commented that women from outwith their wards came to their surgeries for help 'because you're a woman, you'll understand'. This included one councillor who objected to the idea of being perceived as in any way representing women because she was a woman:

People come to my surgery and I say, 'Have you approached
your own councillor?' and they say, 'Oh, he's a man and I can't
really sit down ...' The perception of the public is – it's a
woman, therefore she'll understand. (Liberal Democrat)

This suggests that the idea of a special 'constituency of women'
which women MPs discussed in the 1970s (Currell, 1974; Vallance,
1979) still appears to apply to women in local government in the
1990s. The responsibility to raise equalities issues was also
commented upon:

You have to accept that as a woman – there aren't that many of
us – so when women's issues are discussed, then you do feel
that you have to be kind of representative and think about how
it affects other women – the women you meet in the
playground, for example and how it would affect them ... So
you take on that responsibility as well. (Labour)

You've got a special responsibility as a woman, I think, being
in such a small minority, to try and represent women's views.
(Labour)

Representing only women?

This acceptance by practitioners – that is, women politicians – of a
constituency of women, shifting and partial though the definitions
are, is in contrast to Anne Phillips' tendency to foreclose discussions
about group representation (1993). The majority of women
councillors in this study believed that they both 'stand for' and
that they 'act for' women. However, few women saw themselves as
acting *only* for women. Most women were keen to stress their wish
to serve the whole of the community, although they were aware of
limitations of representation which explained a preference, in many
cases, for additional mechanisms for grassroots consultation and
participation. 'I think women politicians are more likely to have a
philosophy of: "Well, don't ask me what women are thinking – ask
them!"' They were mindful of differences between women and of
diversity more generally. Explicit links were made between an
increase in the numbers of women councillors and an opening up of
the decision-making processes of councils:

If there were more women in politics it would be a lot more accessible ... The amount of people I see in the streets and I say: 'There's something that will interest you, come into the council.' And they say: 'I cannae do that.' I say: 'Of course you can, it's your council!' I think women would promote the attitude of open door politics – that's the way democracy should be. (Labour)

Furthermore, most women in this study believed that the increased presence of women in politics at local authority and national level would make a difference in terms of either style, or content or both.

Empathy or Experience?

Differing conceptions of representation were discussed. It was argued that there was a need for individual representatives to understand, if not experience, the issues in their constituents' lives. It was also contended that representative bodies needed to contain as wide a variety of people as possible. An outspoken Labour councillor and community activist described her reaction when a local politician, attending a meeting about poverty, asked what a 'power card' was:

In an area like [this] where fuel poverty is a huge issue ... practically everyone uses a power card because it is the only way they can cope with their fuel debt ... His lack of insight into the experiences of the people he was representing filled me with horror – how can he purport to represent thousands of people when he is not understanding what their lives are about? But then I'm not saying that everybody has to be poor to understand what it is like to be poor because that's just a silly notion. You need a wide range of people because society is made up of a wide range of people. You need your occasional barm – and you need your personalities, your intellectuals. You need your organizers, you need a wide variety of skills and personalities, I think, to give a balanced group and a balanced government – or else it would all be really boring if we were all Tony Blair.

Representation was seen to be based in part upon ideas of common interests or shared experience and in part upon responsibility and responsiveness. These representative practices were not confined to women, some men who were characterized as careful, empathetic and responsive were included. Sometimes this was based upon an observation that they had personal experience of caring responsibilities.

> If your experience is having to drag the kids to school or not having a nursery school then that's an experience that is worth having but equally a man can know – if he's got a partner who stays at home everyday – he can see what she's going through as well, or women he comes across in his workplace. I'm not saying only women can represent women. (Labour)

Pulling the Strands Together

Most women expressed both symbolic and substantive under-standings of representation. One woman speaking during the school holidays, with her children playing in the corridors of the council headquarters, summed up her view of the symbolic and substantive presence of women in politics:

> I feel the very fact that I am sitting here on the council as a woman – with all my experiences, with my kids outside – that's the best way. That's why I want more women in – not to sit there and go, 'What about women's issues?' Just to *do* it – quietly and without any fuss – get on with the job of being women on the council and putting forward *a* woman's point of view. You don't have to say this is a *women's* point of view; you just have to say this is my view, I'm a councillor – same as you – *listen* to me.

Contemporary claims for women's increased inclusion into political decision-making bodies are premised upon differing conceptions of political representation, differing ideas about the political relevance of gender, and differing expectations as to the consequences of their inclusion. They are part of a more general response by groups hitherto marginalized in the political process who demand that a politics of presence be incorporated into existing ideas about representation.

Overlaid upon these practical and theoretical difficulties is the problem of the issue of particularity in current political 'rules of the game' within specific political systems. In Britain, it is not generally claimed that there is a direct correlation between the presence of individual members of specific groups and the representation of group interests. The most common argument forwarded by British campaigners for reform is that a more socially representative political assembly, like a parliament or a council, will not only be more just and democratic but is also likely to more effectively represent the whole community because it will contain a diverse range of experiences and perspectives. This is the idea of a parliament or council of all talents.

All political parties in mainland Britain have stated their desire to improve the social representativeness of political and public decision-making bodies, whether they are parliaments, assemblies, local councils or other public bodies. However, as discussed in Chapter 2, policies to address under-representation have developed unevenly. Gender is only partially recognized as a legitimate political cleavage in British politics. Notions of formal equality – and equal treatment – are the political and legislative framework within which gender, and indeed race, issues have been mediated and claims by groups can still be regarded as 'particularist'. In particular, positive action has been fiercely contested and, in the case of the Labour Party, uneasily applied.

Although feminist political scientists and political activists do acknowledge a variety of reasons to promote and progress women's increased access to political elites, in Britain they have privileged justice and legitimacy arguments, based upon notions of (individual) fairness and representative proportionality, in preference to justifications which stress women's different interests or different contribution. In part, the reluctance to invoke substantive reasons stems from the potential these arguments have to be used by reactionaries to reinforce stereotypes about women's role. The promotion of symbolic arguments also provides a 'good fit' with dominant notions of gender-neutral equality in British political culture. Increasingly, symbolic arguments about proportionate representation also play to the British government's concern with modernization and democratic renewal post-1997 and the idea that social representativeness may have an important role in this work. These symbolic justifications are a conscious political strategy and are seen as the most straightforward way to argue and most acceptable to men and non-feminist women. Anne Phillips argues: 'The case can be quite adequately prepared in terms of political equality or justice without getting into more troubled waters of representing group interests and concerns' (1993, p. 138).

Distinction perhaps should be drawn between justifications, that is, the claims upon which demands for greater representation are made, and expectations. The competing meanings of representation infuse the various discussions and commentaries. We see, within the British context, equivocation on the part of feminist academics and activists. On the one hand is the intuitive appeal of difference or substantive arguments and, on the other, the pull of symbolic arguments on grounds of both theoretical neatness and pragmatic realism. We see echoes of this in the complex and sometimes contradictory discussions of women politicians. Conflicts, perhaps, between head and heart and between principle and practice.

At present, the primary legitimizing discourse for increasing the number of women in politics is one of 'justice'. However, without the promotion of additional reasonings and discourses which 'dignify' difference and delineate the gendered structure of both political and economic systems as well as ordinary lives, it can be difficult to imbue the exclusion of women with political urgency and the impetus for action. Symbolic arguments present a dilemma in terms of commitment to action. If, achieving equality of representation is seen as an 'ideal' outcome, one of symbolic rather than substantive importance, how hard are parties and systems, who have accepted justice arguments, required to try to 'enable' women's access? Despite the seemingly straightforward appeal to parity – the gendered role of women intervenes to complicate, particularly their unequal burden resulting from the sexual division of labour. This results in one of the features discussed in recruitment studies, the 'supply' problem of aspirant women candidates. In other words, the relatively low numbers of women who put themselves forward as candidates. What price symbolic equality? If women will not necessarily make a difference, then how reasonable would it be to expect political parties and political institutions to make the radical restructuring required to fully include an 'awkward' group of people? Additional justifications may well be required in order to support demands for change.

In terms of how women councillors discuss and explain their practice, the limitations of the equality approach are obvious. To suggest that there may be substantive or difference arguments as well as symbolic or equality arguments does not necessarily mean the debate need drift into the troubled waters of formalized group representation. Multi-valued justifications reflect the realities of women politicians' own experiences and common-sense analysis. This need not create the difficulties Phillips and others fear. We noted at the beginning of Chapter 4 the 'slippery' nature of the concept of representation and the multiple meanings already in play. Politicians are elected primarily on the grounds of geographical representation (constituency or district) and party representation. However, there are other dimensions in play, of which social representation is one. To argue that women parliamentarians or councillors tend to better represent women's interests and to bring different skills and approaches – that is, the substantive argument – provides another reason to 'be there' in fluid models of representation.

Furthermore, it is clear that at popular level the proportionality argument carries implicit messages that the presence of previously marginal groups will have an impact on the promotion of group interests. A clear illustration of this was the expectations that the then new Labour women MPs would vote against benefit cuts to lone parents in 1997 and the derision and disappointment they faced when they voted on party lines. Thus, as a popular discourse, symbolic arguments for proportionate representation can overlap with interests and difference reasonings and therefore lose some of their attraction as the 'safe option'.

Part I: Summary

Explaining women's absence and promoting women's presence

In the first Part of this book we have considered many of the standard accounts relating to women and political representation. We drew upon both empirical and theoretical literatures to consider the explanations as to women's relative absence in councils and parliaments, the nature of the progress made so far and the difficulties outstanding. We also examined the common reasons why it is argued that the more women should be promoted into politics. These issues have also been explored through the accounts of women politicians in Scotland.

The reasons for women's absence in politics are complex and flow largely from the personal, social and structural consequences of women's continued real or assumed responsibility in the domestic sphere. Barriers are also posed by political institutions in the broadest sense by which we mean formal structures and rules and informal practices, norms and values. It is a commonplace point, but worth making none the less, that politics (like much of the world of work) is premised upon others taking care of care. So institutions are designed as if individuals are unencumbered by domestic responsibilities. This presents very real practical difficulties for women who do have such responsibilities. However, the problem of political culture goes deeper and relates to the forms of masculinity entrenched within political institutions. Macho plays out in adversarial and aggressive power politics and zero-sum games. Of course, not all men play by these stereotypical male norms and some women, famously, do. However, many women describe it as alienating and intimidating. It discourages many women who are engaged in party politics from putting themselves forward as candidates and dissuades others from getting involved in formal politics in the first place. On a broader level, distaste for adversarial political culture is sometimes forwarded as a reason why the public (both women and men) feel increasingly alienated and mistrustful of traditional politics and formal political institutions.

The barriers to participation are complex which implies that action is needed on a number of levels: systematic, party political and individual. Additionally, long-term remedies would seem to require fundamental structural changes to gender relations and the gendered division of labour, on the one hand, and to political institutions, on the other.

Political parties have improved recruitment and selection procedures, some have introduced 'weak' positive action, more controversially, the Labour Party has adopted quotas. We argue that all but the most modest of measures bring attendant problems in terms of legitimacy. There are difficulties in imbuing the case for action with urgency and in building and maintaining constituencies of support. Most recently proposals have been forwarded calling upon the government to introduce a new electoral law to clear the way for 'strong' positive action. Activists, and to some extent feminist academics, are pinning their hopes on quotas. Other issues around the need for long agenda transformations of love and politics are barely touched upon.

Women politicians understand barriers to be complex and to relate to the costs of care and the consequences of inimical political culture. Their accounts also reinforce the point that the barriers to women's full participation have proved remarkably resistant and that there have been considerable problems in devising and implementing 'acceptable' mechanisms for change. 'Special measures' to allow more women to gain access have proved hard to justify within dominant political discourses and common understandings of fairness and equality. These reservations are shared by many political women. Many prefer the idea of the long agenda of social transformation, but have little sense of how that can be achieved. There is a sense of progress stalled: of taking two steps forward then one step back. In part, this is as a result of the limitations of operating within narrow definitions of equality as 'sameness'.

Chapters 2 and 3 related to the reasons why women are absent. Chapters 4 and 5 focused upon reasons why women should be present. The arguments for greater gender balance have been well rehearsed: traditionally they have involved issues of justice, equality and the contribution of women's talents; controversially, they have sometimes insisted upon women's different interests. More recently, proportionate representation is being presented as an important plank in strategies to revitalize liberal welfare democracies and renew citizen trust and confidence in political institutions. Women's demands may also be seen as part of a broader movement for the political inclusion and recognition of previously marginalized social groups.

The dominant arguments in the British context relate to symbolic arguments which claim presence on the basis of justice. This rests on demands for modified equality which takes into account social context. This approach finds favour with many feminist academics and feminist campaigners. There are many good reasons for this: on a pragmatic level arguments from justice strike a chord with wider mainstream debates, such arguments make for neater theory, too. Arguments from difference are seen as risky and essentialist. There are also related problems connected with 'stronger' arguments about group representation and identity politics. Feminists are also justifiably anxious that women politicians will face unrealistic expectations. However, there is a paradox: to argue that women's exclusion is an inequality is to accept the difference that campaigners seek to deny. Symbolic arguments do carry implicit messages that the inclusion of women 'makes a difference'.

Although the relationship between 'representation' and 'representativeness' is by no means straightforward and conclusions drawn from research evidence must remain tentative, nevertheless, there is a plausible case that the presence of women may result in substantive as well as symbolic outcomes. Women politicians appear to have different views of power and political process from their male counterparts. There is an apparent difference in terms of policy priorities which can result in an impact on political agendas and policy outcomes. Finally, there is some evidence of a politics of 'connectedness', relating to issues of communication, consultation and responsive responsibility. These differences are conditioned by political party. It is also the case that aggregate differences between women and men mask differences between different sub-groups of women and different sub-groups of men.

The women councillors in the current study perceived themselves to be both equal and different. Neither stance adequately reflected their experience. They understood representation in complex and inclusive ways: sometimes acting for and sometimes standing for women as well as for wider communities. Representation was seen to be based in part upon ideas of common interests or shared experience and in part upon responsibility and responsiveness. These representative practices were not confined to women; some men who were characterized as careful, empathetic and responsive were also included. The limitations of representation led many women to express support for consultation and for enhanced opportunities for women and others to have a greater say in the policy-making process.

Part I establishes the complexity of the issues but leaves us with a number of issues about how to move forward. There are limitations to the ways in which we think, talk and argue about equality and political representation. Political parties are prepared to accept the argument in principle, but in practice there is a reluctance to adopt decisive action. In any event, the strategies for reform do not challenge underlying cultural barriers, gender divisions and political practices. We argue that in order to maintain progress and to tackle underlying social and cultural issues there is a need to search for new arguments and new understandings of women's 'place' in power politics. There is also need to 'tangle' with difference, to look at both the positive and the negative sides of care, and to explore ways in which equality and difference might be provisionally reconciled.

PART II

Challenging Politics? Women and Care

We bring a set of questions and issues from Part I about women and political institutions. Standards accounts of 'getting there' and 'being there' take us so far but the unstable, uneven and contested process of women's more equal inclusion in formal politics highlights the limitations of current political discourse and rhetoric. In Part 2 we look for new understandings of women's experience and roles in politics, and for fresh arguments which challenge 'politics as usual' and support further demands for change.

The initial clues about new directions emerged from the 'stories' of the women politicians in the current study and the paradox of care. We look at alternative discourses and consider some ideas associated with the 'ethic' or 'ethics of care'. Theorists who favour this approach argue that the practice of care results in a 'different voice', a distinctive way of thinking about the world which is rooted in the ties of relationships rather than formal rules. They argue that the values and skills traditionally associated with women should be valued rather than denigrated. Some versions locate the ethics of care in mothering, others broaden their definitions of both care and caretakers. Those who seek to develop the ethics of care in the public sphere of politics and citizenship argue it is a strategic tool or concept which can offer a powerful critique of 'politics as usual' as well as provide a compelling set of reasons why women and men who care should have a political voice.

These ideas are not well known in political science or in political discourse and what does filter through tends to be populist and caricatured – appealing to stereotypical and ultimately disempowering views of women's innate 'goodness' and self-sacrifice. Feminist activists and academics concerned with political representation are inclined to give these ideas short shrift and a wide berth: they are dismissed as the basis of a 'dangerous politics' celebratory of women's traditional self-sacrifice, which would make women somehow responsible for care in the public sphere as well as care in the private or domestic sphere. However, the ethics of care is a broad school and subtle, sophisticated versions exist which emphasize the socially and historically contingent nature of care and seek to develop insights for application in the public sphere.

In Chapter 6 we focus upon a number of thinkers who have considered how to apply the ethics of care to the civil, public space of citizenship and informal politics. They suggest a different view of what politics ought to be about. We ask whether insights derived from this literature can be developed to provide a better understanding of women's experience and role in electoral politics and political institutions. We explore the potential of the political ethics of care as a springboard from which to develop a different rationale for the role of political representatives and to construct new discourses to promote alternative political values and practices. Our aim is to assess the pragmatic potential of these ideas.

In Chapter 7 we consider the extent to which there is an empirical basis to the ideas and arguments. We listen again to the voices of women politicians to establish the parallels and the differences between the practical insights of care theorists and the common-sense theorizing of women politicians. We set out possible new vocabularies and discourses drawn from the previous chapter within which to frame demands for change.

6

The Ethics of Care: A Dangerous Politics?

How do we move beyond the current difficulties in the ways we think, talk and argue about gender and political representation? The gendered realities of women candidates and women politicians expose the shortcomings of dominant notions of equality which underpin approaches to equal opportunities and equal treatment. There are also concerns that to concentrate on difference *only* as disadvantage does not adequately reflect the realities of women's ambivalent and contradictory feelings and experiences of care. Women's real and assumed caring responsibilities present a major barrier to their full participation in public life, however, women are sometimes uneasy that care is characterized as a 'burden' from which they need to be released through 'special treatment'. This is illustrated in the case of women politicians who paradoxically perceive domestic and caring labour to be both a barrier and a resource. They place a high value upon care as an idea and an activity and argue that values and skills which arise from women's experience as carers are useful and desirable in local and national politics.

The aim of this chapter is to explore some of the concepts and arguments to be found within the growing field of moral and political thought which come under the umbrella term of the 'ethics of care'. It assesses their strategic potential and, indeed, their limitations for practical politics and for the discursive contests in which activists seeking to promote women's political equality are engaged. Although care theorists draw upon a range of moral and philosophical traditions, they are all positioned to some degree within 'difference' feminism and use 'care' to challenge existing equality and justice paradigms, in other words, liberal universalist models.

How does this ethic of care compare with the ethic of justice? Different writers operate with varying definitions, but three key differences emerge which are summarized by Sevenhuijsen (1998, pp. 107–8) as follows: first, the ethics of care involves different moral ideas, those of responsibilities and relationships rather than rules; second, the ethics of care is concerned with concrete situations and with problems and dilemmas seen within their socio-economic setting in contrast to an ethics of justice which is concerned with the formal and abstract; finally, the ethics of care is best seen as a deliberative activity rather than as a fixed set of principles.

These recent theoretical suggestions are seen as potential sites in which new directions and new understandings may be found and where alternative political discourses and strategies may be produced. Our main focus is upon the work of Sarah Ruddick (1989), Joan Tronto (1993) and Selma Sevenhuijsen (1998) who each avoids the pitfalls of essentialism and uncritical celebration of 'womanly virtues' by stressing care as a social practice and who have all explored the wider social and political applications of an inclusive version of 'care thinking'. We also consider the work of Susan Okin (1989) who takes a very different starting point but seeks to apply a contextualized ethic of justice to the family and issues of care.

In a Different Voice

Before moving on to consider these works, we briefly need to set out the contemporary origins of the 'different voice' or 'ethic of care' and the polarization it has engendered. The 'ethic of care' was first articulated in the 1980s in Carol Gilligan's hugely influential work, *In a Different Voice*, in which she appeared to have found evidence of parallel but different moral reasoning in women. This reasoning was seen as more contextual, more rooted in ties of relationships and was named a 'Different Voice'. Gilligan suggested that men are more concerned with abstract rights and formal rules which results in an 'ethic of justice' whereas women are concerned with responsibilities and inter-personal relationships which results in an 'ethic of care' (Gilligan, 1982).

Gilligan's model of moral development is made up of three stages: the *pre-social*, the *conventional* and the *post-conventional* perspectives. In the first stage, primary concern is with self and survival. Transition from the first to the second stage is marked by a move from selfishness to responsibility and a recognition of the need to care for others. Women equate 'goodness' with self-sacrifice and care for others. They take on conventional values and norms, speaking with what Gilligan dubs the 'conventional feminine voice' (1982, p. 79). Women are inhibited by modern patriarchal conditions and expectations from moving from this conventional stage to the third, post-conventional stage (McLaughlin, 1997, p. 18). However, despite these difficulties there is a impetus to move beyond the 'conventions of feminine goodness' which confuse self-sacrifice with care and pay little attention to women's own needs. The final post-conventional perspective achieves a balance between the self and others, between autonomy and care. It is seen as an activity or practice and involves a detailed understanding of inter dependence and the dilemmas of achieving that balance in concrete situations (Gilligan, 1982, p. 79; Sevenhuijsen, 1998, p. 51).

In the intervening decade or so, several commentators have attempted to apply Gilligan's insights to a range of spheres and disciplines – including political and moral theory – and in so doing have developed the ideas far beyond Gilligan's original research focus, the moral development of girls and young women. As McLaughlin notes, 'it has taken on a life, meaning and significance which is far wider than that originally intended by Gilligan' (1997, p. 17).

The work of Gilligan and subsequent care theorists has also provoked a fiercely negative response.[1] Critics of this approach argue it is dangerously essentialist, reinforcing sexual stereotypes and of championing a lesser morality which is the product of women and girls' powerlessness and self sacrifice. It is also charged with crudely homogenizing the diverse experiences of women and being inattentive to issues of race, class and sexuality. Others have pointed out that essentialist accounts of an ethics of care tend to celebrate the conventional stage of 'feminine goodness' which Gilligan sought to challenge (McLaughlin, 1997). Indeed, Gilligan has described her reaction to ways in which her work is presented as essentialist or as promoting female moral superiority as akin to losing her voice 'because these are not my questions' (Gilligan, 1993, p. xiii).

Moral Mothers and Maternal Thinking

Despite the ongoing controversy about the ethics of care, the 'different voice' has been developed in different ways. One of the directions has been the exploration of mothering as a 'neglected' form of moral knowledge and important source of women's power. For example, Ruddick has argued that care, in the form of mothering, gives rise to both a mode of thinking and specific skills and strategies that are a resource for peace politics. The notion of distinctive women's values and women's morality, associated in particular with motherhood, is not of course new – nor is the ambivalence of feminists as to whether these ideas constitute an opportunity or a danger for women (Rendall, 1987; Offen, 1992). British socialist feminist Lynne Segal has been deeply critical of what she has termed the 'maternal revivalists' (1987, p. 145). Judith Evans sees this celebration of nurturing qualities as an acceptance of subjugation and asks 'what is the virtue of qualities born of oppression?' (1995, p. 19). However, other feminist reactions have been more ambivalent, recognizing the appeal of an approach that gives worth to 'female values' and 'women's work' in contrast to the low status they are accorded by society,[2] while also being anxious about the potential for such ideas to be co-opted by conservative forces to reinforce sexual stereotypes (Rowbotham, 1985; Okin, 1989).

Reasoning which relies upon women's traditional roles as mothers and carers can easily become essentialist and conservative, a justification to limit and constrain women . In its traditional form, women's morality was confined to the 'right sort' of women and served to exclude many types of women which it classed as 'other' or 'immoral', for example, working-class women, black women, lesbians and 'unfit mothers' (Tronto, 1993). Some versions of maternal thinking, particularly those which stress individualist caring responses (Noddings, 1984; Manning, 1992) are seen to celebrate rather than challenge 'conventional femininity'. Bubeck argues that uncritical or sentimental forms of the 'ethic of care' can function 'as an oppressive ideology which blinds women to their own exploitation' (1995, p. 180). Approaches which romanticize care fail to consider the negative aspects of mothering, such as aggression, resentment and conflict (Flax, 1993; McLaughlin, 1997).

In addition, there is considerable feminist resistance, particularly from those who value universalist notions of citizenship, to the potential application of maternal thinking in the public sphere. Mary Dietz has argued that people must rise above their everyday identities to be citizens. She sees caring work as particularist and insular, and has dismissed the idea that civic virtue can arise from motherhood with the memorable retort: 'When we look to mothering for a vision of feminist citizenship ... we look in the wrong place' (Dietz, 1985, p. 13).

Joan Tronto, a leading theorist of care, acknowledges that essentialist strains of women's different thinking can lead to 'dangerous politics'. However, she, and others, while arguing against giving motherhood a privileged status, have recognized women's experiences as important sources of reflexive reasoning. They have taken the positive aspects of maternal thinking as starting points for developing broader ideas of an ethics of care and its relevance for politics (Tronto, 1993; Sevenhuijsen, 1998).

A Useful Political Tool?

Feminists have, thus, been divided as to whether the 'ethic of care' has inevitably essentialist underpinnings which lead to a 'dangerous politics', celebratory of women's traditional self-sacrifice; or whether it can be used to challenge and transform values and practices in the public and political sphere. Given the size and scope of misgivings, can the 'ethic of care' be seen as a significant political tool or concept?

There are a number of reasons which suggest that a political version of the ethics of care has strategic potential. First, advocates argue that it exposes the relative absence of care as a political value and the lack of regard for issues of care in political decision-making (Tronto, 1993; McLaughlin, 1997). Arguably, the extent to which care is marginalized in politics will vary from political system to political system: so social welfare democracies are likely to be more 'caring' than are unmodified liberal democracies, although care thinkers contend that nowhere is it placed centrally. Second, and closely related to the first point, it challenges politics that 'do harm'

(Green, 1995). So, for example, this would challenge politics where economic imperatives and military goals take precedence over people and the environment. Third, the political ethics of care highlights 'careless' decision-making which may favour formal 'just' solutions rather than effective and context-sensitive outcomes. As such it provides a counterbalance to the ethic of justice. Finally, it seeks to humanize politics by positioning care as a central political value and promoting associated attributes such as attentiveness, responsibility, connectedness, reciprocity and respect for diversity (Tronto, 1993; Sevenhuijsen, 1998).

The preceding points are inter-related and have much in common with other projects promoting radical democracy and citizen deliberation. It is in the next cluster of reasons that we see the significance of the ethics of care for women and for groups of marginalized men.

The ethics of care values the skills that arise and are honed through the practice of care and suggests that these are valuable skills which are needed in the public sphere of citizenship. This emphasis on care as a resource potentially empowers groups of women and marginalized groups of men who characteristically are responsible for caretaking activity, both unpaid and (badly) paid. The public worth attached to 'care thinking' and 'care thinkers' as citizens acts as a powerful form of recognition and validation and also can build or reinforce group solidarity. Taken together, the ethics of care presents a powerful vision of a different sort of politics and a set of reasons to 'be there' (Ruddick, 1989; Tronto, 1993; Sevenhuijsen, 1998).

We move on now to consider some of the ideas which arise from the work of four thinkers who have been influenced by Gilligan. The first, Susan Okin, is labelled by some as a maternal thinker, although her approach is situated firmly within the redistributive justice paradigm and, although influenced by Gilligan's work, is largely critical of the ethics of care. Her critique of justice and her discussion of the requirements for a just society are examined first. A new discourse of gender justice which emerges from her work is outlined.

We then explore aspects of the work of three writers who advocate a socio-political vision of care rather than an individualist one and who anchor the ethics of care within ideas of care as a social practice: American theorists Sara Ruddick and Joan Tronto, and Dutch theorist and political scientist Selma Sevenhuijsen.

Justice, Gender and the Family

Until there is justice within the family, women will not be able to gain equality in politics, at work, or in any other sphere. (Okin, 1989, p. 4)

Okin labels the equal distribution of household labour as 'The great revolution that has not happened' (ibid., p. 4). While women have entered paid employment in greater numbers, this has not been mirrored by an increase in men sharing household labour and the care of children. Even in Scandinavia, where equality between the sexes is highly advanced, women do most housework, men take less parental leave. Women are problematized and penalized, in employment and in politics, because of their caring responsibilities. There is a sense in which domestic arrangements are still seen as a voluntarist agreement, an individual problem, and solutions tend to be characterized in terms of, for instance, the provision of child care. The consequences of the sexual division of labours are not generally dignified as a crisis of justice. Yet women's caring and family responsibilities are singled out by many theorists and by female politicians themselves as an important barrier to women's full political participation. Democracy theorist, Anne Phillips comments, 'As long as the sexual distribution of labour allocates for women the main responsibility for caring for others the time left over for political engagement is necessarily reduced' (1993, p. 15).

In *Justice, Gender and the Family*, Okin (1989) contrasts democratic values of justice and equality with the economic realities of women's lives in the United States: low wages; large wage differentials; the poverty of single mothers and their children; the poverty of elderly women; and women's under-representation in politics and the judiciary. This would be equally true of British society and most other so-called developed nations (see, for example, Rubery, 1988; Glendinning and Millar, 1992; Humphries and Rubery, 1995).

Okin places the unequal division of family and household labour, in particular unequal primary parenting, at the root of social, economic and political inequality and argues that until there is gender justice in the family, women will be unable to gain equality in work, politics or any other area of public life. To underscore the gendered basis of the unequal division of labour, Okin looks at research on couples in the United States by Blumstein and Schwartz.

131

They found that gay couples and lesbian couples were highly unlikely to replicate heterosexual patterns of household labour and were, in general, far more likely to have egalitarian domestic arrangements.[3]

Power relations within the family and the workplace (which both assume a male breadwinner) replicate and reinforce each other. Gendered marriage makes women vulnerable, contends Okin. They are made more vulnerable when they have children and their vulnerability 'peaks' with the breakdown of marriages. Indeed, various studies provide conclusive evidence of the gendered impact of marriage breakdown whereby women and children are impoverished by divorce, while men tend to benefit financially, or recover their former position in a relatively short period.[4]

Okin charts the ways in which the conflict for women between love and work sets them up to be vulnerable: first, socialization, which leads women to expect to be the primary caretakers of children; second, in fulfilling that role women need to attract and keep the economic support of a man – and give priority to his working life; and third, that sex segregation within employment cancels out the educational advances of women in many cases, particularly in administrative and support jobs where pay is lower than comparable male jobs and in which prospects for promotion are limited. Okin characterizes these features as 'vulnerability by anticipation of marriage'. She argues that this phenomenon impacts on women whether they marry or not, and whether or not future support from a male breadwinner is a realistic option (1989, pp. 142–6).

Okin is one of the first liberal theorists to characterize the sexual division of labour in the family – and the resultant inequalities in employment and public life – as a major problem for political and social theory. It is, she suggests, a gender crisis of justice. Justice is, she argues, about whether, how and why people should be treated differently. She asks why, therefore, the gendered injustice within families has not been tackled by social justice theorists. Instead most justice theorists have ignored contemporary gender issues – and seem to have bypassed feminist scholarship and insight in a 'remarkable case of neglect' (Okin, 1989, p. 8). For example, in the work of contemporary justice theorist John Rawls, no mention is made of justice within families. 'Family life is not only assumed, but it is assumed to be just – and yet the prevalent gendered division of labor within the family is neglected, along with the associated distribution of power, responsibility and privilege' (Okin, 1989, p. 9).

Okin's critique has important implications for theories of justice. First, by arguing that relations between the sexes is a matter of justice, she exposes the way that contemporary formulations of justice – even 'progressive' social justice theorists such as Rawls – are unable to deal with injustices arising out of gender, for example, the 'feminization' of poverty and the relative exclusion of women from politics and the judiciary. Second, Okin contends that justice is incomplete without the contextuality of care. As such, her critique demands a reframing of justice to incorporate the reality of gendered lives which she proposes by developing a feminist 'reading' of Rawls which advocates an engaged, rather than a detached standpoint. By this she means that justice cannot be an abstract 'view from nowhere', but must be attentive to the points of view of women as well as the points of view of men (Okin, 1989, pp. 179–80). Her goal is a genderless society in which caring labour and opportunities within the family are redistributed and in which the experience of being brought up within an equal family provides training for citizenship.

'Stretching' justice

Okin's work presents a fundamental challenge to disembodied notions of justice and her arguments have been widely used to make gender equality a 'respectable' or 'acceptable' goal within the paradigm of redistributive justice. However, there are concerns that in 'stretching' mainstream concepts in order to fit care, Okin's work encounters methodological and other problems. Sevenhuijsen contends that Okin takes a problematic and overly simplistic view of gender. Indeed, Okin appears to view gender as entirely the construct of socialization within families and, after Chodorow (1978), the product of unequal parenting. The institutional, symbolic and embodied aspects of gender and gender relations are downplayed or neglected as are other sorts of social division and 'difference'. Sevenhuijsen attributes this weakness, in part, to the Rawlsian framework to which Okin is wedded: she needs to argue that people are all the same if gender is removed, and therefore takes genderless subjects as 'both starting point and aim' (Sevenhuijsen, 1998, pp. 73–5).

According to Sevenhuijsen, the Okin approach gives both too much weight to care and too little. Too much in the respect of presenting the achievement of equality in the family as the solution to all social ills and the unrealistic assumption that a caring perspective gives us the ability to see from 'all points of views'. Too little in that Okin does not accept care as moral reasoning in its own right but only when it can be accommodated within justice reasoning, that is when it can meet the criteria of objectivity which, for Sevenhuijsen, contradicts the whole point of care as a form of situated ethics (ibid., p. 77).

The philosophical and ethical problems inherent in Okin's modification of Rawl's 'Original Position' will continue to provoke debate. However, what is important in terms of our assessment is the extent to which Okin's ideas on gender and justice create strategic opportunities and discursive space for women and to what extent its limitations present 'discursive traps' which may backfire.

The first point to be made is that although conceptual stretching does create all sorts of problems, there are distinct political advantages to framing discourses within existing paradigms. Okin is speaking in the idiom of redistributive justice common in the political discourse of liberal and social democratic welfare states. As such, her voice is more likely to be heard and with it, the justice and gender discourse which emerges from her work.

A new discourse of gender justice

Why has the 'justice crisis' of which Okin speaks been given scant attention? There have been, perhaps, understandable reasons for reluctance to engage in this debate. First, there are difficulties in conceptualizing the sexual division of labour as a mainstream political issue – in liberal feminist terms it is explained as a remnant of traditional social conditioning which will change in time. Second, it is difficult to tackle the issues practically. Although feminists have demanded a renegotiation of gender roles in the domestic sphere, it is difficult to see how legislation could be framed to *require* that men do their share of caring work. In terms of public policy, feminists have tended to concentrate upon means of supporting women to combine care and work by, for example, demands for improved child care provision, flexible working and so on. Paternal leave and parental leave entitlements and access to various 'family-friendly' policies may enable men to do a greater share of caring work but it does not compel them to do so. Many feminists would nonetheless find Okin's family policy suggestions, which include elements of compulsion, an unacceptable state intrusion into families and intimate relationships. Third, the sexual division of labour can be easily interpreted as choice. Because women recognize and value their caring work, it can be viewed that they, as women, choose to have children and choose to spend time with their families and others for whom they care. Finally, because women are only allowed entry to political positions on 'men's terms', changes which take account of women's needs and experiences are delegitimized as special pleading. Male politicians ridicule women politicians' attempts to raise issues of housework or child-care responsibility. Therefore women politicians and candidates are themselves reluctant to complain too publicly, for fear that it is seen as 'bleating', or that it reinforces 'victim' stereotypes.

The idea of a justice crisis of gender is, however, important in its contribution to constructing a discourse which reframes women's common-sense complaints as rational demands for action springing from concerns of justice. We can sketch out three potential features to this discourse: first, that women's domestic and caring responsibilities – and men's resistance to doing their fair share – are re-conceptualized as a crisis of justice with far-reaching social, economic and political consequences; second, that the sexual division of labour would be recast as a concern of social justice in need of remedy and therefore there would be recognition of the need for political action; third, that inequalities in the family would not be characterized as an individualized problem of women's choice, but instead be explained by a complex combination of structural injustices. For instance, Okin demonstrates the ways in which gendered marriages obscure the structural inequalities behind seemingly rational decisions.[5]

Okin's major focus is upon disadvantage, however, in common with care thinkers, she also places public value on nurturing and questions the competence of policy-makers, dealing with issues ranging from family policy to defence, who have had no experience of caring labour:

These are the people who make policy at the highest levels – policies not only about families and their welfare and about education of children, but about the foreign policies, the wars and the weapons that will determine the future or lack of future for all these families and children. Yet they are almost all people who gain the influence they do in part by never having had day-to-day experience of nurturing a child. (Okin, 1989, pp. 179–80)

It is in this respect that the potential limits of her approach become quickly apparent. Although this argument is initially attractive, the notion of care is individualized and conflated with the nurturing of children, while care in its wider forms, as advocated by writers such as Tronto, is neglected. It is constraining and politically dangerous to argue too directly from families to societies, especially if one particular family form is seen to equate with the 'good society'. Okin stakes the development of a just society on equal parenting in equal heterosexual families, and competence as citizens and decision-makers on the experience of caring within families and the training in equality as children growing up in these model families. Sevenhuijsen quickly spots the reactionary political repercussions which would follow for single parents, same-sex parents and for all those who had been brought up in non-standard families (1998, p. 78).

Okin's ideas provide powerful arguments with potential for activists to present the case for equality within acceptable frameworks. Feminists are well used to adopting justificatory stances which have been framed by others but, as Bacchi reminds us, must be attentive to the unintended consequences and theoretical dilemmas these can produce (Bacchi, 1996, p. 121). As such, Okin's work contains both discursive opportunities and political and theoretical pitfalls.

Care as social practice

The ambivalence and considerable resistance to ideas of care thinking have already been noted. However, much of the criticism of 'women's thinking' rests upon a false assumption that talk of an ethics of care necessarily leads to essentialism. An alternative approach is to explore care as a social practice which gives rise to forms of practical wisdom. For some gender is central to the form this wisdom takes (Noddings, 1984; Held, 1990). For others, most particularly Tronto (1993), the gender specificity of such claims needs to be challenged.

Social practice is defined by Frazer and Lacey as 'human action which is socially based and organised, underpinned by formal or informal institutions, usually a combination of these' (1993, p. 17). Practice implies the integration of thought and action directed towards a goal. The idea that specific modes of thinking and problem-solving strategies arise from specific social practices is part of a well-established practicalist tradition in contemporary moral and political thought. By conceptualizing caring as practice, with its emphasis on practical knowledge, the rational activity of caring is stressed. From this perspective it does not seem remarkable nor reactionary to claim that women and certain groups of men who are involved for a large part of their time in a specific practice – in this instance, the practice of caring work – will develop perspectives, skills and insights, and modes of thinking related to that practice.

What must be stressed in work of thinkers like Ruddick, Tronto and Sevenhuijsen is the crucial insistence that care thinking is not just a disposition, a principle or an emotion but a crucial human practice. '[C]aring is not simply a cerebral concern, or a character trait, but the concern of living, active humans engaged in the processes of everyday living. Care is both a practice and a disposition' (Tronto, 1993, p. 104). Tronto argues that to see caring as primarily a disposition renders it individualist and sentimentalized and perpetuates the 'women are designed for caring' arguments. Ruddick suggests the practice of care should be seen as an alternative ideal – a combination of love and knowledge which challenges the traditional separation of emotion and rationality in what she calls 'Love's Reason' (Ruddick, 1989, p. 9).

Despite common characterizations of these arguments to the contrary, these writers do not make any claim that caring and nurturance are innate qualities of women. In contrast to 'feminine ideology' they make no claims that caring is the only activity women should engage in, or that they should be solely defined by it. Ruddick states that she has 'no patience with the idea that a person's identity is wholly formed by her principal work or, still more confining, by the gender identity a particular society expects' (1989, p. 134). Ruddick defines practices as:

Collective human activities distinguished by the aims that identify them and by the consequent demands made on practitioners committed to those aims. The aims or goals that define a practice are so central or 'constitutive' that in the absence of the goal you would not have the practice ... to engage in a practice means to be committed to meeting its demands. (1989, pp. 13–14)

Ruddick uses the example of horse racing to illustrate her definition. Horse racing is a practice, she explains, which is defined by the goal of winning the race: by the shared meaning of a jockey riding a horse over a finishing line. In different cultures meanings may be refined, nevertheless, a riderless horse crossing the finishing line is not a winner and a rider out for a trot is not engaged in the practice of horse racing (Ruddick, 1989, pp. 13–17). Using this schema, maternal practice arises out of a commitment to raise a child. This gives rise to thinking in terms of strategies for dealing with conflicts, which in turn gives way to reflection and modification of practice (ibid., pp. 18–27). Not all mothers are maternal thinkers. Ruddick insists that maternal thinking cannot be idealized, but is instead characterized by struggle and temptation. However, maternal thinking gives rise to important insights, not least the central importance of caring work. It also produces complex and flexible strategies for dealing with need and conflict, which have potential application in social and political contexts. Ruddick's specific purpose is the use of 'transformed' maternal thinking to mobilize women in peace politics.

Ruddick is careful to avoid universalism in her maternal thinking. She stresses the mediating factors of race, class, culture and material circumstances will result in varied practices of mothering within and across cultures; however, she does argue that the demands and goals of the practice are shared. For example, in maternal practice the demands for the preservation of a child's life, its growth and its eventual social acceptability result in the practice of preservative love, nurturance and training (Ruddick, 1989, p. 17).

For Ruddick, three basic claims arise from the framing of caring work as practice: first, that care should be centrally placed in social, ethical and political discourse; second, that practical strategies and intellectual skills which arise from the practice of caring can be 'transformed' and transferred to a wider context of politics; and third, that a potentially superior standpoint arises out of the marginalized practice of care.

The Standpoint of Women

Ruddick and Tronto are among a number of thinkers who use the concept of standpoint in their work. The idea of the visionary standpoint of women was popularized in feminism by Nancy Hartsock (1987). Women's work is seen as rooted in the material world and connected with others. It gives rise to practical knowledge, and because it involves processes of connection, separation, development, change and the limits of control it produces sensitive strategies to deal with change and conflict (Ruddick, 1989, pp. 127–40).

According to this approach, women are involved with work which is central to everyone's lives, but they and that essential work are marginalized. This gives them a point of leverage from which to understand and change society. By virtue of women's marginal experience, especially as devalued carers, they have a greater grasp on reality – this enables them to see and express truths that are obscured from those (mostly men) in a culturally or politically dominant position. For, not only do they have to deal with their own version of reality but they must also negotiate the realities of hegemonic groups, and the way in which these opposing sets of reality relate and contradict each other. In contrast, dominant groups perceive their own reality as 'truth' and are seldom required to acknowledge or consider alternative viewpoints. There is an argued value, or an epistemological advantage, to a marginal position because one has access to different ways of knowing. Hartsock (1987) argues this advantage to the degree that feminist standpoint represents Truth.

Others, such as Patricia Hill Collins caution against claiming too much on the basis of gender or motherhood. She points out that many of the characteristics associated with a 'women's standpoint'– the importance of taken-for-granted knowledge based upon concrete experiences; a standpoint shaped by caring work and relationships; and emphasis upon communication, empathy and dialogue – can all be found in the thinking and practice of men and women in black African-American communities. As such, these practices and values are 'how subordinate groups create knowledge that enables them to resist oppression' (Collins, 1994, p. 86). In turn, Black women practise an 'ethics of caring' which draws from both 'black' and 'feminist' standpoints and also consists of features distinctive to their experience. She stresses the need to recognize multiple realities shaped by gender, race and class.

Ruddick and Tronto use the framework of feminist standpoint to develop their own versions based upon maternal thinking and care perspectives. They argue that their maternal or care standpoints are privileged, but stop short of claims of definitive truths (see also Eisenstein, 1991).

Ruddick sees the value of women's work or maternal practice in its potential to be generalized by society as a whole – and for an ethos of care to imbue society. Ruddick is, however, anxious that these claims are not interpreted to be seen as an aim to create a future that is female – but rather a 'fully human community' where institutionalized gender differences of power and property are eliminated. Indeed, she is careful to include men as potential mothers and maternal thinkers (Ruddick, 1989, p. 134).

Although Ruddick situates women in social movements rather than in elected politics, maternal thinking brings useful insights to the debate on representation. It is useful because it talks about care, a predominant theme in many women politicians' accounts of their lives but of which politics takes scant account. It places value on care, it emphasizes its importance in everyday life, and points to the potential use of 'transformed maternal practice' in public life.

The limits of motherly metaphors

Despite Ruddick's careful definitions, her use of the maternal idiom means her work is often misrepresented as essentialist or as uncritically celebratory of mothering. Ruddick discusses at length what she characterizes as the 'temptations' of maternal practice including parochialism, cheery denial and self-righteousness. She also notes the militarism of some mothers. She is aware that women, organizing as mothers and invoking 'mother's values' can present radical challenges to the state as did the Madres in Argentina in the 1970s, but can also be used to underpin and reinforce reactionary regimes, for example, in Nazi Germany and in Pinochet's Chile (Ruddick, 1989, pp. 223–34).[6] Ruddick does not idealize or privilege mothering in itself. The importance of maternal practice for Ruddick is in its potential, the way in which it can develop rationally, through struggle, into a set of practices and a standpoint with use in the wider world, particularly in pursuit of the politics of peace.

Ruddick's argument is interesting and subtle, and offers many insights. However, many people, both critics and supporters, do not seem to be able to get beyond the 'mother' in maternal thinking (for example, Evans, 1995). Because of this it is unlikely that maternal thinking could pass into everyday political discourse without an undertow of conservatism. Therefore Ruddick's insistence on a specific 'maternal' thinking, rather than a standpoint arising from the general practice of care, is in some respects too partial and contentious for a useful application, although her arguments resonate with many of the accounts of women in political life.

The political vocabulary of care

Tronto in *Moral Boundaries* (1993), perhaps goes furthest in developing the concept of the political ethics of care and answering some of its critics. Her work shares with Ruddick the importance of caring perspectives which reveal the flaws in dominant ways of knowing. She exposes the ways in which dominant discourses obscure the central importance of care; and the structuring of social, economic and political life which fails to incorporate the caring needs and responsibilities of all.

However, Tronto differs from Ruddick in two respects: first, she applies a generic and inclusive definition of caring practice which includes women in their unpaid and paid labours, and also marginal groups of men; and second, she develops the ethics of care into a political idea. She argues that men must be 'persuaded' to give up some their power; and that politics must change in order not only that women may fully participate, but also that politics may more fully reflect the needs and interests of society.

She empties the ethics of care of any biological essentialism by applying a generic and inclusive definition of caring practice which includes women in their unpaid and paid labours, and also marginal groups of men (for example, black and ethnic minority men) who also are required by society to do low-paid caring work (see also, Collins, 1994). She charts the links between 'women's morality' and 'slave's and black people's morality', also noting the similarity between women's morality and the notion of 'sentiment' in the work of thinkers of the Scottish Enlightenment such as Hutcheson, Hume and Smith (see also Sevenhuijsen, 1991). She sees the 'privatization' of virtue as being historically specific to the eighteenth century, in particular, with the expansion of the global economy and the growth of capitalism, and argues that the conditions of the late twentieth century demand that the boundaries between morality and politics be once more redrawn.

Tronto's core argument is that we must stop seeing the clutch of values and concerns about nurturance, compassion and caring as 'women's morality', and start talking about an ethics of care. She argues that care should not be seen as 'merely' morals, but must be placed centrally in politics: 'What I propose to do ... is to offer a vision for the good society that draws upon feminist sensibilities and upon traditional "women's morality" without falling into the strategic traps that have so far doomed this approach' (Tronto, 1993, p. 3). In contrast to Ruddick, Tronto's definition of care, formulated with Berenice Fisher, is comprehensive:

> On the most general level, we suggest that caring be viewed as a species activity that includes everything that we do to maintain, continue and repair our 'world' so that we can live in it as well as possible. That world includes our bodies, our selves and our environment, all of which we seek to interweave in a complex, life sustaining web. (Fisher and Tronto, 1991, p. 40)

Then Tronto develops the ethics of care into a political idea. She argues that 'care' should be introduced as a central political ideal and the practice of care as a political idea because it describes what is necessary for citizens to live together well in a pluralist society.

Care as politics

Tronto takes four basic stages of care practice, which she characterizes as: 'caring about'; 'taking care of'; 'care giving', and 'care receiving' (Tronto, 1993, pp. 106–8). Each phase is analytically separate although inter-related:

- *Caring about*: this phase involves the recognition of the necessity to care and the identification of need. Caring about may be described in individualistic terms or in terms of socio-political responses to issues such as homelessness.
- *Taking care of*: invokes notions of responsibility and agency in the caring process. It involves an acceptance of some responsibility

for the need that has been identified and the consideration of the ways (including the allocation of resources) through which needs claims may be met. So, a government might accept it has a responsibility towards homeless people and allocates resources for policy programmes, for example the provision of hostels or supported accommodation.

- *Care giving*: refers to the provision of care, almost always requiring physical work and direct contact. In both private and public spheres, women are usually over-represented at this stage of the caring process. A range of 'care-givers' might be involved in the area of homelessness such as social workers, health professionals, advocacy workers and volunteers. The programme is likely to be under-funded, the work relatively poorly paid and many of the workers will be women.
- *Care receiving*: the response and participation of the care receiver are crucial parts of the caring process, not least because they provide an assessment of how well and appropriately needs have been met. Homeless people might be involved in the design of projects and be given space to identify their needs and suggest appropriate state agency responses. So, for example, if asked, they might argue that hostels are not an adequate solution. They might point out the need to tackle underlying issues such as poverty, alcohol and drug dependency, abuse and mental health issues.

All four stages have relational aspects, although it is in the latter two phases that most direct and intimate contact takes place and that dilemmas over vulnerability and conflicting demands have to be confronted and negotiated. Power relations and gender relations structure and shape the stages leaving disproportionate numbers of women and disadvantaged groups of men to care for (or, indeed, be cared for) with little or no influence on the powerful preliminary stages which define legitimate need and plan and shape societal responses to those needs. As Sevenhuijsen observes, women often find themselves in the situations where they carry out work 'with great responsibility, but little power' (1998, p. 84).

Tronto goes on to take these elements to formulate an ethics of care (1993, pp. 125–55). The four parts of this ethics of care are as follows:

- *Attentiveness*: this relates to 'caring about'. By this standard, ignoring the needs of others would be a form of a moral failing,

143

and recognizing the needs of those around us would be a moral achievement.

- *Responsibility*: this relates to 'taking care of' and is seen as a central moral category. Tronto argues that responsibility which is contextual is more useful than 'obligation', which arises from a formal response to promises. She uses the riots in South Central Los Angeles as an example of how questions of responsibility can become political debates. She asks, what responsibility has society or government to help in rebuilding an area devastated by riots? This is a different question from 'what obligation?' Governments looking at obligation would look at contracts, formal agreements and previously stated duties, and might conclude they had no obligation to help. However, responsibility goes beyond formal and legal ties and would relate to issues such as the extent to which governments and local politics played a part in creating the conditions for the riot, for instance, through lack of job opportunities, and so on. A responsibility to care would be more flexible than the notion of obligation and, Tronto argues, a better basis for understanding (Tronto, 1993, pp. 131–3).

- *Competence*: this relates to 'care-giving'. Competence of care-giving is framed as a moral notion. Tronto argues for its inclusion in order to deal with the 'bad faith' problem – in short, those who would 'take care of a problem without being willing to ensure the adequacy of the solution'. She uses the example of a teacher in an inadequately funded school being forced to teach a subject even though he is not trained or equipped to do so. Is such a teacher to be morally condemned? Tronto argues that the competence requirement does not condemn the teacher but rather those at the 'taking care of' stage, the authorities, because the competence relates to those responsible for the ensuring adequacy of outcome. She notes that at present, 'especially in large bureaucracies, this type of "taking care of", with no concern about outcome or end result, seems pervasive' (Tronto, 1993, p. 134).

- *Responsiveness*: this relates to 'care-receiving'. Under this heading the care-receiver is required to be responsive to the care received. Tronto challenges the notion of autonomy and self-support – if everyone needs care, then everyone is vulnerable and inter-dependent. The active involvement of care-receivers in interpreting need also minimizes the potential for abuse that arises from vulnerability. Tronto sees responsiveness as engaging from the standpoint of the other – not in assuming the other to be the same as oneself – but accepting the other's position as they express it. She emphasizes that people are not interchangeable, therefore responsiveness values difference. To be responsive also requires one to be attentive, thus all the elements of the ethics of care are intertwined (Tronto, 1993, p. 136).

In addition, Tronto discusses the integrity of political practice, which requires that politics and political action involve the four stages of 'care': 'caring about' (attentiveness); 'taking care of' (responsibility); 'care giving' (competence) and 'care receiving' (responsiveness). Therefore politics which 'takes care of' with 'no concern about outcome or end result' is bad faith. To achieve integrity of practice is not simple, as care involves conflicting needs and scarce resources. Tronto insists that good care practice requires more than good intentions, and requires adequate resources, knowledge, practical strategies and contextual judgement. In addition, there must be attention to and respect for differences. These assessments of need are large social and political questions (Tronto, 1993, pp. 110, 137).

Tronto contends that care, as carers know in reality, is of central importance. However, it has been marginalized in moral and political thought – and in society. Moreover, it has been marginalized because of the contradiction, in both theoretical and practical terms, between the dominant discourses of autonomy and universal equality, and the realities of human vulnerability and interdependence. She challenges ideas about human nature and politics, in particular standard descriptions of the autonomous moral agent or political actor posited by theory, and its everyday equivalent the 'self-made man' as the norm.

She argues because dependence is feared, care is devalued in dominant discourses, care-giving is denigrated and the care needs of the powerful smoothed over. The care work that takes place within the home is trivialized and care work in the public is underpaid and of low status. Using Tronto's reasoning, one can argue that administrative workers like secretaries, whom Okin (1989) sees as being underpaid through processes of 'vulnerability by anticipation of marriage', are further undervalued in order to obscure and trivialize their support of 'self-made' men. The powerful are in reality, care demanders who, because of their resources, can secure more care than others. In what Tronto terms as a 'pre-emptive strike', the powerful adopt strategies which downplay any sense of dependency when their needs are met:

> To treat care as shabby and unimportant helps maintain the positions of the powerful *vis-à-vis* those who do care for them. The mechanisms of this dismissal are subtle; and they are of course filtered through existing structures of sexism and racism. (Tronto, 1993, p. 124)

These 'fragmented conceptions of care perpetuate inequalities of gender, race and class through the construction of "otherness"' (ibid., p. 101). By this Tronto means that the realities of human interdependence are distorted by powerful visions or myths of independence which are created by powerful groups within society. On the one hand, they consume large amounts of care without necessarily recognizing this is the case. On the other hand those who do the caring are unrecognized or undervalued because caring work is seen as inferior. It is no accident then that those who do caring work are predominantly women and marginalized groups of men.

All people are interdependent and at various stages, to various degrees and in various configurations, give and receive care. However, the caring required by the powerful has been rendered invisible – and the 'needy' are problematized and stigmatized. Any form of dependency is seen as weakness – for example, welfare mothers in the United States are seen as lazy because they are dependent – and the only explanation is their 'choice' of lifestyle (Tronto, 1993, p. 123). We also see this played out to some degree in the current political discourse of social exclusion in Britain which focuses on labour market integration as the route to social inclusion. This poses particular problems for women, who have caring responsibilities, and for disabled people who may not be able to take up employment (Bagilhole, forthcoming).

A further consequence of the unbalanced nature of caring burdens is that those who are powerful have the opportunity 'simply to ignore certain forms of hardships that they do not face' (Tronto, 1993, p. 121). Therefore, for example, men, whose caring needs are met and whose caring responsibilities are carried out by others, do not 'see' their privilege nor its relation to the disadvantage of others. Nor do they accept any responsibility for the problem. Tronto terms this *privileged irresponsibility* (ibid., pp. 121, 146–7).

Tronto challenges the centrality of individualist interests in human and political life, which Rawls terms 'life-projects'; and the measuring of human worth only as productive beings embedded in 'the work ethic'. Instead, she posits an alternative view of people as interdependent beings – 'the care ethic' (ibid., p. 102); and an alternative notion of needs not as individual interests but as interpersonal, cultural and contested – and a matter of social concern (ibid., p. 164).

She also contests 'the convenient fiction of human equality' which underpins much political theory. Universalism, which posits people as autonomous and equal citizens, fails to recognize inequalities. This in turn give rise to unequal relationships of power and authority. The starting point of a standpoint of care would be human interdependence, inequality would be recognized – both as part of human experience and also as something to be overcome. The new question, says Tronto, would be how to let equality arise out of inequality:

> What does this transformed account of human nature mean about the way that democratic citizens live their lives? Rather than assuming the fiction that all citizens are equal, a care perspective would have us recognize the achievement of equality as a political goal. At present, we presume that people are equal though we know they are not. If we attempted to achieve some type of equality as a political goal, it would make facts about inequality more difficult to dismiss. Questions such as: at what point do inequalities of resources prevent citizens from equal power? would become important political questions; they would not remain simply theoretical questions. (Tronto, 1993, pp. 164–5)

Tronto accepts there are theoretical difficulties with a move away from universalism, particularly problems of particularity (ibid., pp. 141–5). She attempts to resolve this by suggesting that a theory of care is inadequate unless it is embedded in a theory of justice. In an argument which begins from a very different starting point to Okin, Tronto likewise concludes that the notion of interdependence must be incorporated within adequate theories of justice:

> Because care forces us to think concretely about people's real needs, and about evaluating how these needs will be met, it introduces questions about what we value into everyday life. Should society be organized in a way that helps to maintain some forms of privilege before the more basic needs of others are met? Those kinds of questions, posed in stark form, help us

get closer to resolving fundamental questions of justice more than continued abstract discussions about the meaning of justice. (ibid., p. 124)

Vocabulary of care

Perhaps Tronto's most important contribution to the debate is the articulation of a *vocabulary of care*. She exposes the ways in which dominant discourses obscure the central importance of care; they devalue care and obscure care-giving, especially the care needs of the powerful. Private care is trivialized and public care work underpaid. Moreover, the structuring of social, economic and political life fails to incorporate the caring needs and responsibilities of all. Two key phrases in the vocabulary of care are: *privileged irresponsibility*, which names the advantage powerful groups have as a result of others doing their caring work for them, and *care demanding*, the twin processes of making heavy care demands on others while simultaneously denying or trivializing care and carers.

Tronto argues that the vocabulary of care is a critical and strategic tool with which to reveal power distribution in society and to make visible the 'shabby' treatment of care and carers. She suggests it can serve as a basis for political change and a strategy for mobilizing and organizing. The introduction of the idea of care into political debates would empower women and minority groups, because inequality would be rendered visible and subject to redress; it would thus act as a catalyst for women's political mobilization:

> Care is a way of framing political issues that makes their impact, and concern with human lives, direct and immediate. Within the care framework, political issues can make sense and connect to each other. Under these conditions, political involvement increases dramatically. (Tronto, 1993, p. 177)

We later take Tronto's ideas and further develop them into of a *political discourse of care,* which could potentially empower women in politics. However, we first note some problems.

Tronto has developed a powerful vocabulary, however, she does not address the issue of how care as a political concept becomes legitimized: how does it become an acceptable discourse in a political world in which liberal individualism and the productive/

capitalist vision predominate? It should be noted, for instance in UK governmental discourses during the 1979–97 Conservative administrations, that much social legislation was represented as secondary to free market imperatives. So, for instance, European Union Social Chapter measures were depicted as unaffordable, damaging to jobs, and an unacceptable interference to employer autonomy. Post-1997, while new Labour represents change in terms of its explicit commitment to social justice and democratic renewal, it can be argued these remain secondary to continuity in terms of economic policy, limited public spending and an attachment to market mechanisms.

Tronto is also less than convincing on how the 'powers of the weak' can be used to persuade the powerful to give up some of their power. Does she, for instance, mean they must withdraw their caring labour? (Tronto, 1993, p. 177). Elizabeth Janeway (1980), who coined the phrase the 'powers of the weak', lists among those powers that of disruption. However, she notes that disruption will only work in some circumstances and for a limited amount of time – and Tronto elsewhere discusses the backlash that occurs when carers (like nurses) withdraw their caring labour.

It is disappointing that Tronto does not develop her argument into practical strategy. Tronto, Ruddick and Okin all forward arguments to reinvigorate marginal discourses, but cannot find, indeed, do not seem to be looking very hard for, the answer to three central and related questions: How do we ensure we are heard and listened to? How do we 'persuade' men to give up (some) of their political power? and how do we ensure that men do their fair share of caring and domestic labour?

Judging with Care

The Dutch theorist Selma Sevenhuijsen notes that most discussions of an ethics of care have neglected the political dimension and failed to appreciate the complexity of the interplay between gender, power, care and ethics. Like Tronto, she urges broader conceptions of care which alert us to aspects of care in all sorts of human activity. She tries to situate an ethics of care within a political framework of citizenship and within concrete socio-political settings, most notably through the deconstruction of discourses in public policy documents in the fields of family law and health care. Her analysis is situated in the socio-political context of the Netherlands but her arguments 'speak to a wider audience' (1998, p. ix). Her concern is with public ethics and public debate and the way in which traditional liberal and social democratic frameworks limit the type of issues that can be recognized as public and therefore restrict the range of possible solutions.

She shares Tronto's view about the importance of discourse and political and moral vocabularies and the need to 'test' different 'speaking positions'. As already noted in Part I, the common-sense status of some normative frameworks makes it difficult to think of other ways of thinking and doing things. In *Citizenship and the Ethics of Care* (1998) she challenges the thinking about care and autonomy which is embedded within political debate and policy discussions on current political issues. For example, she demonstrates the way in which changes in family law relating to child custody in the Netherlands – rooted in abstract notions of equal rights and gender-neutral discourses – have reasserted fathers' rights in the Netherlands and neglected the issues of care, power and conflict endemic in concrete situations of relationship breakdown. These reforms are presented as a logical step in the further modernization of society but in reality can serve to disadvantage women and children. She sketches the context sensitive alternatives that would spring from the use of an ethics of care.

Like Tronto (1993) and, elsewhere, Iris Marion Young (1995), she argues that the equation of autonomy with independence within traditional liberal frameworks has led to the privileging of values of self-sufficiency and a denigration of care, dependency or inter-dependency. From there it is but a short step to assertions that the moral judgement of people who care and those who are cared for are undermined by such experiences of connection and they are thus unreliable moral actors. The ethics of care exposes the shortcomings in this version and argues for the recognition of connection and inter-dependence and the norm of diversity rather than uniformity.

She introduces the political idea of 'judging with care' as a concept which works on a number of inter-connecting levels (1998, pp. 4–5): first, to mean careful judgement, emphasizing care as an attitude and a form of action; second, promoting the view of care as a form of social agency; and third, seeing care in a broader political context and the role of citizens in making political judgements about social provision in liberal and social welfare states. She argues that ideas of 'judging with care' create a discursive opportunity, a space in which carers as citizens can 'bring their expertise and moral considerations into public debates without this being associated with a fixed caring identity or with associated claims to moral truth or moral goodness' (ibid., p. 15). Thus, the ethics of care gives rise to a form of deliberative citizenship in which embodied citizens seek to judge with care and use attentive reasoning rather than universalist reasoning as their starting point. She argues this results in a two-fold outcome: first, ideas of citizenship are better able to accommodate diversity and pluralism; and, second, that care is 'deromanticised' which better enables us to 'consider its values as political virtues' (ibid., p. 15).

Sevenhuijsen steers a careful course through the contentious debates and intractable problems which cluster around issues of citizenship, moral identity and identity politics. The ethics of care has often been associated with identity politics and has been seen to share its perceived shortcomings in respect of fixing identities and institutionalizing differences (Voet, 1998). Sevenhuijsen disentangles the ethics of care from identity politics by arguing that political or civic identities spring from what we do, rather than who we are.

Her vision of citizenship is one in which engaged citizens deliberate about significant differences and similarities in society and reach provisional decisions about which values should be promoted as common values. Participation in the public sphere thus provides an opportunity to forge commonalties on the basis of diversity. Universal values are not abandoned, rather, recognized as contingent and renegotiable: ultimately the outcome of politics. The ethics of care and its characteristic practices of attentiveness, responsibility, competence and responsiveness provide the framework for reaching judgements which are attentive to difference and to concrete contexts (Sevenhuijsen, 1998, pp. 14–15, 146). She places her work alongside that of other feminists such as Fraser (1989), Frazer and Lacey (1993), Code (1995) and Bickford (1996) who argue for 'open forms of interpretative and communicative ethics' which provides the space for 'situated forms of political action and judgement' (Sevenhuijsen, 1998, p. 28).

Many of the discussions of moral agency and citizenship take place at a level which seems to be divorced from power politics. Sevenhuijsen, however, insists that the ethics of care is political and that politics is an enduring feature of societies. The goal is not to seek to abolish or render politics redundant but to make it more visible and accountable and to guard against arbitrary public decision-making. Although she argues elsewhere against attempts to integrate the ethics of care with the ethics of justice, she also sees the combination of a political ethics of care with renewed conceptions of social justice and citizenship as potentially most rewarding for dealing with power and conflict in the real world and acting ' "as well as possible" in order to do what needs to be done' (Sevenhuijsen, 1998, p. 68).

Sevenhuijsen is one of the few writers to consider how the ethics of care might work in particular political systems and within particular democratic practices. She argues that the radical pluralism which is suggested by an ethics of care can only work within the framework of democracy and democratic citizenship, with the recognition of human rights and rule of law. However, she says this does not necessarily require a broad participatory model with direct democracy, nor should it need the institutionalized representation of groups. Rather, it should be possible to operate the ethics of care within existing models of well-functioning representative democracy, 'provided that positions of power and decision making are open to representatives of all social groups and provided that there is room for different voices to be heard in the public sphere and for different forms of accountability to be developed' (ibid., p. 146).

Care and gender

In many ways, Sevenhuijsen's work builds upon and further refines the ideas of Tronto. However, she differs in one important respect and that is about the role of gender in the ethics of care. Sevenhuijsen's approach brings gender back into discussions of the ethics of care. In so doing she steers a careful course in which, on the one hand, she refuses to align with maternal thinkers such as Noddings (1984) and Held (1987) who see care and gender as inextricably linked; but on the other hand seeks to counter the tendencies of other care thinkers (for example, Tronto, 1993; Bubeck, 1995) who, in their anxiety to empty care of any essentialism and make it respectable within feminist political philosophy, have sought to sever all connection between care and gender. She argues this is a paradoxical stance: not only because it ignores the large body of empirical work in feminist political sociology which demonstrates the importance of gender for the pattern of public and private care provision and how it is experienced, but also because feminists were first to examine the ethics of care and its potential connection with women's moral experience and values both in intimate relationships and in the public sphere. She argues that speaking of morality and care using gender neutral language and presuming non-gendered subjects is to overlook the reason why the ethics of care was developed in first place. However tricky dealing with gender can be, it cannot be avoided or neglected. There is a need to tackle what she dubs the 'theoretical unease' over gender and sexual difference which emerges in thinking about care and to develop new, more complex, means of thinking about gender which do not slip into 'sophisticated ways of talking about actual men and women' but on the other hand do not underplay the impact of gender in its individual, institutional, symbolic and discursive forms (Sevenhuijsen, 1998, pp. 71, 82).

In addition to the theoretical project of better understanding gender, the insistence that we cannot entirely divorce gender from the ethics of care also means that we cannot divorce real women's experiences from our development of care thinking. Empirical work is needed to complement and inform theoretical work by listening to the different voices (rather than simply the voice) of women. Sevenhuijsen cautions that feminist theory which finds no connection to the everyday practices, goals and dilemmas of women risks becoming 'an empty shell'.

We can take Sevenhuijsen's vision of care and deliberative citizens and develop it within current political debates, particularly concerns about the need to find ways to enhance representative democracy and renew trust between governments and citizens. Care thinking could thus be promoted as a key tool in improving democratic participation, creating meaningful consultation and forging new forms of deliberative citizenship.

The ethics of care, with its starting point of difference rather than uniformity, can act as an 'eye opener' for men who are used to considering themselves the human norm. Thus men would need to start thinking about the political and moral implications of 'being men' and unlearn their 'denial of dependency'. This would further destabilize dominant universalist paradigms and the current domestic, social and political hierarchies of care giving and care receiving (Sevehuijsen, 1998, pp. 19, 50). A related point is that the acceptance that difference, that is difference between individuals and groups and also within one's own sense of self, is a positive fact of life rather than a threat to social stability would promote self-respect and respect for others as crucial social values. In turn, this would give rise to the recognition of responsibility and communication as key political and democratic virtues.

Sevenhuijsen's work is rich in insight and has great potential for 'translation' by feminist activists into popular political discourse. However, there are also a number of outstanding questions. For Sevenhuijsen, argument and deliberation are key elements of political agency, however, we must ask, where does this participation or deliberation take place? Partly, she suggests, through the moral stories people tell themselves and each other. These are seen as crucial mechanisms of communication which operate through everyday interaction, popular culture, journalism and academic research. However, despite elsewhere alerting us to the problems of power, Sevenhuijsen does not explore the ways in which channels of communication are filtered and shaped by power structures which may distort or silence voices. Thus from reading Sevenhuijsen we remain unclear as to the mechanisms by which the ethics of care can be introduced within public discourse. She identifies the role of discursive constraints, but is strangely silent about the institutional barriers which may shape whose voice is heard and the opportunities 'we' may or may not have to be active or deliberative citizens in particular concrete political systems. In short, attention needs to be given to issues of access, to what Iris Marion Young has called 'authoritative speaking positions', and to decision-making processes. Sevenhuijsen sees politics as 'strategic actions within the context of power relations' (1998, p. 68) but her work neglects the issue of how we affect change (and, indeed who *we* are). As such, the dynamic – and the agents – which would turn the ethics of care into a political force are missing from her account.

As noted earlier in this discussion, Sevenhuijsen believes that it is perfectly possible to put the ethics of care into action within existing models of representative democracy, with the proviso that decision-making structures must be open, accessible, responsive and accountable. However, this is not generally the status quo. Where does this leave the ethics of care if everything rests upon an assumption of inclusive, well-functioning democratic institutions which empirically we know is not the case – most visibly through the under-representation of women in social, economic and political decision making which is a feature of all liberal and social welfare democracies? If we accept this, then ethicists of care need to start to pay attention to the levers, mechanisms and agents of change within particular political systems and to issues of access and voice.

To be fair, Sevenhuijsen is more attentive than most to the structures of conventional politics, however, ultimately, she fudges these questions: how can care vocabularies be introduced into political discourse? How do we implement care ethics in concrete political systems with deeply embedded gender and power relations? These details are not side issues or minor inconveniences, but fundamental problems if the ethics of care is to move from words to action and from the undervalued practice of marginalized social groups to the hallmarks of good government and meaningful citizenship.

As noted earlier, although a number of writers have oriented the ethics of care towards politics, the emphasis has been upon citizenship and informal politics. Politicians and political institutions have seldom been a focus. In the following chapter we return to Sevenhuijsen's point that we cannot divorce real women's experiences from our development of care thinking. We explore the parallels and the differences between the practical insights of care theorists and the common-sense theorizing of women politicians. We then consider ways in which some of the ideas, discourses, vocabularies and frameworks of care might be developed and applied to the issue of women's political representation and the reformation of politics. A number of potential political discourses are sketched out.

Notes

1. For a useful overview of some of the debates see J. Tronto (1993), S. Okin (1990) and S. Sevenhuijsen (1998).
2. Sara Ruddick, for example, highlights the contempt with which American society treats caring work by citing a 1975 US Government survey where the complexity of different jobs was rated. Amongst the lowest rated jobs were child care worker, nursery school teachers and foster mothers who scored equal with a parking lot attendant and less skilled than the 'shoveler of chicken offal into a container'; a midwife was considered less skilful than a hotel clerk (Ruddick, 1989, pp. 32–3).
3. American Couples' study cited by Okin (1989, p. 40).
4. Okin, 1989, Chapter 7. For US research see, for example, Weitzman (1985); for British research see, for example, Glendinning and Millar (1992) and Wasoff and Morris (1996).
5. For a discussion of how the gap in earning potential, and therefore

decision-making power, widens during the course of a relationship through 'rational decisions' see Okin (1989, Chapter 7).

6. On a less extreme level, Chapman notes the emergence of the 'Mothers Manifesto' faction in the West German Green movement as constituting a conservative, rather than a progressive tendency with its pro-family, anti-abortion programme (1993, pp. 239–40).

7

Women, Common Sense and the Political Ethics of Care

In Chapter 6 we focused upon a number of thinkers who have considered how to apply the ethics of care to the civil, public space of citizenship and informal politics. They suggest a different vision of what politics ought to be and provide some arguments which promote alternative political values and practices. We ask whether insights derived from this literature can be developed to provide a better understanding of women's experience and role in electoral politics and political institutions.

A central aim of this book is to integrate different approaches and to draw upon women politicians' own experience as an important source of knowledge. We consider the extent to which there is an empirical basis to the ideas and arguments raised in Chapter 6. We listen again to the voices of women politicians to establish the parallels and the differences between the practical insights of care theorists and the common-sense theorizing of women politicians.

Telling Stories of Political Life

We have already established that women politicians discuss care as both a resource as well as a burden. However, do the ideas and values of a political ethics of care have any particular resonance with women politicians? As we have noted, care thinkers have paid little attention to the formal politics of elected office nor have discussions been related to women's own experiences of political life, although a number of writers, most recently Tronto (1993) and Sevenhuijsen (1998), have reminded us that judging with care and about care should form the basis of political judgements. Instead, they have concentrated on developing forms of deliberative citizenship. However, elected politics and the role of political representatives can be seen as an important form of active citizenship. What happens if we take seriously the pleas of care ethicists to situate the ethics of care in concrete situations and listen to the stories of real women – in this case, women who are involved in formal power politics?

Women politicians tell their stories of 'getting there' and 'being there' in different forms for different audiences. The polished after-dinner speech or political address to a mixed audience will sound very different from the stories women politicians share with each other and their confidantes. The questions asked by journalists and academic researchers may shape the answers received. However, gender, care, power and politics are all intertwined in the accounts they give of political life at various levels. Gender is problematized for women in politics. They have to face the contradictions and consequences of being female and politicians on a daily basis. Women may choose to minimize or deny the relevance of gender, but they have to do so consciously, they have to take a position, whereas men are able to 'transcend' their gender. Politics is tied to powerful male cultural symbols and is premised upon male norms and values. It is also premised upon the caring and daily maintenance of male politicians being carried out by women. Male politicians' 'maleness' is unproblematic in contrast to female politicians at times deeply troubling 'femaleness'.

This chapter offers women's own analysis of their political role and practice as an important form of situated knowledge and a neglected resource for seeking new political discourses and new political visions. The use of women's stories is based upon an understanding that women *as women* have to negotiate daily contradictions in both the public and private spheres and this gives rise to complex understandings of gender and politics and possible pointers for change. A narrative approach also 'takes seriously people's stories about what they need to live well' (Sevenhuijsen, 1998, p. 60). A more detailed explanation of this approach can be found in the introduction. Some of the limitations of this approach will be considered later.

Dimensions of Care

The discussions broadly relate to themes of the costs of care and care as a resource. Different aspects were examined: the costs of care for women seeking to enter politics and those encountered once participating in political life; the way in which women councillors' experiences dissonated with dominant ideas of citizens and political actors as autonomous and unencumbered; the ways in which men resist change (and hold on to power) by invoking hegemonic notions of fairness at the level of access; and the way formal institutional rules, as well as informal cultures, undermine women by demanding that they assimilate – or stay at home. On a more general level, women councillors discussed the ways in which gender divisions and gender roles were replicated in politics. Their stories, sometimes contradictory, speak of a complex inter-play between gender, equality, justice and disadvantage.

Of equal importance are women's accounts of the way in which difference is played out in their political roles and values, and the prospects of what might be called 'care thinking' for politics. Most believed that the increased presence of women in local and national politics would have a transformatory potential. There was a widespread perception that women were different in terms of 'doing politics' and that they would make a difference to the outcome of politics by bringing their own perspectives, policy concerns and values. For example, most agreed with the view that women politicians represent the interests of women in the community better than do male politicians; most also agreed with the view that women politicians behaved differently from male politicians (see Chapter 5). These were recurrent themes, although many women held contradictory beliefs. 'Difference' discourses existed alongside 'equality' discourses, which asserted that women were 'as good as' men, and which minimized the political relevance of gender. In some cases women, who in principle espoused equality or 'sameness' arguments in terms of political recruitment, under-scored the relevance of difference when discussing the daily practice of politics.

The parallels and contradictions between women's narratives and the theoretical concepts and models raised in the previous chapter are examined. These include the issues of justice and gender, particularly Okin's concept that gender inequalities in the family are at the root of inequalities in society, work and politics; and that this constitutes as gender crisis of justice. Ruddick's thesis that mothering gives rise to both a mode of thinking and specific skills and strategies that are a resource for politics will be explored for parallels within the present study; as will be the more generalist models refined by Tronto and Sevenhuijsen who argue for an ethics of care to be placed centrally in politics and a vocabulary of care rehearsed to expose the unequal distribution of caring work and the unequal distribution of power. The discussions of the women councillors are examined to see whether experience arising out of practice – the practice of caring – has resulted in new ideas about the practice of politics.

The political costs and dilemmas of care

Turning first to the costs of care: women councillors were clear that the barriers to equal participation in politics were gendered, and perceived them as rooted in the sexual division of labour. They described and discussed a series of constraints which interconnected, and which served to both inhibit potential aspirants at party and candidate level, and disadvantage women as political players once they are inside the system. Domestic responsibilities, time poverty and lack of confidence were identified as the major constraints preventing women from full and fair participation in public life. There was also recognition that the unequal sexual division of labour was inextricably linked to men's resistance as political players, as social actors and as partners to concede their privilege.

Caring burdens were recognized to constitute a major barrier for women seeking to enter politics. These, together with gender role stereotypes, were also seen to further hobble women once they became politicians in terms of opportunities to exercise power and influence. Household labour and issues of caring were seen by female councillors as key factors in both explaining women's relative absence from political institutions, and in justifying the need for their inclusion. Care experience was argued to be a source of insight and strength. However, the expression of these understandings was often ambivalent and hesitant. The paradox of care is a truism – often remarked upon, but less often seen as a legitimate issue of political concern. Women sometimes spoke in a 'conventional feminine voice' marked by a sense of fatalism or an uncritical acceptance of the status quo. Sometimes they spoke in radical 'transformed' ways, which equate to Gilligan's post-conventional 'Different Voice'. More often, however, their common sense contained elements of both.

Equality, Justice and Care

An explicit link was made between equality and the sexual division of family labour, 'Women should have the opportunity equally with men and that cannot happen if they're looked upon as the people who look after the children all the time.' Women were clear that men needed to take more responsibility for household labour and child care and spoke of the disjuncture between some male colleagues' outward commitment to equality and social justice and the concrete realities of their own lives:

> I get amused sometimes at meetings watching the number of men who talk about equality on the agenda, knowing full well that they're there because it is a seven o'clock meeting and the wife is at home looking after the kids and making sure that they get to bed. And I fundamentally believe that some of it has to start in the house. (Labour)

Although these links were made, they were seldom directly expressed as an injustice in the way that Okin suggests that the sexual division of labour within the family is a justice crisis of gender. Domestic arrangements were commonly seen as voluntarist agreements: individual problems to be addressed by individualist solutions. There was little articulation of a crisis of justice; instead it was more often characterized as an unfortunate fact of life which inhibited many able women from entering electoral politics. Without the characterization of justice – or other explanations of the structural nature of inequalities – discussions of the sexual division of labour become rather woman-blaming, especially if individual women have indeed succeeded in negotiating equal terms:

> We've always worked it between us, it's not one of those households where Mummy does everything. Women are their own worst enemy sometimes. They take burdens upon themselves. They think they're the only people that are responsible for child care, they're the only people responsible

for the house and so on. It's guilt. (SNP)

Choice and necessity were, however, seen as inextricably linked in many women's experiences. 'It's very difficult for a woman – because she has got to start by saying, "What is going to happen to the children?"' (Labour). The dilemma for women is that, in the face of men's refusal to do their fair share of caring work, their options are limited. Women recognize the concrete needs of those around them and the necessity of that work because those needs cannot be left unmet, 'the buck stops here'. Their choice becomes that of efficiently managing the double or triple burden – or not participating. As such, the political participation of women with caring responsibilities remains in the gift of her partner or lies in her individual resources to manage conflicting demands:

> If a man is in a political party, then it's the man who goes to the party meetings and the woman who has to stay at home and watch the kids, until the children are up or there are crèche facilities, because the meetings are nearly always at night. If put to the test I think you'd find most men would go to the meetings. They wouldn't say, 'Well, you go this time'. (Labour)

> Along the way we do collect more responsibilities as far as family is concerned so, whereas a man might be able to dump his job for a period of four years to take up something as uncertain as [Westminster] politics, you can't just dump your children for four years, or dump your old mother-in-law. I think there is definitely more difficulty for women and for women the further away from London, then the greater the problem. (Conservative)

The difficulties posed by this 'attribution of final responsibility' within families, even within non-traditional relationships, have been noted in other studies (for example, Saraceno, 1987; Barron *et al.*, 1991). The problem is one that is commonly expressed in the question: where does the buck stop? Men have the psychological and material resources to choose to be present or not, therefore they can 'pass the buck', whereas women seldom even perceive their presence or non-presence in the family as a matter of choice. As a result of a complex combination of psychological and social factors, women see their presence as a necessity, they are acutely aware of the needs

162

within families, especially the care needs of children. Saraceno asks whether women can really *choose* to be absent – to *not* relate; or whether such choice is contingent upon the guaranteed presence of another. It is argued that men have a choice because women's presence is assumed. 'Can one really choose absences, or non-relating, or is that only possible because someone else guarantees *a priori* before any choice is made ... precisely this presence and recognition?' (Saraceno, 1987, p. 199).

An example of this can been seen in the story of one newly elected councillor who spoke about the different approaches men and women take in reconciling family and politics. Although active in local party politics for many years, she had delayed her entry into elected politics. She had first been approached to stand more than six years ago when her children were still young. 'Standing for council then was out of the question.' Her response had been markedly different to that of her husband when he had also been approached:

> Whereas my husband never thought anything about it. Oh, he could do it – and he did do it! *But he'd no other responsibilities.* So that was in my mind then, Gosh, I couldn't do that because who would do this? Who would do that? Now the children are older that's not a problem. (Labour; my italics)

Her comments also revealed her recognition (and apparently uncritical acceptance) of her husband's *privileged irresponsibility*. In addition to child care and domestic labour, she also provided her husband with practical and emotional support in his duties as a councillor, including constituency case work. A number of women had been councillor's wives before they became councillors (see also Barron *et al.*, 1991). Indeed, several women argued that it was not just child care which inhibited women's political activism, but also the care demands and expectations of male partners, 'even if she hasn't got children – the man expects meals at night when he gets home – so there are difficulties put in a woman's way right from the start' (Labour).

Domestic Stability

At the personal level, although several women spoke about the vital support they had been given by family and partners, others spoke of

163

the resistance or acquiescence of partners, which rested on a clear agreement that their lives should not be disrupted by their wife's political work. The reaction reported by a Conservative councillor was far from uncommon, 'My husband thumped the table and said to me, "*Darling*, I don't care what you do – as long as you are *here* when I get home!"' In other words, domestic harmony was conditional upon male demands being met for what Barron *et al.* (1991) have called 'domestic stability'. 'A lot of women have very good partners who are very supportive, but there still is a fine line and edge – where it comes to a point where they say, "No, I've had enough". Because men do expect more' (Liberal Democrat). Several councillors spoke of female colleagues who had left politics over the years because of the accumulation of difficulties in this respect:

> It's difficult some days to pick up the phone and say 'I'm not going to come home, because if I come home, I'm only going to have 15 minutes in the house and then I'll have to go out again – so I'm just going to stay.' Some men have a lot of difficulty with that, and I know of women elected members who have done their stint for four years and had to give it up because it's their marriage or the job. They've been very articulate, very hardworking councillors – but they've been given a choice. (Labour)

Some had personal experience of previously supportive partners withdrawing their support. A number of women attributed the breakdown of their own relationships to factors arising from their involvement in politics:

> I was housing convenor – that's basically what caused my marriage split – I had people phoning me at two o'clock in the morning saying, 'We need a house'. My husband couldn't cope with it – he just flipped.

One recently separated councillor said her husband told her he felt neglected, especially after the birth of their child placed even greater demands on her time. Indeed, some women knew of other colleagues and ex-colleagues who had experienced violence and intimidation from partners who felt they had neglected their domestic responsibilities:[1]

> It's that whole power thing. In some ways I suffered from that myself, not with physical violence, but just the sheer 'I don't

want you to do this, you're supposed to be at home with the children.' (Labour)

Lone parent councillors did not speak directly about whether they felt disadvantaged because they did not have a partner and potential support – or advantaged because they did not have a man's care needs to attend to in addition to those of their children. What can be drawn from interviews, however, is that these women did not appear to think they were disadvantaged in anything other than a financial way (for example, having to bring up a family on benefit, or on part-time or sporadic earnings). There were no openly lesbian councillors in this study, however, research on couples in the USA (cited by Okin, 1989) suggests that lesbian households are far more likely than heterosexual households to share domestic labour equitably. Therefore it can be argued that women in heterosexual partnerships are likely to face the most acute problems of care-demanding and unequal care burdens.

Women's common sense was characterized by an observation, sometimes uncritical, that men's distance from the concrete needs and demands of care afforded them advantages on many levels, while women's care burdens placed them at considerable disadvantage within the family, work and politics. Women in the study frequently described their experience of men, as partners and politicians, as 'care demanding' and exerting what Tronto has characterized elsewhere as 'privileged irresponsibility'. This is where powerful groups can simultaneously consume and benefit from large amounts of care while also celebrating their self-sufficiency and denigrating those who carry out caring work:

It is hard. It's just another thing to juggle with time isn't it? Because you don't become a politician and everything else melts into the background; you still have all the other things to do. . . . The other day the full council started at 10.30 in the morning and finished at 11.30 at night. Now, for the men – they have a wife at home who's made their tea, who's put it in the oven or whatever – so everything's hunky-dory. They haven't had to worry about picking up children from school; they haven't had to worry about putting a meal on the table that kind of thing, but females do. (Liberal Democrat)

There was a clear and common insight into the advantages that this accorded men in general and, in particular, as political players at party and council level. Several women spoke about their experience of male colleagues being impatient with 'excuses' and undermining women who have less time for preparation. 'They forget that we've got the family commitments whether they like it or not. We dinnae get up in the morning and find a shirt ironed and our speech already done, because we had time the night before.' (Labour)

Trailing Domesticity: Men's Reaction to Women and Their Baggage

One of the ways in which men and male-defined systems may be seen to devalue care is in their disregard and discomfort with evidence of 'private' lives and care concerns spilling over into the public world of work and politics. This again relates to a point raised by a number of the care theorists such as Tronto, Ruddick and Sevenhuijsen about the denigration of care. In particular, a number of women highlighted the adverse reactions they had encountered from some of their male colleagues if they had to bring their children into the council – despite the fact that this was generally caused in the first place by the inability of rigid council structures to accommodate the care responsibilities in women's lives.

The flexibility shown in adapting meeting times to accommodate rural councillors, mostly men, travelling in to the headquarters of one council was contrasted with the reaction encountered by councillors who were mothers when they raised the issue of council meetings being held during school holidays. 'They don't even consult with us. We say, "Wait a minute, the kids are on holiday and you've got a meeting here." So we just have to bring them in.'

A young Labour councillor spoke of her experience of child 'unfriendly' practices in her city council. She was first elected when her elder daughter was a few months old, and gave birth to her younger daughter while a serving councillor. Child care has been an intermittent problem for her, and there have been a number of occasions when she has brought both her daughters, as babies, into the City Chambers. She recounts one occasion shortly after she joined the council when she took her six-month-old daughter into a Women's Committee meeting:

The meeting went to 'B' agenda – which is where the public are excluded because it is confidential business. One of the male councillors said my baby daughter ought to be put out of the committee because she was a member of the public! (Labour)

Several years later, acceptance of children was still grudging with little attempt to understand the issues behind the occasionally – and obviously disturbing – appearance of children in the Chamber. One councillor, who was nursing her very young infant during a break in a long, drawn-out meeting of the full Council, was 'shielded' by other women councillors in the corner of the councillors' lounge. She remarked that she had to keep well out of sight of certain male councillors – or they would protest – or even 'manufacture some "shock horror" story about women breast-feeding in the council for the local newspaper'.

Such stories highlight the disregard with which women with child care responsibilities are treated by the system, and by individual men within it. It also underscores the disdain and dislike provoked in some male councillors by the presence of children in the 'public' world – a presence which is seen as illegitimate, disgraceful even. This underlines the distance between some male politicians and the concrete realities of caring labour. These stories at local government level are strikingly similar to the reaction Labour MP Harriet Harman faced when she arrived at the House of Commons for an important vote just nine days after giving birth to her son Joe, as reported by Coote and Patullo:

> She had taken baby Joe to the Whip's Office to be cared for while she voted, but had been spotted on the way in – and in that place a mother and a baby are a rare sighting. As she filed in to vote, the cry went up 'I Spy Strangers' – the curious old phrase used when a non-MP is suspected of going through the division lobby. The MP for Peckham was being accused of smuggling her baby, hidden beneath her cardigan, into the inner sanctum. (1990, p. 255)

Harriet Harman takes up the story:

> Somebody told the Chief Whip in a hysterical sort of way that I had carried him through the Division Lobby. I thought it showed such an unstable approach to this little baby. He was no threat to anyone, yet the very idea of him deeply attacked people's nerve endings. I had come from a cosy home environment, and before that from hospital with all those new

babies. To arrive in the Commons and find it full of anti-social, alien types of men who'd been festering all day before the vote – it really was a culture shock. And then you have to be stripped of your baby in order to exercise your right to vote because that makes you a *real* MP. (Coote and Patullo, 1990, pp. 255–6; italics in original)

This unease which men feel about the presence of women is not confined to political life. Cockburn has charted the way men are disturbed at women 'trailing evidence of domesticity' into the public world of work and has explored the anger and resentment felt by men, both as workers and as managers, at pregnant women and new mothers remaining in their jobs. This relates not only to resentment of 'mother's privileges', for instance, maternity benefits, but also is shaped by powerful perceptions that working mothers are transgressing boundaries (Cockburn, 1991). Evelyn Mahon's research on working mothers in the Irish civil service uncovered cases where women used up their holidays to cover each other's maternity leave because they perceived, in a mixed and highly competitive environment, maternity leave was intensely resented by male colleagues (1991, p. 170).

Scottish women councillors voiced their perceptions that women politicians were seen as untrustworthy, 'there is undoubtedly an ingrained suspicion that women might get pregnant or do womanly things instead of running countries'. Some women were far more comfortable talking about child care as a policy issue rather than their own arrangements. This caution, sometimes irritation, may relate to an unease at being confirmed as the domestic sex, coupled with the sense that women's domestic concerns are delegitimized within political structures:

They have meetings at 3 o'clock – now why do they start a meeting at three? Now if I say – 'It's not fair, you do realize that schools come out at this time and if I am in a meeting, how am I to pick up the kids from school?' – they're not in the least bit interested. In fact, that's better, because that means I can't go to the meeting, and if I'm not there I'm less likely to be a nuisance to them ... and whenever we have tried to get meetings at night or change times they have said, 'Well, you knew what you were coming into when you put your name forward, we all have to make sacrifices and it suits us to come at this time so ... too bad!' (SNP)

Rules of the Game

The rules of the game for politics are characterized by disembodied notions of 'fair play' and appear unresponsive to the needs of others or the messy realities of workaday lives. One of the youngest female councillors in a large regional authority discussed the reluctance of men in political parties to take seriously the issue of the poor representation of women in politics and their failure to recognize the concrete differences between women's and men's lives and the resultant consequences for access to politics. She partly attributed this to a lack of understanding about the ways in which women and their lives have changed. She argued many political men were uneasy with women who do not easily fit stereotypes:

> They have a real problem because, in the main, they're '50s' men – so women are cute and malleable, or they are their wives, or their Ma. And then there is this new breed of woman that they don't really have a *scoobie*[2] how that works and they don't try to understand.

She argued that the view still prevails that if women are interested in politics they will enter, and that their responsibilities are their own concern. She also suggested that this reluctance to understand may stem, at least in part, from an unwillingness to share power and an understanding that sticking to the rules benefits men:

> They don't try to understand, and I think that's the pitiable thing. They can't grasp that feminism, for want of a better word, is nothing more than fairness. It's about applying the logic that you would apply in any other situation to half the population! That's how simple it is for me, and yet they can't grasp it. They are reluctant to share power. They are reluctant to give up any of their practices. They are reluctant to change what we do as a party; and they still think that if women are that interested they'd join anyway – no question of any other responsibilities that women will have, no question of crèches, etc. They don't try to understand any of the things that are going on in women's lives to try and encourage them to come into the party. (Labour)

Formal justice and political rules of the game emphasize procedural fairness and do not require that needs be addressed nor adequacy of solutions assessed. There is little space within such commonplace

169

definitions of equality for other arguments which assert that to treat people as equals may require that they be treated differently; ideas that 'we merit equal though not identical treatment; equal in the sense of equally good, and more appropriate to us' (Evans, 1995, p. 3). This explains why there is so little impetus for rules to be bent – as it is commonly seen – to accommodate the needs of women to be treated as equals. This results in women being faced with the choice of managing disadvantage or being caught in what another Labour councillor called the 'Excuse me, I need extra because ... ' trap which labels women as needy and 'other':

> We need to be looking at what structures are in place that suit women. It always amazes me when we have long meetings, for example, they always talk about comfort breaks and – how can I put this in a way that makes sense? – OK, they'll have a comfort break and they'll say, 'Five minutes' and I'll say, 'How about quarter of an hour?' Maybe women have got their period and need slightly longer to do certain things – and men don't realize. So you need to make sure that whatever you are organizing has to take account of the women there and women's needs. And that's what's missing: women have as much right to access to everything as men have without having to say, 'Excuse me, I need extra because ... ' (Labour)

Research has demonstrated that, in organizational life, it is often the case that the only option women are given is assimilation. To be an equal of men in the public sphere, women are required to become 'indistinguishable' from men (Cockburn, 1991, p. 164). Similarly, to be taken seriously in political life there is an expectation that women put aside 'womanly things'; that they leave their baggage – the kids, the elderly relatives, the laundry and the shopping list at home – out of sight. As one councillor asked with exasperation: just what are the priorities of local government when, as a councillor, her petrol and travel expenses are allowed against tax, but the cost of child care when she goes to council meetings is not?

> If I'm going to a meeting and the family can't watch the boys then I have to pay for a childminder – and that's not a non-taxable allowance. I can get my petrol expenses but I can't get anybody to watch my kids! (SNP)

Trivializing Care

Others discussed the ways in which male councillors trivialized care – and the problems women faced as carers. This disregard for the cost of caring sometimes extended to women in the community:

> We take it [the problems of women as carers] more seriously than men – whether it's because we've been there and we know what other people, other women, are being faced with. Men are apt to push it to one side: 'Ah, it's a woman's *job* – women are *supposed* to worry; women are *supposed* to feel stress'. (Labour)

> Women in general have had a tough time for so long anyway that they really need us to be on their side. I mean just a simple thing, although it's not a simple thing it's a huge complex problem, like providing child care. It is so important and there are men who sympathize – I'll give them that some of them do – but I don't think they fully understand what a hold back it is for women not to be able to have child care they can afford and can count on. And that's just one thing, there are so many more. (Labour)

Some women spoke about feeling they were hamstrung by men's trivialization of women and women's issues, when instead they sought to have women's traditional concerns incorporated into the mainstream:

> They are sidelined and there's a great deal of, 'Och, well, what do you expect of a bunch of women, they would suggest that'; but I want the lives of women to be *part of the process*. (SNP)

The common-sense discussions of women politicians' experiences reveal a commonplace assessment that political parties and political institutions are constructed for men – and that women's presence is contingent on women playing by male rules. Women's common sense is also characterized by an observation, sometimes uncritical, that men's distance from the concrete needs and demands of care affords them privileged irresponsibility on many levels, while women's care burdens place them at considerable disadvantage within the family, work and politics. However, at present caring issues and concerns are seen as trivial and apolitical. Women who are excluded from politics are seen to be 'failing to come forward';

women politicians who point out the structural disadvantages of female responsibilities are seen to be 'bleating about child care'.

Revaluing care

On the one hand, the costs of care were well recognized at both a practical and symbolic level. On the other hand, care was also understood to be a source of strength and value. There was a desire to place what Tronto has characterized as an 'ethics of care' centrally in political and social life, 'Care should be central to everyone's lives, not just women's.' However, there was a struggle to see this as a wholly legitimate political issue and uncertainty as to how to an 'ethics of care' might be introduced into current political systems:

> The parameters are always set, have been set, by men – and feminists have tried to beat men at their own game ... to succeed in business, and to succeed in politics, and to get to the top, and to be Mrs Thatcher, and so on. And I don't think that is necessarily the answer, because I think society needs carers, and needs people doing the things that traditionally have been done by women – they don't have to be done by women. But I think until that work is equally valued you won't get the change ... Women will be expected to do all the men's things *and* all the women's things as well. (Liberal Democrat)

Although sometimes couched in terms of 'what women know', rather than a sense of legitimate political discourse, nevertheless women politicians did use notions of 'difference' and 'care' to challenge hegemonic values. In particular, many women saw their experience of care-giving and their ability to juggle competing roles and demands as valuable political resources both in terms of policy-making and as general competencies which deserved recognition. They perceived women to have valuable managing skills, and argued that women were generally more practical, 'They bring a more common-sense approach', and were better organized, more adaptable and more responsive than many male councillors.[3]

> I think women look at things in a totally different way from men. You can even see it in your own home, the way a woman will look at the practical side of life, the way her husband

doesn't. She'll plan ahead for the future, she'll always see things coming. And I think women do that in politics as well. (Labour)

I think women tend to get to the point more quickly in their own heads because they deal with so many things at the same time. Particularly if they've got children and things like that – they have to be able to get rid of the chaff and get to the point. (Conservative)

Men tend to jump in without stopping to think, whereas women – I think because of their background, probably having brought up a family, having to budget and juggle housekeeping money – women tend to draw back a wee bit and think before they act and also look through to any end product ... Not just see things as black and white. (SNP)

It is interesting to note that although ideas can be contradictory women councillors do see a characteristic approach arising from care work. Women also argued that they made good politicians because they 'have other lives outside the council' in contrast to many male politicians:

It always amazes me the number of men who sit around here for hours on end, and you think: God, do they do nothing else? Have they not got another life? Have they not got a family? Have they not got a home? Have they not got a shopping list? (Labour)

The relative absence of women in politics and the law was seen to account for many of the deficiencies apparent in social policy and judicial workings. It was argued that men encountered difficulties in recognizing and dealing with the complexity of everyday social policy problems such as housing and child care, 'I think men actually think the answer to a lot of the problems is purely a mechanical one.' In contrast, women brought valuable skills and specialist knowledge to politics, strengths drawn from their experience at the 'coal face' of family and community life and recognized the 'bothersome' complexity and implications of everyday issues:

Talking about children, the answer is not necessarily for more and more child care or nurseries it's really for a much more equal society, where men and women don't have to work forty or forty-five hours a week – a much shorter week, flexible so that we can raise our children *and* have a satisfying career. (Labour)

Women councillors appeared to have supportive attitudes to a range of policy areas which affect women more than men, for instance, child care, nursery provision, community safety, community care, housing and transport policy, health, violence, equal opportunities and greater political representation for women. Women across different political parties found the term 'women's issues' problematic for a number of reasons, in the main because they perceived these issues to be human or society issues rather than narrowly defined women's issues. Some introduced the idea of a women's perspective or angle across all policy areas which 'refocuses the agenda'. For example, the issues of child care and work flexibility figure prominently in women's understandings of economic development. Women councillors, irrespective of their political standpoint, shared some core understandings about the gender-differentiated impact of certain policy areas and saw such issues as, at the very least, 'worthy of debate' and sometimes the basis of working in alliance to promote gender-sensitive policy and service delivery.

According to the women councillors, male politicians were often headstrong, unpredictable in temperament, emotional and demanding. They were prone to 'tantrums' and 'shouting and bawling' when contradicted. They characterized (some of their) male colleagues in terms of rigidity of thinking and an unwillingness to consider different and differing viewpoints. This was expressed, for instance as 'Men have set ideas, women are more open and receptive to opposing views'; in terms of policy-making men were seen as, 'glossing things over' or, 'going with the tide', or of, 'engaging in confrontational politics which means that underlying issues are not resolved'. This contrasted with perceptions that women possessed qualities of patience and flexibility, 'Women in politics bring an even keel to things' which gave rise to strategies to 'cool down' heated situations by, for instance, listening and by seeking compromises:

I think a lot of women have got this capacity for being able to see both sides of an argument and to be able to articulate that

174

and bring a certain amount of common sense – and cool the thing down. (Liberal Democrat)

I think we're mair open to discussion to resolve an issue. (Labour)

Am I generalizing here? I'm basing a lot of what I say on what I see personally – so it's my experiences I'm obviously going on. I do think that women have a civilizing effect and they can bring a higher quality to arguments – even if they're just sitting there listening half the time – that is a quality in itself. (Liberal Democrat)

It is interesting to note in these discussions that, in parallel with care theorists, openness and the ability to listen are forwarded as a political virtues. A number of women also suggested that empathy was a political quality:

I think that's one of the things women bring to politics, they take a little time, take a little patience, they think things out – thinking ahead to the future, thinking how something is going to affect somebody else. (Labour)

In one of several emerging discussions about alternative criteria, a single parent understood her life experiences as well qualifying her to seek election as a councillor:

I had children, they were my first priority. I had experience of life, experience as a single parent after divorce – I knew what it was go from having money to not having money and wondering where the kids' next pair of shoes is coming from, the next meal on the table etc. I had experience from work in personnel and of debt counselling – so I was in position to help other people. (Labour)

Judging with Care?

There are parallels between women politicians' concerns with care as a political idea and value and the ideas of care thinkers. The councillors discussed their desire to practise a politics in which context-sensitive and effective solutions would be negotiated. These ideas are strikingly similar to Tronto's 'integrity of practice' and

Sevenhuijsen's 'judging with care', both of which feature key components of attentiveness, responsibility, competence and responsiveness.

Women spoke of their preference for informality 'as a positive force for relaxing people' and for 'freeing up thought and discussion' among colleagues as well as promoting greater accessibility and participation for members of community groups. A distinction was made between 'formal' solutions and 'women's solutions' and between people and structures:

> I hesitate to mention character things, but I think women on the whole would like to look deeper into why things are happening and therefore are prepared to discuss solutions other than just ordinary formal solutions. Women *are* more interested in people, and politics is about people and not structures and therefore women are more likely to get solutions and decisions that are correct than men. Now, that is a totally sweeping statement and you can understand why I was reluctant to make it, but I think there is something in there that you can glean, because other women will say the same thing – and I think it's a positive thing, to be more interested in people than structures. (Labour)

In another example, one councillor argued that the implementation of quotas to improve political access for women was not an adequate solution on its own, because it did not tackle the underlying issue of discriminatory structures and thinking:

> You see, I'm no sure where I stand on quotas because I think they have to go hand in glove with the whole thinking process. I think it is very easy – the easy way out – to say: 'Fifty-fifty, aren't we good? We agree with equality!' Forty-sixty, fifty-fifty – whatever line they draw. 'We're for women, we're for equality, we've done it, we've achieved it!' Absolute rubbish, because it's the easy way out! If they forgot about the numbers game and were prepared to say, 'OK, our thinking is changing, we're prepared to think about the *barriers* to politics for *everybody*', because there *are* barriers to certain men, disabled, black, gay, whatever – and the thinking was, 'We want to be open access'. I would rather that happened instead. (Labour)

The preference for 'people' has been noted before and is usually posited in opposition to policy. However, in terms of this study women did not see the two in contrast and were very clear that policy was about people. Political science has tended to present this as evidence of women as being community-minded rather than political. However, the implications of this discussion, which is echoed in varying forms in many of the interviews, is that women are concerned with care as a central political idea and as a standard, and work towards what Tronto and Sevenhuijsen have called an *integrity of practice*, where context-sensitive and effective solutions are negotiated. Another highly experienced politician, whose discussions also contain embryonic frameworks of care, used the crisis over health as an example of how traditional (male) politics – particularly at Westminster – do not work to create meaningful solutions:

> The health service is at a point of crisis, we have to find ways of financing the kind of care that technology is able to provide and the kind of care our ageing population requires and this is a matter of extreme and acute importance to everybody in society. There are different ways of looking at that, but does anybody sit down and discuss this rationally? No. Nobody is saying, 'this is difficult, there are hard decisions to be made – we can't afford everything.' Who is to make these hard decisions about what kind of care we are going to provide and who is going to pay for it, and how? I would like to believe that if there were more women involved at a much higher level there would be more of that kind of approach. (Liberal Democrat)

Most women were keen to stress their wish to serve the whole of the community, although they were aware of limitations of representation, which explained a preference, in many cases, for grassroots consultation and participation. Women said they viewed politics differently from men, for example, seeing it in terms of problem solving, or for the common good of the community, and that they preferred consultation and compromise as means of working. They perceived the traditional view of politics as being about pursuit of power with more emphasis on winning and less emphasis on workable solutions.

This argument was in emerging form in the councillors' discussions, it was not highly developed and it was contested, particularly by those women, albeit a tiny minority, who believed that power politics was the only way politics can be done. There was ambivalence, therefore, it is important not to over-emphasize difference. Although some women councillors were aware of the complex difficulties, and the considerable potential pitfalls of the 'distinctive contribution' or 'women's values' justification, the 'difference' and 'making a difference' arguments, in general, resonated with the experiences and opinions of almost all the women in the study. This included women who elsewhere in their interviews were more reluctant to concede the political relevance of gender.

These ideas are reinforced by the empirical literature. As we saw in Chapter 4, comparative research suggests that women politicians are more likely than male politicians to value citizen participation and consultation in the policy-making process and in service delivery, and to be more likely to be concerned with political action in terms of problem solving, service delivery and developing policy, rather than measuring their success by their bargaining position in power structures.

Emerging Discourses of Politics and Care

A number of women outlined what they saw as women's particular concern for issues relating to 'the human life cycle in all its forms':

> Women – it may be because of the way they are traditionally brought up – but I don't think it is only that, I think there is an interest in people and in relationships – and what people make of those – is of particular importance to women. Whether, on one level, it's things like contraception and abortion, and what sort of provision is made there for young women and older women as well; right through to things like nurseries and education broadly, ... the care of the elderly in the community, and health. I mean they are all along that string of the life cycle. It's not that men *aren't* interested in those sorts of things, because of course they are – but I think women have a particularly strong wish to make all that better. (Labour)

Women's discussions of the conflict between 'love' and politics, particularly at national Westminster level, served as a critique of the political values of the system. Structures which forced female – and male – politicians to be separated from their families and divorced from care were seen as problematic and undesirable, not just inconvenient:

> The thing about Westminster is not just the distance – but also the absolutely ridiculous hours, the times meetings are held at. A lot of women don't want to miss so much of their children's lives in any event. It is not purely a decision to send your children to boarding school, you've made a decision about what you want out of family life anyway. It's not *just* who is going to look after them, it is not just the practicalities, it's, 'Well, I don't actually *want* to be away from Monday night to Friday morning' or whatever it is, 'I don't want to *do* that every week (Labour)

> Really, I think that takes you back to issues of child care and things like that – that's a big problem being a woman and in politics if you want to pursue that career – I mean what's the Houses of Parliament? It's incredible – that's presumably why a lot of {women} are not there because what do you do with your kids for heavens sake? (Conservative)

This echoes the themes raised by women politicians in a number of other countries. Political scientist Jenny Chapman remarks: 'The fact that the family still comes first for most women is not just a cultural hangover but a reflection of the values women want to see preserved' (1993, p. 225). These concerns about the value of care, relationships and family life and the inter-connection of private and public at the common-sense level, arising from everyday experience, articulate similar positions to care theorists like Tronto, who argues for a society which values care and where people can care and do other things:

> In all, a society that took caring seriously would engage in a discussion of the issues of public life from a vision not of autonomous, equal, rational actors each pursuing separate ends, but from a vision of interdependent actors, each of whom needs and provides care in a variety of ways and each of whom has other interests and pursuits that exist outside the realm of care. (1993, p. 168)

It is possible in this debate to see an intersection between theory and practice – where women are recognizing, negotiating and articulating the contradictions they experience when they try to combine the different elements of their lives, and the sense in which they find contemporary political values and political fora as out of tune with their own needs and values.

Playing the Game

As discussed in Chapter 4, and in the evidence from other studies world-wide, many women contend that they view politics differently to men. For example, it is claimed that women see politics as problem solving, aimed not at sectional interests but for the common good of the community. Women are said to prefer consensus and consultation as means of working. These claims resonate with many of the women here. Those who spoke of their desire for a different way of doing politics also spoke about the constraints under which they currently operated. As such, they faced a dilemma – because there was a need to somehow get women 'in there' on men's terms, before they can do things on their 'own terms':

> It's how you get from here to there that is the difficulty. If there are only individual women, they really perhaps have to fight men on their own battlefield. And, to some extent these women, Thatcher *et al.*, have managed to succeed so far because they have been good at the man's game. The women who are not good at the man's game don't get through at the moment, and I think that is the difficulty of how you get from here to there; of how to make a major break-through on our *own* terms. (Liberal Democrat)

Women may argue that they have little time and appetite for power politics but, as one young councillor noted, they have little choice:

> You have to use the games that are in play and they *are* games – and that's another thing, women don't generally have the time to play games! But unfortunately it's a case of, 'Is this what the boys are up to today? Oh dear!' Sleeves up and get in.

She argued that until politics can be changed to reflect what women want it was, 'the only game in town'. Women politicians were faced with a hard choice: to start playing the 'boys' games' or to be marginalized:

Now, it's not the way women operate. It is completely alien to what it is that you feel you need to do, but if you're faced with that kind of choice? I have to say, if you decide you're not going to play that game, then you're dead in the water – absolutely dead in the water. I've seen it happen in here and I can tell you women who will be coming back [after the elections] who will be no further on, who will be marginalized further because of their support for the wrong candidate, because of an inability essentially to grasp that the big boys are not going to give up power, and we can't change anything unless *we* are holding power.

Like other women, she had made the conscious choice to operate in the system as it currently is rather than as she would ideally like it to be:

I am here primarily to do a job, but I'm very well aware that I can't do that job to the best of my ability unless I have power – so, it's the only game in town in here. It's not my choice of a game, it's their game, but I will bloody well use it to my advantage. And then, when I have power, if it falls into my lap [laugh] *Then* you can call the shots! So it means *nothing* unless you're holding all the cards. Regardless of what it is you want to do, it is *completely* unachievable unless you have the clout to do it. Unfortunately, the only game in town is not one I'm particularly fond of, but I'll bloody well beat them at it just to make sure. I have decided clearly that what is important at the end of the day to me is that I can deliver what I have set out to deliver.

Another councillor explained the approach as the 'borrowing of men's clothes':

I think sometimes you have to borrow men's clothes and you have to be able to get inside the mind of a man – particularly in all the qualities that are admired in men: putting things across, being forceful, being determined, being decisive, which perhaps sit less naturally on women. (Conservative)

However, a few women in this study were sceptical about the possibility or credibility of 'different politics'. A Labour veteran and former Lord Provost sounded a cautious note:

It's very easy to hide behind a wall of saying 'Well, women

would do it differently.' You have to tackle the world as it exists and saying women behave differently is no different from – you know most *men* don't behave like power politicians – most *people* don't live their lives like that.

She argued that it is the nature of power politics that determines the way male and female politicians operate – if they are to be effective. She believed in pragmatism, and that it was the ends – effecting social change – that were crucial, not the means:

> Everything is do-able differently if at the end of the day you know what you want to achieve. But what I want to achieve is a better life for the very poor, and I could hang around being nice or I could say 'Bugger you! I'm sorry, Director of Housing, I'm not listening to the claptrap you're giving me. You are *not* going to put the rent up.' And not putting up the rent is more important than how I say it – or 'Repair that roof.' So, yes, of course it's possible for us to interact differently. But at the end of the day we are here to take power and give it to people who are powerless, and contemplating my navel isn't going to help too much in that! (Labour)

A Conservative councillor for a rural community, who classified herself as 'a well-kent face' rather than a political councillor, observed, 'I don't think that they behave differently, no. Women are the same as men. There are many people in this world, be they males or females, where a little power and they just get fair carried away with the whole thing' (Conservative).

The issue of the nature and desirability of power politics is controversial, as is the contention that women are less conflictual and more consensual than men in politics. Examples of the personal styles of women leaders such as Margaret Thatcher would seem to counter these suggestions. However, it is clear from the stories recounted here and elsewhere that there is a strong perception that adversarial politics are perceived as alien and alienating to women. The devaluing of care and current styles of politics are also seen as somehow linked: 'Until caring work is equally valued you won't get change in the way that politics is organized', although this connection is seldom further articulated.

Getting from Here to There?

How is change to be effected? Although many women did perceive their presence to make some difference, it is clear that there is still far to go. The question of how long individual women can work for change within male systems without being changed and incorporated by the system has been widely discussed. Individual women within political institutions live with large degrees of dissonance between what is and what ought to be (Eisenstein, 1991; Lovenduski and Randall, 1993). The operation of *realpolitik* together with *institutional sexism* creates a system whereby women who want to advance must play by male-defined rules and identify with male-defined political goals. Several women in the study argued that structures had to be changed first, rather than expecting women to change things from within. 'It's too much to ask women – the number of women who have been ground down and left by the system not even trying to alter it, just trying to fit in' (Labour). The danger of incorporation was discussed by another woman who argued there were three sorts of women in politics:

I think there are women who are still committed to radical change within politics – they're not looking for power, they're looking for change. Now obviously you can't get change without power. But there are the other women who have already got the power who were women who at one time were very committed to changing but who now want the status quo, because they've got it. Then there are women who don't believe in change in the first place, but have benefited from a degree of change – but that doesn't seem to have induced them at all to support the other women who are struggling to get in. (Labour)

There was a striking uncertainty about how to get 'from here to there' and a general reluctance to invoke 'special measures'. While there is no doubt that sometimes this is a strategy for doing nothing (for instance, there is no point pursuing immediate short agenda measures when what is needed is some vague and far distant transformation of gender relations); it also illustrated the difficulties many women have in dealing with contradictory notions of equality and difference (see Chapters 2 and 3).

Getting from Here to There: Societal Value Changes?

Wider social and economic change was seen to hold out prospects for value change: through the changing attitudes of younger generations and through the dramatic changes in women's participation in the labour market:

> Young men are quite different, whatever Mrs Thatcher may or may not have done for this country, she changed a lot of attitudes – and a hell of a lot of attitudes have changed among young men who would see things quite differently and understand women in the workplace, and understand women's issues. There's hardly a birth takes place that a man isn't standing there with his wife or partner. (Conservative)

Women saw a gradual improvement with shifting patterns of social and economic life, and argued that there was evidence of a degree of value change among some younger male politicians. Several pointed out that a number of their male colleagues shared child care with their partners, although this was still unusual enough to be commented upon. The visibility meant some of the problems of child care were perhaps seen as more legitimate – less as a special favour or a 'mother's privilege'. For example, a number of women were careful to use male examples when talking about the problems of child care, for instance, male colleagues who had missed meetings because of caring commitments. Women saw the growing domestication of men as progressing their understanding of care roles and care issues and providing the potential for alliances. This underlines the point that for most women, caring was not an essentialist identity but rather a practice. A number of councillors saw the greatest gap in attitudes and policy priorities between generations rather than genders.

> The only way we'll get it changed is by involving our male colleagues and about letting them see the difficulties. I mean, OK, there are two or three guys in here who are great, and there's one who doesn't work now but he's got a boy of fourteen and his wife works – and he has the same problems ... But they're not all like that because there are so many old men who've never had to face the problem. (Labour)

I've tried changing the older ones' minds and you get nowhere.
You can't even have a decent argument with them because
they won't debate with you at all, they just think you are a
silly female. (Liberal Democrat)

On a personal level, several women, feminist and non-feminist,
spoke about the way they had tried to avoid gender stereotyping
when they raised their own sons and daughters. They spoke of their
boys accepting a greater domestic role. 'As far as household chores,
my son had to do every bit as much as the girls – he could iron his
shirts and wash the dishes, and even cook mince and tatties as well
as the girls could.' Women spoke about their daughters being more
confident and assertive than they had been when they were girls,
'they're not frightened to do anything'; 'There's none of this only
boys can do that'; 'It's different from when I was at school.'

Helen Wilkinson of the independent think-tank Demos, in an
argument drawn from analysis of a longitudinal survey of British
values, asserts that there has been a convergence of values between
men and women in the 18–30 generation including a positive
attitude to gender equality (1994, pp. 19–27). However, other
research is more ambivalent, showing for example that traditional
ideologies can reassert themselves in equalitarian relationships once
couples have children (for example, Brannen and Moss, 1991), and
that fathers spend markedly less time with their children than
mothers, even those women who work full-time. One survey in the
mid-1990s found that more than half of the fathers of under-15 year
olds spent five minutes or less a day in one-to-one contact with their
children. It suggested that men preferred hobbies and sport to
spending time with their children.[4] Indeed, some councillors in the
current study were pessimistic. Several interviewees spoke about the
sexist attitudes of their own sons, 'I think they'll grow out of it – at
least I hope so.' Others spoke about the persistence of sexist
attitudes among younger councillors, 'trying hard to be the big
boys'. A number of councillors believed that talk of change at
societal level was over-stated, especially the evolving role of men, 'I
don't think the *New Man* bleedin' exists outwith what my son calls
the luvvies.' Others believed that change had occurred but that
'New Men', who were more positive about alternative values, were
marginalized in a society which still equated *machismo* with success.

It is quite interesting too that the men who seem to be more
accepting of women having an equal role in society, men who

seem to be more interested in working in a more co-operative way are, on the whole, *less* successful in the men's world. And men who in many ways seem to be overgrown small boys, fighting over the biggest desk and whatever, seem to be the achievers. (Liberal Democrat)

It is also clear that in many cases thinking about progressing women was blocked by a lack of alternative common sense about equality – the way in which many women felt they had to make a choice between love and politics – that is, to decide on political participation on men's terms or to save their energies for family life. This leads to a strand of biological fatalism:

> Someone asked me if I was optimistic and I said, No, I really am not. Sometimes I despair of the fact that women like me who have worked so hard for so long and have made such a little impression on these male-dominated structures in society. But I don't think legislation is going to change it, I honestly don't. Not as long as you have the biological function of the woman which whether she chooses to marry and/or have children or not is still an inescapable factor in this whole business. (Conservative)

Where to from Here?

The common-sense stories of these women politicians' experience of fragmented lives, managing contradictory aspects of their work and identity as women, mothers, wives, workers and politicians are rich with insight. We see a vision of transformed politics, albeit ill defined rather than well elaborated. We can hear new discourses, albeit tentative, contradictory and contested, in these stories as well as voices which are reactionary and fatalistic about women's 'inevitably domestic personae'.

Common themes emerge, themes which are strikingly similar to the central themes of care theorists: the way present political and social systems and value structures obscure the central importance of care; and the means by which certain powerful groups and actors benefit from, while simultaneously devaluing, care; recognition that practical strategies and intellectual skills which arise from the practice of caring such as attentiveness, connectedness, responsibility and reciprocity can be 'transformed' and transferred to a wider context of politics; and demands that politics change, not only that women may fully participate, but also that politics may become more fully human and reflect the needs and interests of all groups in the community.

We set out below some possible new vocabularies and discourses drawn from Chapter 6 within which to frame demands for change. Okin brings ideas of a gender justice of crisis and Ruddick introduces the insight that skills gained from mothering might have broader application in the public sphere. However, we focus predominantly on the work of Tronto and Sevenhuijsen who stress the generic nature of care beyond narrow definitions of motherhood. Tronto and Sevenhuijsen see care thinking as a form of situated knowledge and reflective practice. They develop tools which expose the costs of care and the privileged irresponsibility of those who demand care while simultaneously denigrating it and those who care-take. Care also provides an alternative vision of political values and political practices based upon attentiveness, responsibility, competence and responsiveness. These crucial skills are seen to be developed in the practice of caring.

In particular, Tronto's 'vocabulary of care' is a critical and strategic tool. If introduced and rehearsed, it would build upon women's common-sense analysis and further expose the uneven distribution of power in society. It would identify male politicians and party officials – as well as men in general – as *care demanders* exercising *privileged irresponsibility*. It would also make visible the ways in which care is denigrated and the disadvantages experienced by carers.

Tronto and the political vocabulary of care

Tronto exposes the ways in which dominant discourses obscure the central importance of care; they devalue care and obscure care-giving, especially the care needs of the powerful. Private care is trivialized and care work in the public sphere is underpaid. Moreover, the structuring of social, economic and political life fails to incorporate the caring needs and responsibilities of all. Her insights could be used to underscore the way that political systems are premised upon the false autonomy of political actors. In reality that autonomy is based on an assumption that women will do the care work for men: every politician needs a wife. Two key phrases in the vocabulary of care are, 'privileged irresponsibility' (which names the advantage powerful groups have as a result of others doing their caring work for them) and, 'care demanding' (the twin processes of making heavy care demands on others while simultaneously denying or trivializing care and carers). Tronto argues that the vocabulary of care can be used to reveal the power imbalances in society and to make visible the disadvantages experienced by carers. She suggests it can serve as a basis for political change and a strategy for mobilizing and organizing.

If we take Tronto's ideas and further develop them, we can argue that that the introduction of a *political discourse of care* could potentially empower women in politics in a number of ways. First, the notion of 'care as practice' would legitimize many women's experiences, and would link caring to citizenship, and for the purposes of our argument also to political office.[5] Although we have earlier noted the double-edged nature of such arguments. Second, the skills of *attentiveness, responsibility, competence* and *responsiveness* can be proffered as transferable skills vital in a politics where needs are discussed and where there is, 'an honest intersection between needs and interests' (Tronto, 1993, p. 167). In societies where governments grapple with increasingly complex and intractable policy problems and, sometimes, incommensurable demands, such skills should be at a premium. Third, the care debate exposes inequalities and could potentially empower and mobilize members of marginalized groups. The vocabulary of care would expose 'costs' of care and the inequalities which arise from the way in which politics (like much of the world of work) is premised upon others taking care of care.

There is an opportunity to progress the representation debate by drawing upon these new insights and new discourses. For example, if Tronto's four elements of care were to be applied to the problem of access to power, then political systems would be exposed as lacking 'integrity of practice'. Political systems and parties would be judged as merely complying with the most formal and detached elements of the political ideal of care, without following through with the specifics required for effective resolution of the democratic deficit. Just as in Tronto's earlier examples of large corporations who formally tackle a problem with no concern for the end result, political structures would be exposed as acting in 'bad faith'. For although they display some formal attentiveness ('caring about') and responsibility ('taking care of') in respect of the issue of women's under-representation, in that they all, in principle, support the idea of increasing the number of women and have, in most cases taken some steps to encourage more women candidates to come forward (for a range of measures and actions see Chapter 2), there are serious failings in competence ('care-giving'), that is in ensuring that adequate, appropriate and effective action is taken. Measures may be half-hearted and ineffective, for example, policies for balanced panels and shortlists may be introduced without any monitoring to ensure women are regarded as 'real' rather than token candidates. Meanwhile little is done to tackle the underlying problems of political parties and institutions where adversarial and aggressive power politics dominate and where political actors are assumed to be unencumbered. Finally, there has been little progress in progressing responsiveness ('care-receiving'), which in this context would mean securing the involvement of women in the process, and incorporating women's own understanding of their needs and what is required to effect their inclusion.

Tronto's typology could prove to be a useful tool of analysis to expose the shortcomings of current political systems. Continuing the analysis, in order to achieve integrity of practice, radical restructuring of politics would be needed. Politics would, thus, have to fit in with caring lives whilst also enabling citizens to combine care with other human activities.

Sevenhuijsen's 'judging with care'

Sevenhuijsen's analysis further develops and systemizes ideas about political vocabularies, building upon the work of Tronto. We can draw upon her idea of 'judging with care' as a potentially useful concept. The political idea of 'judging with care' works on a number of inter connecting levels (1998, pp. 4–5): first, it means careful judgement, emphasizing care as an attitude and a form of action; second, it promotes the view of care as a form of social agency; and, third, it sees care in a broader political context and the role of citizens in making political judgments about social provision in liberal and social welfare states.

Sevenhuijsen argues that ideas of 'judging with care' create a discursive opportunity and a space in which carers can be empowered to deliberate and to analyse public policy as critical citizens.

The introduction of the phrase 'judging with care' into popular political discourse has great potential. First, by coupling justice and care it can both sit within the 'norms' of political debate and also act as a channel through which the ethics of care can gain a political space. Second, the idea of 'judging with care' is one in which care is not a 'bolt-on' but rather where its inclusion works to transform existing ideas about political judgement. Third, by emphasizing that the skills honed in care practice are also those needed to practise 'good' or 'responsible' politics, 'judging with care' can be used to give further weight to arguments which promote greater access and voice for women and other carers. 'Judging with care' provides an alternative rationale for women to be present in political decision-making bodies. To extend Sevenhuijsen's logic we need care thinkers inside political institutions as well as outside as critical citizens.

Together their arguments present an emerging alternative criteria for public office and represent a questioning of the competence of politicians and other decision-makers (mostly men) who have little or no experience of hands-on caring. For, if caring was recognized as a central practice and core value of political and social life, then caring work would seem an essential 'life experience' and those divorced from care would seem deficient in their ability to make political decisions based on complex judgements about competing needs. Furthermore women and minorities would appear more competent, better rehearsed in the practices and thinking required for exercising political power.

A Dangerous Strategy?

Do the common insights discussed above avoid some of the potential pitfalls of which critics of the 'ethic of care' warn? Or, in listening to the voices of women are we celebrating what we should be challenging? I confess to some anxiety when I hear the note of populist female supremacy – complaining yet complacent about the status quo – in some of the accounts here and elsewhere. It is also important to note that the invocation of the traditional skills of women's work and women's values has been used in politics – sometimes quite cynically. The housewife imagery employed by former British Prime Minister Margaret Thatcher is a striking example of this (Webster, 1990).

We must ask whether championing a sense of difference powers change, or whether it reinforces stereotypes. Can we speak of difference without reducing political discourse to a sex war of words more apt for the school playground? How can we talk of different values without the danger of reproducing dualisms and making women responsible for caring in the politics as well as care in the private or domestic sphere? In short, are we fostering dangerous politics?

On the one hand, we must not underplay the reactionary and divisive undertow to populist or simplistic versions of 'women's values' or the ethics of care. On the other, it simply will not do to write off women's stories as unsatisfactory – the product of 'false consciousness' or 'feminine ideology'. It is significant that many have critically reflected upon practice and experience of themselves and other women and have thought seriously about the inter-connection of issues of care, the sexual division of family labour, the gendered patterns of work, and unequal access and influence in political decision-making. The point made by supporters of the care standpoint is that these skills, strategies and values are transferable to politics – not in their narrow or traditional application – but in their *transformed* version. It must also be emphasized that to argue that women's political values and activities are informed by an ethics of care is not to claim that women are essentially more caring then men, rather that their life experiences and social location give them an awareness of the importance of care. If care is an approach rather than an identity it can move beyond the limitations of difference.

Listening again to these women politicians' stories, I am struck by the qualifications and provisos which serve as 'book ends' around talk of care and difference; the unease felt by many women straying onto this ground. In part, I attribute this to the lack of available metaphors or conceptual frameworks for women activists to discuss and understand gender and their experiences of the collision of care and gender in politics. In the absence of clear and well-rehearsed models, women have to fall back upon the language of individualized women and men and sex differences to express their understandings. To be sure, it is real men who trivialize, patronize, undermine and exclude women in politics, but it not all men and not only men. Women become tongue-tied trying to express the institutional, symbolic and discursive elements of gender and gender divisions and the specific forms of masculinity which are embodied in conventional politics. Furthermore, it becomes

191

difficult to widen the debate to include different forms of care and to see ways in which men might be part of the project to 'think care'.[6] To reinforce Sevenhuijsen's plea: there is a pressing task to find ways to explain the multi-levelled complexity of gender and gender relations.

It is, therefore, important to be cautious and to maintain a realism about the costs of care, to be alert to the possible political repercussions as well as the potential opportunities that giving these ideas a wider circulation might bring. Further empirical investigation is needed: which listens to varied women's voices and indeed to listen anew to the stories male politicians tell. Crucially, there must be recognition of the heterogeneity of women and the implications of this.[7]

Any strategic use of the 'ethics of care' must be careful to keep these real problems in sight and must involve giving attention to the political relevance of care, as both a disadvantage and as a distinctive resource and value. However, not withstanding these provisos, the careful and selective use of the common insights of care theorists and women politicians could be used to promote greater understanding of women's political role, re-invigorate discourses and political campaigning around women's more equal representation; and act as a lever for political change.

Notes

1. Barron *et al.*'s study found that the irritation or resistance expressed by the male partners of several women councillors rested on an objection to their wives 'not being there' and to the expectation that women, whatever their other responsibilities and interests, provide domestic stability. They recount instances where 'male irritation at domestic disruption' resulted in sabotage, for instance, one man threw his wife's council papers in a nearby skip; and another used his wife's absences to justify his extra-marital affairs (1991, pp. 95–7). See also Martlew *et al.*'s study of Scottish activists (1985, p. 55).
2. Scoobie: West of Scotland rhyming slang for 'clue'.
3. These perceptions are similar to the findings of a large number of studies in the field of organization and employment studies. Brannen and Moss (1991) argue that working mothers have developed sophisticated time management strategies in response to their multiple roles and responsibilities, which are a valuable resource and result in increased efficiency and productivity. For a survey of British studies on employment

and family life see Brannen *et al.* (1994).

4. NOP poll for the charity, Care for the Family, June 1995.

5. The potential utility for public life of lessons learned in the family find some parallel in Okin, who suggests that the family is a crucial site where children (and adults) learn about justice and fairness (1989, pp. 156–9). Sara Ruddick discusses the training of children as one of the aspects of maternal practice (1989, p. 177).

6. Sevenhuijsen suggests the development of multi-layered model of gender. This allows for more variation than dichotomous models and makes it is easier to understand instances of mismatches between 'institutionalised ideologies of gender and care on the one hand and the way in which people express their self image, experience and desire for change on the other' (Sevenhuijsen, 1998, p. 82).

7. Among this group of women were variations in age and class, however, all but one councillor was white and none was openly lesbian. This might explain why gender is seen as of most importance rather than other social divisions – although several did address race and other differences. Political party was still the strongest predictor of attitude although women from all parties addressed issues of difference. The preponderance of quotations by Labour councillors owes as much to their numerical dominance in Scotland and in this study than to any monopoly of care thinking. There were some differences between feminists and non-feminists: women who defined themselves as feminists were sometimes reluctant to step outside the androgyny, or sameness, framework which worked as a justification for participating on equal terms with men. However, those whose discussions most clearly articulated elements of transformed care thinking were both feminist and non-feminist.

Conclusion: Doing Politics, Speaking Care: Sharpening the Vision?

The voice metaphor is a powerful image which runs through discussions of gender, power, politics and democracy and seems ever more elastic. To employ it again, this book is an attempt to start up some conversations: between feminist political science and feminist moral and political theory; and among feminist academics, feminist activists and women. In particular, it seeks to give voice to some of the experiences and insights of female local politicians. These women cannot claim to speak for all women – indeed, they would be horrified if their stories were used in such a way; but they can offer us practical insights and theorizing 'from below' from which generalizations can be made and new directions sought. By listening to women's voices and also finding ways in which complex ideas from feminist theory can enter into popular discourse we find mutual benefit: theory finds context and practical wisdom finds system.

The book points to the strategic importance of discourse and rhetoric, arguing that current limitations in the ways of thinking, talking and arguing about gender and political representation have resulted in a sense of faltering progress – or, indeed, closure – in debates and campaigns for gender equality in elected politics. New versions of political discourses are needed to reinvigorate the debate and to progress action. We need new ways of speaking about women and politics, and equality and difference; new political vocabularies with which to express alternative visions of politics and political practices. It is also necessary that we choose our words strategically and construct compelling arguments for feminist activists and feminist insiders to use to promote change. These discursive strategies will be informed by the concrete contexts and political realities within which we operate at any given time. Two key sources for new ideas and alternatives are to be found: in recent theoretical work on the political ethics of care; and in the common-sense discussions of women politicians.

In this final chapter we bring the arguments to a close and work towards demonstrating that care thinking and concrete experience provide a nexus between different levels of debates around citizenship, equality and representation, difference and democracy. We also examine some the difficulties that continue to grumble away without apparent resolution.

In the Way of Women?

Certain barriers are common to all outgroups or outsider groups, particularly in terms of access to political and social resources. However, there are certain gender-specific impediments: sexist cultures and practices create obstacles, and the consequences of the sexual division of labour are far-reaching. At one level, there are two simple and competing explanations about the under-representation of women in political elites: the first accounts for their absence in 'supply' terms, in short, women fail to come forward in sufficient numbers; the second points to 'demand-side' factors and argues that it is masculine culture within organizations and the attitudes and practices of individual men which, in Cockburn's phrase, 'stand in the way of women'. In reality, neither explanation stands alone.

Models of recruitment which demonstrate that barriers can operate at different levels and are inter-related are important to any understanding of under-representation in political systems. Systematic, party political and individual factors work together in complex ways to shape the social composition of political elites. The exclusionary process is multi-faceted as research which moves beyond candidate studies reveals. The stories of women councillors in this study add support to other in-depth studies: barriers to equal participation in politics were seen as gendered and, in part, rooted in the sexual division of labour. They described and discussed a series of constraints which interconnected, and which served to both inhibit potential aspirants at party and candidate level, and also disadvantaged women as political players once they were within the system. An interlocking triangle of domestic responsibilities, time poverty and under-confidence was identified by many as the major barrier preventing women from full and fair participation in public life. The unequal domestic and caring burden of women is often characterized as a truism, but it is a fundamental force which impedes, restricts and shapes women's entry and presence in both the worlds of work and of politics.

However, it must be recognized that at each level these factors interact with demand-side factors such as exclusionary and alienating structures, rules and informal practices and the resistance of men as political players, as social actors and as partners to give up some of their power. Barriers are also posed by political institutions in the broadest sense by which we mean formal structures and rules and informal practices, norms and values. It is a commonplace point, but worth making none the less, that politics (like much of the world of work) is premised upon others taking care of care. So institutions are designed as if individuals are unencumbered by domestic responsibilities. These understandings reveal the flaws in models of recruitment which tend to posit supply and demand factors as separable for analysis; instead women's own stories portray a picture of multiple and multi-layered inter-connections.

Thinking about Action

It follows that if barriers are multi-dimensional, then proposed measures to address them will be likewise complex. Discussion of possible measures to improve the proportion of women in national and local politics takes place within concrete political and organizational frameworks. These frameworks tend to privilege ideas of formal equality and equal treatment, and seldom take into account the concrete reality of everyday lives: of the caring responsibilities (of, in the main, women) and the care needs and interdependence of all human lives. Women councillors' gendered realities exposed the limitations of dominant constructions of equal opportunities and 'fairness', however, their discussions were contra-dictory. Although there was recognition that women's unequal access to power was in part the consequence of the sexual division of labour, there was also acceptance of the legitimacy of dominant constructions of justice and equality which stress sameness not difference. Women sometimes felt that the way we currently argue about equality leaves them little alternative but to emphasize their sameness with men – or opt out.

There was broad agreement about many practical measures to tackle the under-representation of women, such as encouragement and support with child care. However, 'strong' positive action – which guarantees results – was contentious. Many women councillors expressed a preference for what Cockburn has termed the long agenda project of transformatory change, involving societal change and the reformation of politics, but there were considerable difficulties in constructing acceptable strategies to achieve such change. There was a sense of closure in many of the discussions, emanating from a distaste for 'unfair privileges' or special treatment. This makes it difficult to see how strong constituencies of support for positive action can be built and maintained in current conditions. However, women did challenge (albeit in muted voice) existing political criteria and constructions of merit, and argued that women brought distinctive values and skills to politics.

The pursuit of the short agenda and the marginalization of other discourses have resulted in a sense of closure in terms of progressing the debate and the reality of women's representation in power politics. Women knew what they wanted but were flummoxed about how to bring about a politics more inclusive and more relevant to women – the long agenda project of transformatory change.

Political parties are important players in any attempt to change the social composition of parliaments and councils and they remain crucial channels through which women seek political office. Within the British system, ideas which invoke difference and challenge male hegemonic values are in opposition to dominant discourses within all the parties but may resonate with the contradictions of women politicians' lived realities. Women politicians, at the practical level, have to combine caring responsibilities with political lives and have to deal with the lack of 'fit' between their own lived realities and personal political agendas, and dominant political discourses. However, longer agenda measures are likely to cause problems in terms of, at an ideological level, finding the vocabulary to justify the type of radical, political and cultural change needed in order to ensure women's equal access, presence and influence in political assemblies; and, on a practical level, in terms of political stomach for intervention.

Women and Representation

In Chapters 4 and 5, we asked two questions: why should there should be more women in politics; and, what difference would more women in politics make? Theories of political representation and competing claims of equality and difference were examined and discussed in relation to empirical evidence and women politicians' own understandings of representation and political practice.

The meaning of political representation is shifting and 'slippery' – at once both a core concept of democracy and also the site of fundamental disagreement. Representative democracy is built on a paradox: citizens are both present and absent, and the degree of their inclusion or exclusion from the process of decision-making is dependent upon differing democratic expectations and conventions, and variations in conceptions of citizenship and ideas about the role of their political representatives. The relationship between 'representation' and 'representativeness' is by no means accepted but concerns about the skewed composition of parliaments, councils and other political decision-making bodies have been a persistent thread of debates on democracy. The near monopoly of white males in political institutions has given rise to increasingly urgent calls for more proportionate understandings of representation. These concerns are expressed in terms of a democratic deficit and the need for a 'politics of presence'. Demands by women and by member of minority ethnic groups for a 'place' in political assemblies are fuelled by an increasing sense of political exclusion, frustration at the slow pace of change and a contention that who we are has an impact on what we think and what we do.

Contemporary claims for women's greater presence in democratic institutions are based upon differing conceptions of political representation, differing ideas about the political relevance of gender, and differing expectations in terms of end goals and outcomes. There are symbolic and substantive arguments for more proportionate political representation. Symbolic reasonings are concerned with issues of, first, justice and equity and, second, those of legitimacy and recognition. Substantive arguments rely on contentions of interests and resources. The symbolic dimensions to arguments for proportionate representation do not rest or fall on whether the inclusion of women will make a difference. In contrast, substantive arguments become entangled with complex issues of identity and difference.

The empirical evidence, although suggestive that women politicians in current political systems may make a difference, far from settles any arguments about the nature and extent of any 'women's politics'. Research also highlights institutional constraints that may prevent women politicians from acting 'differently' in conditions where they form a small minority. These insights make it difficult to assess 'potential difference' on the basis of actual experience in current political systems.

Although feminist political theorists, political scientists and activists do acknowledge a variety of reasonings to promote and progress women's increased access to political elites, in Britain they have privileged justice and legitimacy reasonings, based upon notions of (individual) fairness and representative proportionality, in preference to justifications which stress women's different interests or different contribution. This is partly because symbolic arguments are seen as respectable and acceptable within dominant notions of gender-neutral equality in British political culture. Post-1997, the British government's drive to modernize political institutions and reinvigorate democracy has provided another timely peg upon which to hang symbolic arguments. In part, there are also fears that 'speaking difference' may unleash a dangerous politics which stereotypes women and is vulnerable to backlash.

Everyday Practices of Representation

In terms of how women councillors discuss and explain their practice, the limitations of the equality approach are obvious. Representation held complex and contested meanings for women councillors. They used notions of equality, parity and fairness to promote their claim for an equal presence in the polity *and* also notions of difference. Most believed that they both 'stand for' and that they 'act for' women. However, few saw themselves as acting only for women. Most were keen to stress their wish to serve all groups within the community, although they were aware of the limitations of representation and therefore supported, in many cases, mechanisms for grassroots consultation and participation.

Furthermore, it is clear that at the popular level the proportionality argument carries implicit messages that the presence of previously marginal groups will have an impact on the promotion of group interests. A clear illustration of this was the expectations that the then new Labour women MPs would vote against benefit cuts to lone parents in 1997 and the derision and disappointment they faced when they voted on party lines. Thus, as a popular discourse, symbolic arguments for proportionate representation can overlap with interests and difference reasonings and therefore lose some of their attraction as the 'safe option' of representation formulations.

At present, the only legitimizing discourse for increasing the number of women in politics is one of 'justice'. However, without the promotion of additional reasonings and discourses which 'dignify' difference and delineate the gendered structure of both political and economic systems as well as ordinary lives, it can be difficult to imbue the exclusion of women with political urgency and the impetus for action. Additional justifications may well be required in order to support demands for change. We therefore need to explore and systemize ideas of difference.

Justice, maternal thinking and ethics of care

How do we move beyond the current difficulties in the ways we think, talk and argue about gender and political representation? What happens if we tangle with difference? Is work which explores women's moral reasoning and the ethics of care inevitably dangerous and unavoidably essentialist? Or might we find ideas with potential use in the sphere of power politics with relevance to and resonance for women as political actors?

Theorists who favour this approach argue that the practice of care results in a 'different voice', a distinctive way of thinking about the world which is rooted in the ties of relationships rather than formal rules. They argue that the values and skills traditionally associated with women should be valorized rather than denigrated. Those who seek to develop the ethics of care in the public sphere of politics and citizenship contend that it can be used as a strategic tool or concept which can offer a powerful critique of 'politics as usual' as well as provide a compelling set of reasons why women and marginalized men who care should have a greater political voice.

In Chapter 6, we went fishing, carefully – dipping into only those pools where the implications of 'difference' or 'care' approaches for politics were being systematically and sensitively developed – and we netted some new ideas and new arguments. Although Okin is not a care theorist, her work also promotes a reconciliation of justice and care. Her idea of a justice crisis of gender is important in its contribution towards constructing a discourse which reframes women's common-sense complaints as rational demands for action springing from concerns of justice. It presents a compelling feminist analysis of the sexual division of labour in terms acceptable to mainstream debate. Women's domestic and caring responsibilities – and men's resistance to doing their fair share – are re-conceptualized as a crisis of justice with far-reaching social, economic and political consequences. The sexual division of labour becomes an issue of social justice in need of political remedy. Inequalities in the family are not to be explained away as the result of nature or choice, but instead result from a complex combination of structural injustices. These arguments are not new to feminists but Okin has framed and developed the ideas within the language of social justice which provides the potential for activists to present the case for equality within acceptable frameworks. We also noted the limitations of Okin's work and the potential pitfalls of loading too much onto families: that inequality within the family is the whole of the problem; and that equal parenting within equal families is the whole of the answer. This model has simplistic notions of gender and oppression, it also fails to take difference and diversity into account.

We also examined the work of writers (Ruddick, 1989; Tronto, 1993; Sevenhuijsen, 1998) who are central to the development of the political ethics of care. Part I demonstrated the importance of discourse and political and moral vocabularies: the hegemonic status of some frameworks makes it difficult to think of other ways of thinking and doing things. Ideas from care theorists can be taken and developed into, in Tronto's phrase, a 'political vocabulary of care' with which to voice new arguments in the debate about the representation of women and women's 'concerns'. The introduction of care speaking in politics – or a *political discourse of care* – would work for women in a number of ways: first, the notion of 'care as practice' would legitimize many women's experiences, and would link caring to citizenship and political office. The skills of care practice – attentiveness, responsibility, competence and responsive-ness – could be presented as crucial political attributes in an inclusive politics which addressed needs and interests. 'Judging with care' and about care should form the basis of political judgements and creates the opportunity for carers as citizens to bring their expertise into political life. A focus upon care exposes existing inequalities and could potentially empower marginalized groups. These writers have been concerned with citizenship rather than with conventional politics or legislative and decision-making bodies. However, their insights have potential for broader application. We suggested ways in which these new insights could be employed as tools of analysis to expose the shortcomings of current political systems and the need for a radical restructuring of politics. The vision of a transformed politics is one in which politics is more inclusive, accessible and responsive. As such, it would have to fit in with caring lives and reflect the concerns of a society which placed care at its core while also enabling all its citizens to combine care with other human activities.

Challenging Politics: Care as a Cost and a Resource

We had noted earlier the high profile women councillors gave to care as both a cost and a resource. In Chapter 7 we examined the parallels and contrasts between the ethics of care and the common-sense theorizing of female local politicians and asked whether these ideas and values had resonance with women who are currently engaged in traditional political structures.

Domestic and caring labour was perceived by many women politicians to be both a barrier and a resource. Political parties and assemblies were commonly seen to be constructed for men – and women's presence is contingent on them playing by the 'male game'. Women's common sense was also characterized by an observation, sometimes uncritical, that men's distance from the concrete needs and demands of care afforded them 'privileged irresponsibility' on many levels, while women's care burdens placed them at considerable disadvantage within the family, work and politics. Many also placed a high value upon care as an idea and an activity; they argued that values and skills which arise from women's experience as carers were useful and desirable in local and national politics. At present caring issues and concerns are seen as trivial and apolitical. The 'carelessness' of much conventional politics and political practice was also commented upon and criticized. Women argued for a different sort of politics in which the importance of care and carers' perspectives was recognized; and in which politicians exercised careful judgement. Many were convinced that the presence of women was a crucial element of such a process of rethinking and change. However, the expression of these understandings was often ambivalent and hesitant. The paradox of care is a truism – often remarked upon, but less often seen as a legitimate issue of political concern. Some accounts were marked by a sense of fatalism or an uncritical acceptance of the status quo. Women sometimes spoke in traditional, potentially reactionary terms, with little impetus for change; sometimes in radical 'transformed' ways. More often, however, their common sense contained both strands of thinking.

These discussions of politics, representation and power pose an emerging challenge to existing gender-blind constructions of political equality and equal opportunities; a challenge which has the potential to subvert traditional constructions of political criteria and privileged power forms by advancing alternative models based on women's experience and values, and a nascent political ethics of care.

Common themes emerged which found parallel in the work of the theorists examined: the way present political and social systems and value structures obscure the central importance of care; and the means by which certain powerful groups and actors benefit from, while simultaneously devaluing, care; recognition that practical strategies and intellectual skills which arise from the practice of caring can be 'transformed' and transferred to a wider context of politics; and demands that politics change, not only that women may fully participate, but also that politics may be more responsive and responsible and that it may more fully reflect the needs and interests of the whole community.

New Political Discourses of Justice, Merit and Care

Activists and academics involved in debates and campaigns to increase the numbers of women in politics have been chary of invoking difference or referring to 'women's distinctive contribution' to back their claims. This is understandable in the context of what is politically acceptable. It has also been the case that some of the versions of 'difference' in common currency have been populist and crudely supremacist, playing into the hands of those who would trivialize the issues or, indeed, use ideas of difference to reinforce gender stereotypes and women's inequality. There is also wariness in a world without guarantees, and a political system with party discipline and competing loyalties, that such claims set women politicians up for a fall; that they will inevitably fail to live up to ideals of 'sisterhood' (or indeed all-caring motherhood) and romanticized notions of moral superiority.

However, there are other points to counterbalance these concerns. It is clear from our discussions that other versions of 'difference' thinking exist – particularly work on the political ethics of care – which deserve a fair and full hearing. These versions, using generic definitions of care, move away from debates about equality versus difference and provide the possibility to craft discourses which expose models of politics which devalue care as the problem rather than women and other carers. These frameworks also provide a vision of inclusive politics, more usually developed at the level of citizenship, and create discursive space within which women and marginalized groups of men can be present with recognized expertise and competence. To be sure, problems remain but these ideas should not be discounted out of hand.

We must also take seriously what women say: their own 'common-sense' analysis of their political role and practice is as an important form of situated knowledge and a neglected resource. Many women position care as a central political idea, and see its transformatory potential. Their stories demand that care be reassessed as a meaningful practice with application in the public and political spheres. That does not mean we cannot challenge and disagree with elements of women's stories: in many cases these themes intertwine with strands of hegemonic ideology which serve to obscure and maintain women's oppression and disadvantage. However, there must be recognition of the situated knowledge they bring to these debates. In the study many women had critically reflected upon practice and upon their own experience and those of other women. They had thought seriously about the interconnection of issues of care, the sexual division of family labour, the gendered patterns of work, and unequal access and influence in political decision-making.

We also have to admit that present strategies have only served women up to a point in their campaign for equal presence in the polity in Britain, and have contributed to problems of legitimacy over the introduction and implementation of special measures, such as quotas and all-women shortlists. In contrast, Scandinavian countries, notably Norway, have used multi-valued justifications which invoke both equality (justice) and difference (interests and resources). There are issues of how well political strategies travel and differences of political culture need to be taken into account. However, a 'credo of difference' would seem to offer strategic attractions. The addition of discourses on difference, presented in an accessible way, have positive potential to 'free up' discussion, and action, on women's representation in Britain. It is clear from the current study, and also empirical findings in many other countries, that the discourses of difference resonate strongly with the perceptions and experiences of women politicians. Women politicians already call upon a much wider range of reasonings and justifications than those of justice and proportionality; however, at present, these *common-sense* alternatives lack legitimacy.

The integration of arguments about justice, difference and care, and the insights of women politicians result in several emerging challenges to dominant ideology and contemporary debates and political practices. Several potential discourses emerge: first, 'justice' discourses which reconceptualize the unequal distribution of power in politics and the sexual division of labour as a 'justice crisis'; second, 'criteria' discourses, which challenge existing constructions of political merit and desirable political skills; and, finally, 'long agenda' discourses which challenge existing political paradigms and values, and which promote transformatory change. Each works in a different way to make the needs of equality more 'transparent' and imbues debates about women's representation with political urgency and moral legitimacy. Taken together, they provide an explanation of the status quo, a prescription for change and the means for empowerment.

Power and politics

Moral and political theory can offer insights and lessons for feminist political science and political activism on representation, but it is not a one-way process. Feminist theorists have too often overlooked or excluded political and state institutions and conventional power politics from their considerations. Vogel (1998) notes that, particularly in Anglo-American feminist theory, the state is sidelined: partly as a result of the historically and culturally specific conceptions of politics as diffuse and decentred, and partly as a result of feminism's radical critique of narrow visions of politics and its discovery of 'private' and 'civil society' as significant sites of political power.

We may recognize the scope and variety of politics in a multiplicity of domains, but we cannot dismiss the importance of the state: whether we conceive it to be instrumental or chaotic, monolithic or differentiated, closed or permeable, the state and its institutions are a significant locus of power. Ideas about care and citizenship need to be considered and developed within specific political systems. In addition, the dynamics of change are conspicuously absent from many accounts. What combination of factors together with individual or groups as agents of change will turn the ethics of care into a political force? Although clearly a matter for empirical investigation, it is plausible to suggest that women inside and outside 'the machine' may play a pivotal role in such a dynamic. Before returning to the theme of women's presence, we first turn to look at two inter-related issues: first, the role of gender in the political ethics of care; and second, the issue of identity politics.

Can Men Think Care Too?

What role does gender play in all this? Carver (1998) rightly notes that 'gender is not a synonym for women'; however, real women often disappear from gender neutral accounts. Theoretical insights which underline women's moral competence give crucial support to women and counteract powerful cultural assumptions of women as suspect and untrustworthy. The starting point must be the here and now: where we can say, with all sorts of provisos about heterogenity and diverse experiences mediated by other social divisions, that real women (or individuals with the gender category 'women') are practised in care and judging with care. This practical expertise must be recognized and emphasized although we must guard against populist or 'untransformed' versions which translate into 'mother knows best'. We are talking about practice not goodness; about sets of the skills and modes of thinking which can be used to judge with care, rather than a source of all the answers. The insistence that we cannot entirely divorce gender from the ethics of care, also means that we cannot divorce real women's experiences from our development of care thinking. Empirical work is needed to complement and inform theoretical work by listening to the

206

different voices (rather than simply the voice) of women. The voices in this book speak for themselves, rather than for all women, although their common sense raises issues and ideas that may be generalizable. The composition of the group was shaped by a particular set of political and social contexts, there are gaps and absences. The voices of black women, lesbians and disabled women are needed to more systematically explore these ideas. If care is socially contingent, each will experience and understand their practice in a different way. This book represents a starting point, rather than a last word.

Where do these discussions leave men? Can men think care too? Or will we be left with two sorts of politicians: women who do 'care' and men who do 'power'? Clearly, this scenario would play to the worst fears of those who warn against speaking of the political ethics of care: where women become responsible for care in the public realm as well as the private while men get on with the 'real' business of politics. We already see manifestations of this in the concentration of women politicians and women ministers in areas of health, family and social welfare. The ethics of care must challenge men if it is to transform values and practices in the public and political sphere. It may also create the opportunity for different sorts of men to enter politics.

The framework of the ethics of care includes generic definitions which allow the debate to be widened to include different forms of care and to see ways in which men might be part of the project to 'think care'. There is also recognition that certain groups of men do care work and 'think care.' Care theorists argue that the ethics of care can act as an 'eye opener' for men who are used to considering themselves as the human norm. Models of inclusive politics which highlight differences can provoke thought about the political and moral implications of 'being men' (Sevenhuijsen, 1998).

It could also be argued that the concrete presence of women in substantial numbers in political assemblies disrupts politics as usual. Political practices, values, rules and ideas are shaped by gender relations and are loaded with powerful gender symbolism; symbolism which equates power, authority and leadership with the 'male' (Jones, 1993). This has presented particular problems for women, where 'female' and politician have hitherto been seen as a contradiction in terms. This has also constrained the range of acceptable masculinities for men to practise. The presence of women and the ideas of the political ethics of care potentially allow new forms of political practice to evolve and also potentially allow men to behave in different ways. The presence of women may act as a catalyst of change – even though not all women may act as intentional agents of change.

Identity Politics and Category Politics

Demands for the presence of women as 'gender-categorized' individuals in politics are related to broader questions of identity politics, that is the growth of social movements around race, women, sexuality and more recently disabled people. We touched upon this in Chapter 4. A number of writers have critiqued politics based upon identities and questioned how far they can form the basis for political action. Rian Voet (1998) calls identity politics a 'politics of indignation' and warns of its shortcomings in respect of essentialism, fragmentation, fixing identities and setting groups up in opposition to each other. Others raise questions of authenticity: who can claim to speak for whom; and caution that politics of identity can foreclose possibilities of communication, dialogue, coalition or advocacy (Phillips, 1993, 1995; Sevenhuijsen, 1998). However, recognition of the problems of identity politics has not, as Phillips notes, sent people 'scurrying back to the safety of the politics of ideas, rather it has underlined the importance of presence to contest representations' (1995, p. 241).

Bacchi's discussions of 'category' politics are useful for under-standing and promoting claims for presence. She coins the phrase 'category politics' to describe the central role of concepts and categories in political practice, particularly in respect of the relationship between politically mobilized social groups and the state. Such politics requires the invocation of identity categories (for example, 'black', 'women', and so forth) and conceptual categories (most particularly 'equality') to justify claims for access to political and other resources. She highlights the power of 'insiders' to name, misname or rename for political purposes and the struggle between various actors to control the meaning of 'essentially contested concepts' such as equal opportunities. Categorizers, she notes, are almost always white men.

Category politics takes place at many levels, but the state (and the political and organizational actors within the state) constitute a key site of contestation. Furthermore, the outcome of these contests has consequences for policy. Bacchi concludes that feminists need to give attention to the political meanings of categories and the material consequences which result from category politics. This is a complex politics which is in a constant state of flux. Meanings can be appropriated and reappropriated in ways never intended by the original categorizers. An analysis of the ways in which conceptual and identity categories are constructed and their implications for affirmative action and 'women' is seen as an essential precondition for developing strategies of change. At present, women's absence from spheres of influence means that feminists are often forced to adopt justificatory stances which have unintended consequences. This leads Bacchi to argue, 'What follows is the importance of having more women in politics and in positions of influence to engage in examining the uses of "women" and other categories. Those whom the category is deemed to represent need to be present in numbers to debate its uses' (1996, p. 13).

These and related arguments reinforce the claims for the presence of women in decision-making bodies; not necessarily to 'represent' some fixed notion of women, but rather to be actively engaged in contesting meanings and categorizations: processes which have material consequences for women's lives. Bacchi's model allows women presence and the possibility of agency which is lacking in many other accounts. It is reinforced by Cockburn's insistence that it is for women to decide what differences matter. Her aim is:

> *parity* for women as a sex or for groups of women in their specificity – to counter the claims that you can't be equal and different. This counter strategy involves acknowledgement and assertion of bodily and cultural specificity. (Cockburn, 1991, p. 13)

Being There – Making a Difference?

Phillips speculates that 'politics is more formative than sex, and that the contrast between those who get involved in politics and those who do not is deeper than any gender difference between those who are elected' (1995, p. 75). Is this the case? At one level this is a plausible point: very few men or women participate in party politics, still fewer go on to elected office; therefore, as a group they are extraordinary. However, we also know that gender plays out in complex ways in political life. To claim otherwise is to close our ears to what women politicians say; and to close our eyes to the evidence of gender politics played out on a daily basis in parliaments and councils. Phillips' remark fails to recognize the gender systems of politics and political practice; these restrict the versions of masculinity present to be sure – but place women in a double bind – where women and politics are seen as contradictions in terms.

Does this scepticism about the potential impact of women's presence protect female politicians from unrealistic expectations or does it serve to feed into powerful cultural constructions of women as untrustworthy and suspect? Women's presence brings no guarantees. We can think of few instances of cast-iron guarantees and watertight accountability in public and political life, but it is not the case that the strategy to achieve equal representation is, as Phillips suggests, 'a shot in the dark'. The metaphor suggests a wild gamble with the outcome a matter of luck or chance. We see, in this study and in other research, women representing women in the sense of representation as responsibility and representation as responsive-ness. They feel responsible for a 'constituency of women' and tend to more often speak for and act upon matters of sex equality and other women's 'concerns'. They are responsive in terms of their preferences for consultation and communication and, in many cases, their relations with women's organizations and community groups. There are important issues of accountability in any system of representa-tive democracy, but we should not discount ideas of substantive representation because we cannot envisage conditions for perfect accountability. These should ideally be matters for empirical investigation. The role of feminist organizations as bridges between women office holders and the women in the community and their concerns may offer one sort of accountability (see, for example, Carroll, 1992).[1]

We can draw from the theoretical literature, the empirical evidence – inconclusive though it may be in many respects – and the suggestions of practitioners (that is, women politicians) a set of reasons for women to 'be there'. It is almost impossible to disentangle theoretical points from political points in the debates around women's access and presence in political assemblies. Justifications inevitably intertwine with expectations. The political ethics of care makes explicit what form of difference women's presence might make in terms of opening up political institutions and political practices and introducing the political idea of judging with care. Again, these ideas need to be tested empirically in concrete settings.

Desperately Seeking Solutions and Provisional Settlements

This book took as its starting point the problems of political equality in the specific context of local and national electoral politics in Britain. The counsel of safety or perfection does not take us very far, and seems increasingly divorced from the world as we now accept it: full of uncertainties, ambiguities and risk. We cannot expect to find all the answers in one theoretical model, or one strategy, or in one set of political practices. Sevenhuijsen describes this acceptance of modest ambitions when she speaks of finding ways to act 'as well as possible in order to do what needs to be done' (1998, p. 68). Settlements are provisional and contingent upon the political circumstances and the discursive contests from which they result.

Constitutional change in the UK, with the creation of new political institutions and the reform of old ones, the experimentation with different forms of electoral systems, and the reworking of relationships between the centre and the constituent nations, has created new conditions and new opportunities. Systematic changes are, in part, the response to widespread political concerns about democratic renewal, low levels of trust and public confidence, and demands for relationships between political institutions and civil society to be renegotiated. These concerns are part of a wider phenomenon experienced by many liberal or social democratic states.

These circumstances have also created conditions for the renegotiation of gender relations in politics and the unprecedented opportunity for feminist activists to promote gender balance in political institutions, and to press for new ways of thinking about and doing politics which would incorporate the values and concerns of women. Explicit links have been made between democratic renewal and the participation of women. We see such claims voiced, for example, by women ministers of the EU member states in the Charter of Rome in 1996[2] when they declared that balanced participation of women and men in politics would 'bridge the gap between citizens and politicians, revitalize democracy, and increase citizen confidence in the institutions of democracy'. This is a particularly important time to develop multiple strategies to gain a greater understanding of women's political activity, to promote more women into politics, and to press for new ways of thinking about and doing politics which would incorporate the values and concerns of women.

Women politicians' stories of political life and insights from care theorists provide keys for better understanding gender and elected politics and a basis for creating powerful new discourses to promote political equality in terms of access and transforming political values and practices.

It is important to temper any claims with realism and to be alert to the possible political repercussions as well as the potential opportunities that giving these ideas a wider circulation might bring. It is important not to claim too much for difference. It is a contested notion in the stories of women politicians in this and other studies. 'Women's politics' in action are not permanent or fixed, but shifting and provisional. Further empirical investigation is needed, which listens to varied women's voices and indeed listens anew to the stories male politicians tell. Crucially, there must be recognition of the heterogeneity of women and the implications of this. Therefore any strategic use of the 'ethic of care' must be careful to keep these real problems in sight and must involve giving attention to the political relevance of care, as both a disadvantage and as a distinctive resource and value.

It is also clear that the presence of women can only be a part of the solution. There needs to be consideration of supplementary channels of participation and communication. We have already noted the similarities between aspects of the political ethics of care and ideas of radical pluralism. We can see elements of radical plural democratic practice in operation in new sorts of social partnership or citizen participation arrangements in a number of countries (see, for example, USGS, 1998a, 1998b); and in more radical versions of 'mainstreaming' in which gender equality and other equalities perspectives are incorporated into policy making (see Council of Europe, 1998; USGS, 1998a, Mackay and Bilton, 2000). In the following section we want to briefly speculate about the Scottish Parliament as a potential site in which strands of the political ethics of care and wider radical pluralist ideas may play out.

The Scottish Parliament – A Window of Opportunity?

Although this book has taken as its focus debates about women, politics and representation at national, devolved and local levels in the UK, it draws upon wider debates and comparative literatures. It is also grounded in a specific set of political circumstances in Scotland. As we noted in earlier chapters, the constitutional debate in Scotland opened up a 'window of opportunity' for more equal gender representation. In addition to arguments about the 'democratic deficit' and social justice, the belief that women would 'make a difference' triggered a pluralist coalition of women politicians, party activists, trade unionists and members of women's groups in Scotland to campaign for gender balance and family-friendly practices in the new Scottish Parliament.

It has been argued that gender equality became an intrinsic part of the broader debates of democracy, accountability and representation in Scotland in the 1990s. Striking optimism was expressed by women councillors, party activists and women in various groups and organizations in Scotland about the idea of the Scottish Parliament and the role that women might play. The Scottish Parliament was seen by many women as a 'long agenda' measure, which held the promise of a more inclusive and appealing politics. Brown argues that it was this vision of difference which was important in bringing women together (Brown, 1996).

The many twists and turns of the contemporary campaign for devolution in Scotland, and in particular women's long, uneven and eventful struggle for equality of representation are charted elsewhere. (Brown, 1996, 1998, 1999; see also Breitenbach and Mackay, 2001). What needs to be said here is that long road to devolution allowed substantial time for reflection, deliberation and public debate about the nature of democracy, participation and consultation. This process was characterized by a civil society/cross-party coalition working towards consensus on the shape and character of constitutional change: the defining theme of which was a determination to 'break the mould' of politics. Wide-ranging consultation was undertaken and a great deal of preparatory work done through a Scottish Constitutional Convention, which brought together civil society groupings and political parties (SCC, 1990, 1995). Women as key individuals, as members of political parties and organizations such as trade unions and voluntary organizations, and as members of women's groups were vocally present in these discussions and their ideas and expectations fed into the blueprints for the parliament. Women argued for measures which would overcome barriers to participation: changes in the electoral system and recruitment procedures; 'family friendly' working practices in the parliament including sensible working hours and child care provision, and cultural changes with the promotion of less adversarial, more consensual politics. Getting more women MSPs into a Scottish Parliament was, however, seen as only one aspect; women also campaigned for structures which would provide greater access to government and the policy-making process for individual women and diverse groups of women.

Alliances were made not only between women but also with the broader movement for constitutional change. In turn, gender representation became an intrinsic part of the consensus about a new constitutional future.[3] These visions of a new democratic system and wider participation were reflected in the Scotland Act 1998 and informed the work of the cross-party Consultative Steering Group (CSG) on the Scottish Parliament (Brown *et al.*, 1998 and 1999a; CSG, 1998). Common purpose was forged around the desire for a different kind of politics now encapsulated in the key principles of the new parliament: power sharing, accountability, accessibility and equal opportunities. This power-sharing model involves partnership between the executive and the legislature; strong, all-purpose parliamentary committees have powers to scrutinize and initiate legislation, call enquiries and consult widely. Power sharing also extends to ideas of sharing power with the people of Scotland with multiple points of access and increased opportunities for consultation and participation in policy-making as individual citizens and as members of social partner organizations, broadly defined. A key role of the new parliament is its responsibility to promote openness, participation and consultation. It has also been agreed that equality perspectives will be 'mainstreamed' into all aspects of the work of the parliament and the Scottish Executive.

We can therefore see considerable promise in the early stages of a new political institution of both the representation of women in terms of their presence as elected MSPs, and also the representation of women's interests and concerns through increased access to the policy and legislative process and enhanced opportunities for consultation, participation and deliberation through consultative structures. These include the Women in Scotland Consultative

Forum, established in 1997 and the Scottish Civic Forum (formerly the Civic Assembly) both of whom emphasize their role as 'gateways not gatekeepers' to channel and promote dialogue on issues of public policy in an inclusive and participative way.

It is early days yet but we may speculate that there are certain similarities between the political ethics of care and a set of new institutions and practices in whose creation women's voices and women's ideas have played a substantial role. Conscious attempts have been made to promote a different political culture and more responsive political practices. We can suggest tentative similarities between the vision of the political ethics of care with its recognition of diversity and interdependence and its dimensions of attentiveness, responsibility, competence and responsiveness; and the Scottish Parliament's attempt to move beyond 'power politics' towards a problem-solving approach and its undertakings to improve democratic participation, creating meaningful consultation and forging new forms of deliberative citizenship. We also see recognition of the importance of care in the parliament's practical operations around a set of family-friendly policies. Women have played a part in envisioning the reformed politics of Scotland; they also have a concrete presence in the new institutions in which this reformed politics will play out. There are high expectations but also considerable anxiety and scepticism that the parliament will be able to deliver what it promised. Although well planned and discussed these ideas and practices are essentially being transplanted into an existing political culture: there has been early disappointment at the persistence of adversarial party politics – the legacy of the Westminster model should not be underestimated. There are also difficulties in creating meaningful new models of power sharing which are representative and empowering – rather than merely creating new sets of insiders. Until systematic research is undertaken these observations remain speculative. However, the new Scottish Parliament provides a concrete opportunity to test ideas of the political ethics of care.

A Modest Proposal

This book has taken as its starting point the concrete contexts and political realities for women in the political institutions of Scotland and the UK. We have argued that in order to maintain progress and to tackle underlying social and cultural issues there is a need to search for new arguments and new understandings of women's 'place' in power politics, and new political vocabularies to express alternative visions of politics and political practices.

This is not a proposal for feminists and other women activists to 'ditch' the arguments of justice and equality. Rather, it suggests that multi-valued justificatory strategies should be used, which reflect the complexity of everyday experience and discourse and which draw upon the strategic insights of care theorists. New discourses do not, of course, necessarily equal action. However, notwithstanding these provisos, the careful and selective use of some of the insights from these debates can promote reinvigorated discourses and political campaigning on women's equal representation, and act as a lever for political change. Eventual action is contingent upon having the necessary vocabulary to justify and legitimize women's political participation at both ideological and practical levels. We have to be able to 'speak' care if we are to do new sorts of politics.

Notes

1. Alternative forms of accountability are offered through women's units, feminist policy machinery and other sorts of state feminist institutions which institutionalize women's concerns.
2. The Charter of Rome was signed on 18 May 1996 by women ministers of 13 member states at the 'Women for Renewal in Politics and Society' conference in Rome. The text of the Charter is published in Leijenaar (1996).
3. Although Brown (1998) is clear that this consensus needed the constant pressure of women activists to shore it up.

Bibliography

Ackelsberg, L. and Diamond, I. (1987) 'Gender and political life: new directions in political science', in B. Hess and M. Farree (eds), *Analysing Gender: A Handbook of Social Science Research*. Beverly Hills, CA: Sage.

Adonis, A. (1993) *Parliament Today*. Manchester: Manchester University Press.

Amos, V. and Parmar, P. (1984) 'Challenging imperialist feminism', *Feminist Review*, 17.

Antolini, D. (1984) 'Women in local government: an overview', in J.A. Flammang (ed.), *Political Women: Current Roles in State and Local Government*. Beverly Hills, CA: Sage.

Ås, B. (1975) 'On female culture: an attempt to formulate a theory of women's solidarity and action', *Acta Sociologica*, 18 (2–3).

Bacchi, C.L. (1990) *Same Difference: Feminism and Sexual Difference*. London: Allen and Unwin.

Bacchi, C.L. (1996) *The Politics of Affirmative Action: 'Women', Equality and Category Politics*. London: Sage.

Bagilhole, B. (1997) *Equal Opportunities and Social Policy: Issues of Gender, Race and Disability*. London: Longman.

Bagilhole, B. (2001, forthcoming) 'Divide and be ruled? Multiple discrimination and the concept of social exclusion', in E. Breitenbach, A. Brown, F. Mackay and J. Webb (eds) *The Changing Politics of Gender Equality*. Basingstoke: Palgrave.

Banks, O. (1993) *The Politics of British Feminism, 1918–1970*. Aldershot: Edward Elgar.

Barrett, M. (1987) 'The concept of "difference" '. *Feminist Review*, 26.

Barron, J., Crawley, G. and Wood, T. (1991) *Councillors in Crisis: The Public and Private Worlds of Local Councillors*. Basingstoke: Macmillan.

Barry, J. (1991) *The Women's Movement and Local Politics*. Aldershot: Avebury.

Beetham, D. (1992) 'Liberal democracy and the limits of democratization', *Political Studies*, 40 (5).

Bers, T.H. (1978) 'Local political elites: men and women on boards of education', *Western Political Quarterly*, (3).

Bickford, S. (1996) *The Dissonance of Democracy: Listening, Conflict and Citizenship*. Ithaca, NY and London: Cornell University Press.

Bochel, C. and Bochel, H.M. (1996) 'The "careers" of local councillors in Scotland', paper delivered at Elections, Public Opinion and Parties conference, September.

Bochel, C. and Bochel, H.M. (2000) *The Careers of Councillors: Gender, Party and Politics*. Aldershot: Ashgate.

Bochel, J. and Denver, D. (1983) 'Candidate selection in the Labour Party: what the selectors seek', *British Journal of Political Science*, 13 (1).

Bock, G. and James, S. (eds) (1992) *Beyond Equality and Difference*. London: Routledge.

Boneparth, E. and Stoper, E. (eds) (1988) *Women, Policy and Power: Toward the Year 2000*. Oxford: Pergamon Press.

Bono, P. and Kemp, S. (eds) (1991) *Italian Feminist Thought: A Reader*. Oxford: Basil Blackwell.

Brannen, J., Meszaros, G., Moss, P. and Poland, J. (1994) *Employment and Family Life: A Review of Research in the UK (1980–1994)*. London: Department of Employment.

Brannen, J. and Moss, P. (1991) *Managing Mothers: Dual Earner Households after Maternity Leave*. London: Macmillan.

Breitenbach, E. (1995) *Quality Through Equality*. Glasgow: Equal Opportunities Commission (Scotland).

Breitenbach, E. (1996) 'The Women's Movement in Scotland in the 1990s', *New Waverley Papers*. Edinburgh: Department of Politics, University of Edinburgh.

Breitenbach, E. and Mackay, F. (eds) (2001) *Women and Contemporary Scottish Politics: An Anthology*. Edinburgh: Polygon at Edinburgh.

Bristow, S. (1980) 'Women councillors: an explanation of the under-representation of women in local government', *Local*

Government Studies, 6 (3).

Brown, A. (1996) 'Women and politics in Scotland', in J. Lovenduski and P. Norris (eds), *Women in Politics*. Oxford: Oxford University Press.

Brown, A. (1998) 'Deepening democracy: women and the Scottish Parliament', *Regional and Federal Studies*, 8 (1).

Brown, A. (1999) 'Taking their place in the new house: women and the Scottish Parliament', *Scottish Affairs*, 28 (2).

Brown, A. and Galligan, Y. (1993) 'Changing the political agenda for women in the Republic of Ireland and in Scotland', *West European Politics*, 16 (2).

Brown, A. and Galligan, Y. (1995) 'Why so few seats in the house for Irish and Scottish women? Women's views from the periphery of Europe', paper presented to Women and Politics in Ireland, the Second National Conference of the PSAI, Dublin, March.

Brown, A., Jones, A. and Mackay, F. (1999a) *The 'Representativeness' of Councillors*. York: Joseph Rowntree Foundation.

Brown, A., McCrone, D. and Paterson, L. (1996) *Politics and Society in Scotland*. (1st edn) Basingstoke and London: Macmillan.

Brown, A., McCrone, D. and Paterson, L. (1998) *Politics and Society in Scotland*. (2nd edn) Basingstoke and London: Macmillan.

Brown, A., McCrone, D., Paterson, L. and Surridge, P. (1999b) *The Scottish Electorate: The 1997 General Election and Beyond*. Basingstoke: Macmillan.

Brown, L.M. and Gilligan, C. (1992) *Meeting at the Crossroads: Women's Psychology and Girls' Development*. Cambridge, MA and London: Harvard University Press.

Bryson, V. (1992) *Feminist Political Theory: An Introduction*. Basingstoke: Macmillan.

Bubeck, D. (1995) *Care, Gender and Justice*. Oxford: Clarendon Press.

Burness, C. (1995) 'Will Scotland lead the way for women?', *Parliamentary Brief*, March.

Bystydzienski, J. (ed.) (1992) *Women Transforming Politics*. Bloomington: Indiana University Press.

Campbell, B. (1987) *The Iron Ladies*. London: Virago.

Carby, H. (1982) 'White woman listen! Black feminism and the boundaries of sisterhood', in Centre for Contemporary Cultural Studies, *The Empire Strikes Back: Race and Racism in 70's Britain*. London: Hutchinson.

Carey, J.M., Niemi, R.G. and Powell, L.W. (1998) 'Are women state legislators different?', in S. Thomas and C. Wilcox (eds),

Women and Elective Office: Past, Present and Future. New York and Oxford: Oxford University Press.

Carroll, S. (1984) 'Women candidates and support for feminist concerns: the closet feminist syndrome', *Western Political Quarterly*, 37 (2).

Carroll, S. (1985) *Women as Candidates in American Politics*. Bloomington: Indiana University Press.

Carroll, S. (1992) 'Women state legislators, women's organizations, and the representation of women's culture in the United States', in J. Bystydzienski (ed.), *Women Transforming Politics*. Bloomington: Indiana University Press.

Carver, T. (1998) 'A political theory of gender', in V. Randall and G. Waylen (eds), *Gender, Politics and the State*. London: Routledge.

Cavarero, A. (1992) 'Equality and sexual difference: amnesia in political thought', in G. Bock and S. James (eds), *Beyond Equality and Difference*. London: Routledge.

Center for the American Woman and Politics (CAWP) (1978) *Women in Public Office*. Metuchen, NJ: Scarecrow Press.

Center for the American Woman and Politics (CAWP) (1983) *Women Make a Difference*. Rutgers, NJ: Eagleton Institute of Politics.

Chapman, J. (1986) 'The political motivations of women candidates for local political office: a generational comparison', paper presented to the Annual Conference of the Political Studies Association, Nottingham, April.

Chapman, J. (1987) 'Adult socialisation and out-group politicization', *British Journal of Political Studies*, 17 (3).

Chapman, J. (1993) *Politics, Feminism and the Reformation of Gender*. London: Routledge.

Chodorow, N. (1978) *The Reproduction of Mothering: Psychoanalysis and the Sociology of Gender*. Berkeley, CA: University of California Press.

Cockburn, C. (1977) *The Local State*. London: Pluto Press.

Cockburn, C. (1983) *Brothers: Male Dominance and Technological Change*. London: Pluto Press.

Cockburn, C. (1985) *Machinery of Dominance*. London: Macmillan.

Cockburn, C. (1987) 'Women, trade unions and political parties', *Fabian Research Series*, 349, London: Fabian Society.

Cockburn, C. (1989) 'Equal opportunities: the short and long agenda' *Industrial Relations Journal*, 20 (3).

Cockburn, C. (1991) *In the Way of Women: Men's Resistance to Sex*

Equality in Organizations. Houndmills and London: Macmillan.

Cockburn, C. (1996) 'Strategies for gender democracy: strengthening the representation of trade union women in the European social dialogue', *European Journal of Women's Studies*, 3 (1).

Code, L. (1991) *What Can She Know? Feminist Theory and the Construction of Knowledge*. Ithaca, NY, and London: Cornell University Press.

Code, L. (1995) *Rhetorical Spaces: Essays on Gendered Locations*. New York and London: Routledge.

Collins, P.H. (1994) 'The social construction of black feminist thought', in M. Evans (ed.), *The Woman Question*. (2nd edn) London: Sage.

Consultative Steering Group on the Scottish Parliament (1998) *Shaping Scotland's Parliament*. Edinburgh: Scottish Office.

Coote, A. and Patullo, P. (1990) *Power and Prejudice: Women and Politics*. London: Weidenfeld and Nicolson.

Council of Europe Rapporteur Group on Equality between Women and Men (1998) *Gender Mainstreaming: Conceptual Framework, Methodology and Presentation of Good Practices. Final Report of Activities of the Group of Specialists on Mainstreaming*. Strasbourg: Council of Europe, EG-S-MS (98) 2.

Currell, M. (1974) *Political Women*. London: Croom Helm.

Cuthbert, J. and Irving, L. (2001) 'Women's aid in Scotland: purity versus pragmatism?', in E. Breitenbach and F. Mackay (eds), *Women and Contemporary Scottish Politics*. Edinburgh: Polygon at Edinburgh.

Dahlerup, D. (1988) 'From a small to a large minority: women in Scandinavian politics', *Scandinavian Political Studies*, 11 (4).

Darcy, R., Welch, S. and Clark, J. (1994) *Women, Elections and Representation*. (2nd edn) Nebraska: University of Nebraska Press.

Davis, K. (1992) 'Towards a feminist rhetoric: the Gilligan debate revisited', *Women's Studies International Forum*, 15 (2).

Denver, D. and Bochel, H. (1994) 'The regional elections of 1994', *Scottish Affairs*, 9 (3).

Diamond, I. and Hartsock, N. (1981) 'Beyond interests in politics: a comment on Virginia Sapiro's "When are interests interesting? The problem of the political representation of women"'. *American Political Science Review*, 75.

Dietz, M.G. (1985) 'Citizenship with a feminist face: the problem with maternal thinking', *Political Theory*, 13 (1).

Dietz, M.G. (1987) 'Context is all: feminism and theories of citizenship', *Daedalus*, 116 (4).

Dolan, K. and Ford, L.E. (1998) 'Are all women state legislators alike?' in S. Thomas and C. Wilcox (eds), *Women and Elective Office: Past, Present and Future*. New York and Oxford: Oxford University Press.

Duverger, M. (1955) *The Political Role of Women*. Paris: UNESCO.

Eagle, M. and Lovenduski, J. (1998) 'High time or high tide for Labour women?', *Fabian Pamphlet*. 585, London: Fabian Society.

Edwards, J. (1995) *Local Government Women's Committees*. Aldershot: Avebury.

Eisenstein, H. (1991) *Gender Shock: Pracitising Feminism on Two Continents*. Sydney: Allen and Unwin.

Evans, J. (1995) *Feminist Theory Today: An Introduction to Second Wave Feminism*. London: Sage.

Fawcett (1997) *Winning Women's Votes*. London: Fawcett.

Finer, S.E. (1985) 'The contemporary context of representation', in V. Bogdanor (ed.), *Representatives of the People? Parliamentarians and Constituents in Western Democracies*. Aldershot: Gower.

Fisher, B. and Tronto, J. (1991) 'Towards a feminist theory of care', in E. Abel and M. Nelson (eds), *Circles of Care: Work and Identity in Women's Lives*. Albany, NY: State University of New York Press.

Flammang, J.A. (ed.) (1984) *Political Women: Current Roles in State and Local Government*. Beverly Hills, CA: Sage.

Flammang, J.A. (1985) 'Female officials in the feminist capital: the case of Santa Clara County', *Western Political Quarterly*. 38 (1).

Flax, J. (1993) *Disabled Subjects: Essays on Psychoanalysis, Politics and Philosophy*. New York and London: Routledge.

Franzway, S., Court, D. and Connell, R.W. (1989) *Staking a Claim: Feminism, Bureaucracy and the State*. Cambridge: Polity Press.

Fraser, N. (1989) *Unruly Practices: Power, Discourse and Gender in Contemporary Social Theory*. Cambridge: Polity Press.

Frazer, E. and Lacey, N. (1993) *The Politics of Community: A Feminist Critique of the Liberal-Communitarian Debate*. Hemel Hempstead: Harvester Wheatsheaf.

Gallagher, M., and Marsh, M. (eds) (1988), *Candidate Selection in Comparative Perspective: The Secret Garden of Politics*. London: Sage.

Gelb, J. (1990) 'Feminism and political action', in R.J. Dalton and M. Kueuchler (eds) *Challenging the Political Order*. Cambridge: Polity.

Gelb, J. and Palley, M.L. (1987) *Women and Public Policies*.

Princeton, NJ: Princeton University Press.

Gill, B. (1999) *Winning Women: Lessons from Scotland and Wales*. London: Fawcett.

Gilligan, C. (1982, new Preface, 1993) *In a Different Voice: Psychological Theory and Women's Development*. Cambridge, MA and London: Harvard University Press.

Gilligan, C. (1995) 'Hearing difference: theorising connection', *Hypatia*, 10 (2).

Githens, M. (1984) 'Women and state politics: an assessment', in J.A. Flammang (ed.), *Political Women*. Beverly Hills, CA: Sage.

Githens, M., Norris, P. and Lovenduski, J. (eds) (1994) *Different Roles, Different Voices: Women and Politics in the United States and Europe*. New York: HarperCollins.

Githens, M. and Prestage, J. (eds) (1977) *A Portrait of Marginality: The Political Behavior of the American Woman*. New York: Longman.

Glendinning, C. and Millar, J. (eds) (1992) *Women and Poverty in Britain*. London: Wheatsheaf.

Goss, S. (1984) 'Women's initiatives in local government', in M. Boddy and C. Fudge (eds), *Local Socialism?* London: Macmillan.

Green, K. (1995) *The Woman of Reason*. Cambridge: Polity.

Gregory, J. (1999) 'Revisiting the sex equality laws', in S. Walby (ed.), *New Agendas for Women*. Basingstoke: Macmillan.

Gross, D.A. (1978) 'Representative styles and legislative behavior', *Western Political Quarterly*, (3).

Guadagnini, M. (1990) *Unfinished Democracy: What Kind of Strategy for a Real Change?* Report no. CPL/CEEG (90) 12. Strasbourg: Council of Europe.

Haavio-Mannila, E. *et al.* (eds) (1985) *Unfinished Democracy: Women in Nordic Politics*. Oxford: Pergamon Press.

Halford, S. (1988) 'Women's initiatives in local government … where do they come from and where are they going?', *Policy and Politics*, 16 (4).

Halford, S. (1992) 'Feminist change in a patriarchal organisation: the experience of women's initiatives in local government and implications for feminist perspectives on state institutions', in M. Savage and A. Witz (eds), *Gender and Bureaucracy*. Oxford: Blackwell.

Harding, S. (ed.) (1987) *Feminism and Methodology*. Milton Keynes: Open University Press.

Hartsock, N. (1987) 'The feminist standpoint: developing the ground for a specifically feminist historical materialism', in S. Harding (ed.), *Feminism and Methodology*. Milton Keynes: Open University Press.

Hedlund, G. (1988) 'Women's interests in local politics', in K. Jones and A. Jonasdottir (eds), *The Political Interests of Gender*. London: Sage.

Held, V. (1987) 'Feminism and moral theory', in E. Feder Kittay and D.T. Meyers (eds), *Women and Moral Theory*. Totowa, NJ: Rowman and Littlefield.

Held, V. (1990) 'Feminist transformations of moral theory', *Philosophy and Phenomenological Research*, 50 (1).

Hernes, H.M. and Voje, K. (1980) 'Women in the corporate channel in Norway: a process of natural exclusion?', *Scandinavian Political Studies*, 3 (2).

Hills, J. (1981) 'Candidates: the impact of gender', *Parliamentary Affairs*, 34.

Hills, J. (1983) 'The lifestyle constraints on women councillors', *Electoral Studies*, 2 (1).

Holsti, O. and Rosenau, J. (1982) 'The foreign policy beliefs of women in leadership positions', in E. Boneparth (ed.), *Women, Power and Policy*. New York: Pergamon.

hooks, b. (1981) *Ain't I a Woman? Black Women and Feminism*. Boston: South End Press.

Hosykns, C. (1996) *Integrating Gender, Women, Law and Politics in the European Union*. London: Verso.

Houston, B. (1985) 'Prolegomana to future caring', *Hypatia*, 7.

Humphries, J. and Rubery, J. (1995) *The Economics of Equal Opportunities*. Manchester: Equal Opportunities Commission.

Innes, S. (2001) 'Quietly thrilling: women in the Scottish Parliament', in E. Breitenbach and F. Mackay (eds), *Women and Contemporary Scottish Politics*. Edinburgh: Polygon at Edinburgh.

Janeway, E. (1980) *Powers of the Weak*. New York: Morrow.

Jennings, M.K. and Thomas, N. (1968) 'Men and women in party elites: social roles and political resources', *Midwest Journal of Political Science*, 12 (4).

Jonasdottir, A.G. (1988) 'On the concept of interest: women's interests and the limitations of interest theory', in K. Jones and A.G. Jonasdottir (eds), *The Political Interests of Gender*. London: Sage.

Jones, K.B. (1990) 'Citizenship in a women-friendly polity', *Signs*. 15 (4).

Jones, K.B. (1993) *Compassionate Authority: Democracy and the Representation of Women*. New York and London: Routledge.

Judge, D. (1999) *Representation: Theory and Practice in Britain*. London: Routledge.

Kanter, R. (1977) *Men and Women of the Corporation*. New York: Basic Books.

Karvonen, L. and Selle, P. (1995), *Women in Nordic Politics*. Aldershot: Dartmouth Press.

Kathlene, L. (1998) 'In a different voice: women and the policy process', in S. Thomas and C. Wilcox (eds), *Women and Elective Office: Past, Present and Future*. New York and Oxford: Oxford University Press.

Kelly, E. (1992) 'The future of women in Scottish local government', *Scottish Affairs*, 1 (3).

Kelly, E. (1995) 'Sweeties from the boy's poke?' unpublished MSc thesis, University of Strathclyde.

Kelly, L. (1988) *Surviving Sexual Violence*. Cambridge: Polity Press.

Kelly, L., Burton, S. and Regan, L. (1994) 'Beyond victim or survivor: sexual violence, identity and feminist theory and practice', paper presented to the British Sociological Association Conference, Preston.

Lee, M.M. (1976) 'Why few women hold public office: democracy and sex roles', *Political Science Quarterly*, 91 (2).

Leijenaar, M. (1989) *De Geschade heerlijkheid (politiek gedrag van vrouwen en mannen in Nederland, 1918–1988)*. The Hague: SDU-uitgeverij.

Leijenaar, M. (1996) *How to Create a Gender Balance in Decision Making*. Brussels: Commission of the European Communities.

Leijenaar, M. and Mahon, E. (1992) 'Power to what end?', *Nijmegen Political Science Reports*. Nijmegen: University of Nijmegen.

LeLohe, M.J. (1976) 'Sex discrimination and under-representation of women in politics', *New Community*, 5 (1–2).

Lieberman, S. (1989) 'Women's committees in Scotland', in A. Brown and D. McCrone (eds), *The Scottish Government Yearbook 1989*. Edinburgh: Unit for the Study of Scotland, University of Edinburgh.

Lister, R. (1997) *Citizenship: Feminist Perspectives*. Basingstoke: Macmillan.

Local Government Management Board (1998) *Local Authority Councillors Census, Exit and Newly Elected Councillors Surveys*. London: Local Government Management Board.

Lorde, A. (1984) *Sister Outsider*. Trumansberg: The Crossing Press.

Lovenduski, J. (1986) *Women and European Politics*. Brighton: Wheatsheaf.

Lovenduski, J. (1993) 'Introduction: the dynamics of gender and party', in J. Lovenduski and P. Norris (eds) *Gender and Party Politics*. London: Sage.

Lovenduski, J. (1996) 'Sex, gender and British politics', in J. Lovenduski and P. Norris (eds), *Women in Politics*. Oxford: Oxford University Press.

Lovenduski, J. (1997) 'Gender politics: a breakthrough for women?' *Parliamentary Affairs*, 50 (4).

Lovenduski, J. and Norris, P. (1989) 'Selecting women candidates: obstacles to the feminisation of the House of Commons', *European Journal of Political Research*, 17 (3).

Lovenduski, J. and Norris, P. (1993) *Gender and Party Politics*. Sage: London.

Lovenduski, J. and Randall, V. (1993) *Contemporary Feminist Politics: Women and Power in Britain*. Oxford: Oxford University Press.

Lovenduski, J. and Stephenson, S. (1998) *Overview State of the Art Study of Research on Women in Political, Economic and Social Decision Making in Europe*. Brussels: European Commission.

Mackay, F. (1996a) 'Getting there, being there, making a difference? Gendered discourses of access and action in local politics', unpublished PhD dissertation, University of Edinburgh.

Mackay, F. (1996b) 'The zero tolerance campaign: setting the agenda', in J. Lovenduski and P. Norris (eds), *Women in Politics*. Oxford: Oxford University Press.

Mackay, F. (2001) 'The case of zero tolerance: women's politics in action?', in E. Breitenbach and F. Mackay (eds), *Women and Contemporary Scottish Politics*. Edinburgh: Polygon at Edinburgh.

Mackay, F. and Bilton, K. (2000) *Learning from Experience: Lessons in Mainstreaming Equal Opportunities*, Edinburgh: Governance of Scotland Forum, University of Edinburgh.

Mactaggart, F. (2000) *Women in Parliament: Their Contribution to Labour's First 1000 Days*. Fabian research paper posted at: www.fabian-society.org.uk/publications/extracts/womeninparliament.html

Mahon, E. (1991) 'Women and equality in the Irish civil service', in E. Meehan and S. Sevenhuijsen (eds), *Equality Politics and Gender*. London: Sage.

Manin, B. (1997) *The Principles of Representative Government*.

Cambridge: Cambridge University Press.

Mann, L. (1993) *Public Policy and Participation: The Role of Women in the Highlands*. Report to Barail, Easter Ross: Lorraine Mann Research and Consultancy.

Manning, R.C. (1992) *Speaking from the Heart: A Feminist Perspective on Ethics*. Lanham, MD: Rowman and Littlefield.

Martlew, C., Forrester, C. and Buchanan, G. (1985) 'Activism and office: women and local government in Scotland', *Local Government Studies*, 11 (2).

Maud, Sir J. (Chairman) (1967) *Report of the Committee on the Management of Local Government, Volume 2: The Local Government Councillor*. London: HMSO.

McGrew, A. and Bristow, S. (1984) 'Candidate to councillor: a study of local political recruitment', in S. Bristow, D. Kermode and M. Mannin (eds), *The Redundant Counties?: Participation and Electoral Choice in England's Metropolitan Counties*. Ormskirk: G.W.A. Hesketh.

McLaughlin, J. (1997) 'An ethic of care: a valuable political tool?' *Politics*, 16 (1).

McLean, I. (1991) 'Forms of representation and systems of voting', in D. Held (ed.), *Political Theory Today*. Cambridge: Polity Press.

Meehan, E. and Sevenhuijsen, S. (eds) (1991) *Equality Politics and Gender*. London: Sage.

Mellors, C. (1978) *The British MP*. Saxon House: Farnborough.

Merritt, S. (1980) 'Sex differences in role behavior and policy orientations of suburban office holders: the effect of women's employment', in D. Stewart (ed.), *Women in Local Politics*. Metuchen, NJ: Scarecrow Press.

Mezey, S.G. (1978) 'Does sex make a difference? A case study of women in politics', *Western Political Quarterly*, 31 (4).

Morris, J. (1991) *Pride Against Prejudice*. Harmondsworth: Penguin.

Neuse, S.M. (1978) 'Professionalism and authority: women in public service', *Public Administrative Review*, (3).

Nicholson, L. (1995) 'Interpreting gender', in L. Nicholson and S. Seidman (eds), *Social Postmodernism: Beyond Identity Politics*. Cambridge: Cambridge University Press.

Noddings, N. (1984) *Caring: A Feminine Approach to Ethics and Moral Education*. Berkeley, CA: University of California.

Noddings, N. (1990), 'Ethics from the standpoint of women', in D. Rhode (ed.), *Theoretical Perspectives on Sexual Difference*. New Haven, CT: Yale University Press.

Norris, P. (1985) 'Women's legislative participation in Western Europe', *West European Politics*, 8 (4).

Norris, P. (1994) 'Introduction', in M. Githens *et al.* (eds), *Different Roles, Different Voices: Women and Politics in the United States and Europe*. New York: HarperCollins.

Norris, P. (1996) 'Women politicians: transforming Westminster?', *Parliamentary Affairs*, 46 (1).

Norris, P. (ed.) (1997) *Passages to Power: Legislative Recruitment in Advanced Democracies*. Cambridge: Cambridge University Press.

Norris, P. and Lovenduski, J. (1995) *Political Recruitment: Gender, Race and Class in the British Parliament*. Cambridge: Cambridge University Press.

Offen, K. (1992) 'Defining feminism: a comparative historical approach', in G. Bock and S. James (eds), *Beyond Equality and Difference*. London: Routledge.

Okin, S.M. (1989) *Justice, Gender and the Family*. New York: Basic Books.

Okin, S.M. (1990) 'Thinking like a woman', in D. Rhode (ed.), *Theoretical Perspectives on Sexual Difference*. New Haven, CT: Yale University Press.

Okin, S.M. (1992) *Women in Western Political Thought*. Princeton, Guilford: Princeton University Press.

Perrigo, S. (1995) 'Gender struggles in the British Labour Party from 1979–1995', *Party Politics*, 1 (3).

Perrigo, S. (1996) 'Women and change in the Labour Party', *Parliamentary Affairs*, 49 (1).

Phillips, A. (1987) *Divided Loyalties: Dilemmas of Sex and Class*. London: Virago.

Phillips, A. (1991) *Engendering Democracy*. Cambridge: Polity Press.

Phillips, A. (1993) *Democracy and Difference*. Cambridge: Polity Press.

Phillips, A. (1995) *Politics of Presence*. Oxford: Clarendon Press.

Phillips, M. (1980) *The Divided House*. London: Sidgwick and Jackson.

Pitkin, H. (1967) *The Concept of Representation*. Berkeley, CA: University of California Press.

Potter, E. (1998) 'Political representation of women in Northern Ireland', *Politics*, 18 (1).

Pringle, R. and Watson, S. (1992) ' "Women's interests" and the post-structuralist state', in M. Barrett and A. Phillips (eds), *Destabilizing Theory: Contemporary Feminist Debates*. Cambridge:

Polity Press.

Pugh, M. (1992), *Women and the Women's Movement in Britain 1914–1959*. Basingstoke and London: Macmillan.

Putnam, R.D. (1976) *The Comparative Study of Political Elites*. Englewood Cliffs, New Jersey: Prentice-Hall.

Radice, L. (1985) 'Winning women's votes', *Fabian Tract*, 507, London: Fabian Society.

Randall, V. (1987) *Women and Politics*. (2nd edn) Basingstoke: Macmillan.

Randall, V. and Waylen, G. (eds) (1998) *Gender, Politics and the State*. London: Routledge.

Rao, N. (1998) 'Representation in local politics: a reconsideration and some new evidence', *Political Studies*, 46 (1).

Rawls, J. (1971) *A Theory of Justice*. Oxford: Oxford University Press.

Rendall, J. (1987) *Equal or Different: Women's Politics 1800–1914*. New York: Basil Blackwell.

Rhode, D. (ed.) (1990) *Theoretical Perspectives on Sexual Difference*. New Haven, CT: Yale University Press.

Rhode, D. (1992) 'The politics of paradigms: gender difference and gender disadvantage', in G. Bock and S. James (eds), *Beyond Equality and Difference*. London and New York: Routledge.

Rich, A. (1980) 'Compulsory heterosexuality and lesbian existence', *Signs*, 5 (4).

Roseniel, S. (1999) 'Postmodern feminist politics: the art of the (im)possible?', *European Journal of Women's Studies*, 6 (2).

Rosenthal, C.S. (1998) *When Women Lead: Integrative Leadership in State Legislatures*. New York and Oxford: Oxford University Press.

Rowbotham, S. (1985) 'What do women want?' *Feminist Review*, 20 (2).

Rowbotham, S., Segal, L. and Wainwright, H. (1979) *Beyond the Fragments*. London: Merlin Press.

Rubery, J. (ed.) (1988) *Women and Recession*. London: Routledge and Kegan Paul.

Ruddick, S. (1980) 'Maternal thinking', *Feminist Studies*, 6 (2).

Ruddick, S. (1989) *Maternal Thinking: Towards a Politics of Peace* (UK edition: 1990 Women's Press) Boston: Beacon Press.

Rush, M. (1969) *The Selection of Parliamentary Candidates*. London: Nelson.

Russell, M. (2000) *Women's Representation in UK Politics: What Can Be Done Within the Law?* London: The Constitution Unit,

University College London.

Saint-Germain, M.A. (1989) 'Does their difference make a difference?' *Social Science Quarterly*, 70 (4).

Sapiro, V. (1981) 'When are interests interesting? The problem of the political representation of women', *American Political Science Review*, 75 (3).

Saraceno, C. (1987) 'Division of family labour and gender identity', in A. Showstack Sassoon (ed.), *Women and the State*. London: Hutchinson.

Scott, J. (1986) 'Gender: a useful category of historical analysis', *American Historical Review*, 91 (5).

Scottish Constitutional Convention (1990) *Towards Scotland's Parliament*. Edinburgh: Scottish Constitutional Convention.

Scottish Constitutional Convention (1995) *Scotland's Parliament: Scotland's Right*. Edinburgh: Scottish Constitutional Convention.

Scottish Local Government Information Unit (1995) 'Scotland's councillors: a profile', *Scottish Local Government Bulletin*, 75.

Scottish Local Government Information Unit (1999) 'Council election results 1999', *Scottish Local Government Bulletin*, 113.

Scottish Office (1997) *Scotland's Parliament*. Cmd. 3658, July. Edinburgh: HMSO.

Segal, L. (1987) *Is The Future Female?* London: Virago Press.

Sevenhuijsen, S. (1991) 'Links between contextualised moral thinking and the Scottish Enlightment', in E. Meehan and S. Sevenhuijsen (eds), *Equality, Politics and Gender*, London: Sage.

Sevenhuijsen, S. (1998) *Citizenship and the Ethics of Care: Feminist Considerations on Justice, Morality and Politics*. London: Routledge.

Shaul, M. (1982) 'The status of women in local government', *Public Administration Review*, 6.

Short, C. (1996) 'Women and the Labour Party', in J. Lovenduski and P. Norris (eds), *Women in Politics*. Oxford: Oxford University Press.

Showstack Sassoon, A. (ed.) (1987), *Women and the State*. London: Hutchinson.

Skard, T. and Haavio-Mannila, E. (1985) 'Women in Parliament', in E. Haavio-Mannila *et al.* (eds) *Unfinished Democracy: Women in Nordic Politics*. Oxford: Pergamon.

Skjeie, H. (1988) *The Feminization of Power: Norway's Political Experiment (1986–)* Oslo: Institute for Social Research.

Skjeie, H. (1991a) 'The rhetoric of difference', *Politics and Society*, 19 (2).

Skjeie, H. (1991b) 'The uneven advance of Norwegian women', *New Left Review*, 187.

Skjeie, H. (1993) 'Ending the male political hegemony: the Norwegian experience', in J. Lovenduski and P. Norris (eds), *Gender and Party Politics*. London: Sage.

Skrede, K. (1992) 'From access to integration: women as agents of change in the decision-making process of public policy', paper presented to the Gender and Power Workshop at the ECPR Joint Sessions of Workshops, Limerick, 30 March–4 April.

Stokes, W. (1998) 'Feminist democracy: the case for women's committees', *Contemporary Politics*, 4 (1).

Stoper, E. (1977) 'Wife and politician: role strain among women in public office', in M. Githens and J. Prestage (eds), *A Portrait of Marginality: The Political Behavior of the American Woman*. New York: Longman.

Studlar, D. and Welch, S. (1987) 'Understanding the iron law of andrachy: effects of candidate gender on voting in Scotland', *Comparative Political Studies*, 20 (2).

Thomas, S. (1991) 'The impact of women on state legislative policies', *Journal of Politics*, 53 (4).

Thomas, S. (1994) *How Women Legislate*. Oxford: Oxford University Press.

Thomas, S. and Welch, S. (1991) 'The impact of gender on activities and priorities of state legislators', *Western Political Quarterly*, 44 (2).

Thomas, S. and Wilcox, C. (1998) *Women and Elective Office: Past, Present and Future*. New York and Oxford: Oxford University Press.

Tronto, J. (1987) 'Beyond gender difference to a theory of care', *Signs* 12 (4).

Tronto, J. (1993) *Moral Boundaries*. London: Routledge.

Tronto, J. and Fisher, B. (1990) 'Towards a feminist theory of caring', in E.K. Abel and M. Nelson (eds), *Circles of Care: Work and Identity in Women's Lives*. Albany, NY: State University of New York Press.

Unit for the Study of Government in Scotland (1998a) *'Mainstreaming' Equal Opportunities*. Edinburgh: Scottish Office Constitution Group.

Unit for the Study of Government in Scotland (1998b) *Citizen Participation and Social Partnerships: Involving Civil Society in the Work of Parliaments*. Edinburgh: Scottish Office Constitution

Group.

Vallance, E. (1979) *Women in the House*. London: Athlone Press.

Vallance, E. and Davies, E. (1986) *Women in Europe*. Cambridge: Cambridge University Press.

Voet, R. (1998) *Feminism and Citizenship: Feminist Critiques of the Concepts of Social-Liberal Citizenship*. London: Sage.

Vogel, U. (1989) 'Is citizenship gender-specific?', paper presented to the PSA Annual Conference, Warwick, 4–6 April.

Vogel, U. (1998) 'The state and the making of gender: some historical legacies', in V. Randall and G. Waylen (eds), *Gender, Politics and the State*. London: Routledge.

Wahlke, J., Eulau, H., Buchanan, W. and Ferguson, L. (1962) *The Legislative Process: Explorations in Legislative Behavior*. New York: John Wiley.

Wainwright, H. (1987) *Labour: A Tale of Two Parties*. London: The Hogarth Press.

Wasoff, F. and Morris, S. (1996) 'The Child Support Act: a victory for women?' in J. Millar and H. Jones (eds), *The Politics of the Family*. Aldershot: Avebury.

Watson, S. (1992) 'Femocratic feminisms', in M. Savage and A. Witz (eds) *Gender and Bureaucracy*. Oxford: Blackwell.

Webster, W. (1990) *Not a Man to Match Her: The Marketing of a Prime Minister*. London: The Women's Press.

Weitzman, L.J. (1985) *The Divorce Revolution: The Unexpected Social and Economic Consequences to Women and Children in America*. New York: Free Press.

Welch, S. (1985) 'Are women more liberal than men in the US Congress?' *Legislative Studies Quarterly*, 10 (1).

Whicker, M.L. and Jewell, M. (1998) 'The feminization of leadership in state legislature's', in S. Thomas and C. Wilcox (eds), *Women and Elective Office: Past, Present and Future*. New York and Oxford: Oxford University Press.

Wilford, R. (1996) 'Women and politics in Northern Ireland', in J. Lovenduski and P. Norris (eds), *Women in Politics*. Oxford: Oxford University Press.

Wilford, R. and Galligan, Y. (1999) 'Gender and party politics in Northern Ireland', in Y. Galligan, E. Ward and R. Wilford (eds), *Contesting Politics: Women in Ireland, North and South*. Boulder, CO and Oxford: Westview Press.

Wilford, R., Miller, R., Bell, Y. and Donoghue, F. (1993) 'In their own voices: women councillors in Northern Ireland', *Public*

Administration, 71 (3).

Wilkinson, H. (1994) *No Turning Back: Generations and the Genderquake*. London: Demos.

Witt, L., Gaget, K.M. and Matthews, G. (1994) *Running as a Woman: Gender and Power in American Politics*. New York: Free Press.

Yeatman, A. (1993) 'Voice and representation in the politics of difference' in S. Gunew and A. Yeatman (eds), *Feminism and the Politics of Difference*. Sydney: Allen and Unwin.

Young, I.M. (1989) 'Polity and group difference: a critique of the ideal of universal citizenship', *Ethics*, 99 (2).

Young, I.M. (1990) *Justice and the Politics of Difference*. Princeton, NJ: Princeton University Press.

Young, I.M. (1994) 'Justice and communicative democracy', in R. Gottlieb (ed.), *Tradition, Counter Tradition, Politics: Dimensions of Radical Philosophy*. Philadelphia: Temple University Press.

Young, I.M. (1995) 'Mothers, citizenship and independence: a critique of pure family values', *Ethics*, 105 (3).

Index

equality   2–3, 4, 38, 74, 75, 117, 121,
   125, 147, 196–7
and difference debate   8–11, 159
and sexual division of family
   labour   161
ethics of care   3, 4–5, 6, 89, 123–55,
   200–2, 207–8, 210, 212, 215
caring responsibilities as barrier to
   women's political
   participation   131, 160
and citizenship   149–50, 151, 153,
   158, 188, 202
compared with ethics of
   justice   126
criticism of   127, 136
and democracy   152, 154
and 'difference' discourse   153–4,
   190–1, 204
empowering of women in politics by
   political discourse of care   188–9
and gender   152–5, 206–8
greater grasp on reality   139
and identity politics   151
and judging with care   150–5, 158,
   175–8, 189–90, 201–2
justice, gender and the
   family   131–6
marginalization and trivialization of
   care   145–6, 148, 150, 166,
   171–2, 186, 187, 203
and men   166–8, 171–2, 207
motherhood and maternal
   thinking   128–9, 138, 140–1
origins and engendering of
   polarization   126–8
as political tool   129–30, 142–8,
   148–9, 151–2, 155, 175–6, 177,
   200
political vocabulary of care   141–2,
   148–9, 160, 187–9, 201
and the powerful   145–6
and Scottish Parliament   215
skills transferable to politics
   172–4, 186–7, 188, 191,
   201, 202, 203
as social practice   136–8, 188, 201
and standpoint of women   139–40
Tronto's stages and elements
   of   142–5

and women councillors   157–8,
   159–61, 172–4, 175–6, 177,
   202–3, 204
European Parliament   26–7, 97
European Union Social Chapter   149
Evans, Judith   9, 128

family, *see* sexual division of labour
family law   149, 150
family responsibilities   3, 25, 29, 30,
   31–2, 57–60, 64, 162–3
Fianna Fáil   34
'first past the post' (FPTP)   26
Fisher, Berenice   142
Flammang, Janet   93
foreign policy   92
Fraser, Nancy   84
Frazer, E.   137

Galligan, Yvonne   29, 35
gay couples   132
gender   117, 158, 209–10
   and ethics of care   152–5, 206–8
   justice crisis of   131–6, 160, 161,
      187, 201, 205
   political interests of   85–6
gender role stereotypes   25, 29, 30
general election (1997)   38–40
Germany   91
Gilligan, Carol: *In a Different
   Voice*   126–8, 161
Githens, M.   91, 98
Goss, S.   14
group representation   100, 114,
   118–19, 121
Guadaginini, Marila   90–1

Harman, Harriet   167–8
Hartsock, Nancy   83–4, 139
Hedlund, G.   113
Held, V.   152
Hills, J.   30, 94
Holsti, O.   92
homeless   143
household labour   131, 160, 161

'ideal candidate syndrome'   26, 31,
   56–7
identity politics   151, 208–9